THE RENAISSANCE

F. FUNCK-BRENTANO

The Renaissance

GEOFFREY BLES: THE CENTENARY PRESS
TWO MANCHESTER SQUARE, LONDON, W.1

TRANSLATED BY F. C. FLETCHER

FIRST PUBLISHED IN APRIL 1936

MADE AND PRINTED BY
BUTLER AND TANNER LTD.
FROME AND LONDON

CONTENTS

CONTENTS

I

THE GOTHIC NIGHT

IN the course of the ninth and tenth centuries successive
waves of barbarian invaders swept over the former
Province of Gaul, leaving death and devastation in their
wake. The Saracen invasion submerged the South of France,
the Hungarians ravaged the West.

The Normans, " sailing the ocean like pirates ", used the
rivers to strike at the very heart of the land. As the chronicler
Richer says, " These aliens committed the most cruel ravages,
sacking towns and villages, laying waste the fields, burning
churches and departing laden with slaves."

In the ninth and tenth centuries of our era every single
town in France was destroyed. This fact alone shows the
extent of the destruction of life and property.

Adrevald, a monk of Fleury-sur-Loire, laments thus over
Paris : " This city, once crowned with honour and wealth,
fertile of land, whose people lived in perfect safety, this city,
which might justly have been called the treasury of kings
and the warehouse of nations, is now but a heap of ashes."

Amid this scene of anarchy began the work of social recon-
struction which made France a nation.

The sole institution remaining intact was the family, firm
on its foundations of human instinct. Amid the storm the
family strengthened and drew closer its ties. The younger
branches clustered round the head of the family—the *cap
d'hostel* of Southern France—forming a small state whose

9

influence spread gradually from the purely social to the political sphere, so that the State in its final form was merely the product of this gradual metamorphosis of private into public institutions. This work, a marvellous example of laborious vigour, occupied the period from the beginning of the ninth to the end of the eleventh century, the greatest in French history. The France of the twelfth century owed its existence to institutions which were the creation of the people themselves, every detail appropriate to its purpose, every institution pregnant with meaning, each one of the infinite variations of practice conforming easily and naturally to the national genius.

At this time, too, the " Chansons de Gestes " sprang anonymously to life, to spread, not only throughout France, but throughout the civilized world.

The oldest, and certainly the finest, have perished : even the " Song of Roland ", the earliest to survive, is only a recasting of " the ancient lay " as the minstrel sang it. Nevertheless it takes a worthy place among the masterpieces of French literature beside the " Song of William of Orange ".

With these arose in that Ile-de-France, which is the very heart of France, that purely " French " style which Rafael, incapable of comprehending, called " Gothic ", a synonym for barbarous, wild and incoherent.

We in our day cannot imagine the splendours of the churches of the eleventh and twelfth centuries,

> " Clad in their white robes of virginity ",

though even now, deformed and mutilated as they are by inconsequent additions and tasteless restoration, they remain perhaps the finest works of man.

Imagine Notre-Dame unspoilt, pure white, with its host of

statues (which the Revolution in great measure destroyed), with its wealth of lucent glass (which the eighteenth-century chapter condemned to be broken up), with its portals flaming with gold and colours, its giant St. Christopher and its equestrian figure of Philippe le Bel under the porch. Its proportions are perfect in their grandeur and harmony, in the infinity of rich detail, so that the whole transcends even Greek art of the best period.

Viollet-le-Duc maintains that civil architecture, as exemplified in towers and castles, in town halls and markets, is at least equal in æsthetic value to the ecclesiastical.

Gaston Paris, after an exhaustive study of thousands of texts, writes as follows :

In the Middle Ages, the relations of man to man were fixed by rules whose justice none presumed to question. No one thought to protest against the society in which he lived, or dreamed that a better could be constructed : every man desired only to bring it closer to its own ideal.

As an example we may take the guild regulations drawn up in the reign of St. Louis by the guildmaster Etienne Boileau. They have the same grand outlines, the same perfect harmony that pervades their neighbour and contemporary, the church of Notre-Dame.

The Middle Ages in France reached their highest state of vigour in the thirteenth and fourteenth centuries. Early in the fourteenth, the first cracks appeared in the building, and the decay of society began with the decay of the bonds which cemented it, the unity of landlord and tenant on the land, of patricians and craftsmen in the towns.

It was still a proverb, till the thirteenth century, that " Lordless loon liveth but ill ".

Discord appeared first in the great towns of Flanders and

the cities of Gascony, in Bruges, Ghent and Ypres, and in Bordeaux and Bayonne.

The patrician class owed its wealth and prosperity to the labour of the artisans, but this very wealth, the reward of the leadership and protection given by the patricians to the workers, tended more and more to alienate it from the people who had raised it to its proud position, while on the other hand the workers, whose own progress was largely due to the patricians, had so developed their organization that they no longer felt the need of the initiative and protection of the great. The same process of division and disruption took place, though more gradually and peacefully, on the land, between landlord and tenant. There ensued a great social crisis culminating in more than a hundred years of war, for what is called the Hundred Years War was rather a civil than a foreign war.

Throughout Europe the struggle was fought between the same parties under various names : craftsmen against patricians, guilds against lignages ; Burgundians against Armagnacs in France, "clauwaerts" and "leliaerts" in Flanders: in Italy "popolo minuto" against "popolo grosso", Guelph against Ghibelline, "Whites" against "Blacks".

The Latin texts divide them summarily into " majores " and " minores ". In France, the popular party is usually known as the " commons ".

In a precious manuscript of the eleventh century the monk Paul speaks of a collection of charters going back to the ninth century.

What changes ! [he writes]. The rolls in the abbey chest show that the peasants of to-day live another life than those of former days. Even the words they use are changed. I have found [he says in another place] the names of places and even of common things so changed that they are not only lost, but impossible to identify. Instead of preserving, men have destroyed them.

The men of the end of the fifteenth century perhaps still possessed most of the words which were current at the beginning of the fourteenth, but the customs, practices and, above all, the ideas of which those words were the expression had undergone in a critical century a change at least as great as that lamented in the eleventh-century document we have quoted.

II

CHRISTOPHER COLUMBUS AND
COPERNICUS

CHRISTOPHER COLUMBUS and Copernicus are
the two men who had the greatest influence on the
new society which was in process of formation at
the end of the fourteenth century.

Columbus was born in 1446 at Genoa, of a family of poor
weavers. His schooling was naturally rudimentary, but he
filled out its gaps by later hard work. He was certainly a
great sailor, but solely by force of character and determina-
tion, for even in the realm of practical nautical science
his store of knowledge was always very limited. Much
is made of the foreknowledge of eclipses, with which he
astounded the Indians of the New World, but this he took
direct from the almanac. He foresaw a storm which has
become famous, and saved his ships while those of other
captains were lost. As a matter of fact, this storm had
been foretold to him not by astronomy, but by astrology,
through the opposition of Jupiter and the Moon and the
conjunction of Mercury and the Sun. In other words, his
foresight was nothing but a happy coincidence. His studies
of the Pole Star led him to the conclusion that the earth
was pear-shaped, with the point towards the equator, on
which he placed the Earthly Paradise, on the banks of the
Orinoco.

Though born in Italy, what culture Columbus possessed

was purely Spanish. All his letters, even those addressed to Italians, are in that language.

When he set out on his first voyage, Columbus had no thought of discovering a new continent, and he had never any conception either of the nature or the worth of his success. His aim was to discover a new and direct route to the East Indies, but primarily to enrich himself. He sought treasure, gold, pearls and diamonds. He took care to reserve for himself, in the contract which placed him in command of the expedition, ten per cent of the pearls, precious stones and metals, spices and any other articles of commercial value that might be obtained.

The first sailor to sight land had been promised a pension of 10,000 maravedis. On the thirty-second day of the voyage, on leaving the Canaries, Columbus took care to bespeak this for himself.

The Metropolitan Museum of New York possesses a fine portrait of the great sailor from the brush of Sebastian del Piombo. It shows a person of dignity, tall and broad-shouldered with strongly marked features. His eyes are large and their expression grave, even sorrowful. The vertical lines on the forehead betray indomitable energy. The hair, cut like that of a woman of to-day, falls in heavy masses. The hands are well-shaped, and their pose adds to the dignity of the whole figure.

Columbus first reached land at the island now called Haiti, which he named Hispaniola, " Little Spain ", and which the buccaneers, who conquered most of it afterwards, rechristened San Domingo. Hispaniola was inhabited by Indians, whom Columbus thus describes :

" They love their neighbour as themselves. They smile when they speak, and their words are friendly and gentle."

A people in the true spirit of the Gospel.

Columbus writes further of them :

I am on terms of close friendship with the King, who is proud to call me brother and to treat me as such. Even if his feelings should change to enmity, neither he nor his people could use weapons, which are completely unknown to them, so that the men I have left there could lay waste the whole island without danger to themselves.

Las Casas, before the throne of Charles V, paints this picture of the Indians :

They know neither pride nor ambition nor blasphemy nor many other vices for which they have not even words. Can we pride ourselves on anything but the advantage of a certain intellectual superiority, which in them is balanced by a great gentleness, uprightness and simplicity. From their simplicity it might be assumed that they cannot rule themselves ; how then have they lived so long under their caciques without trace of those disorders so frequent among us ?

Their sole safeguard for private property consisted of stakes stuck in the ground, a sort of immobile policeman. The five small kingdoms into which the island was divided dwelt together in peace. The tribes were ruled by caciques whom they revered and obeyed by a natural impulse of affection and respect. Columbus had proof of their magnanimity on the day of his arrival. The largest of his caravals, the " capitana ", was wrecked on a reef and the natives spared no pains to save crew and lading.

In return for this kindness, the man who could speak of the Indians the words quoted above embarked on a policy of utter treachery and cruelty, which culminated in the enslavement, under the vilest conditions, of this gentle people, and finally brought about their destruction.

Hispaniola was rich in gold. " Gold," says Columbus,

" is the greatest earthly good. Its possessor can do as he will, even to despatching souls to paradise."

He had dangled the most alluring baits before the eyes of Ferdinand and Isabella, the " Kings " of Castile and Aragon. A courtier and greedy by nature, he determined that the gold which was the price of the favour of the Court of Spain should be provided by the Indians themselves, and that they should be enslaved to toil in the mines.

The chief of one of the five provinces of the island was a certain Coanabo. To him Columbus proposed a treaty on terms which were readily accepted. His confidence thus gained, he was kidnapped and placed aboard a ship leaving for Europe. The ship was lost on the voyage. When they learnt of this piece of treachery, his subjects revolted, but their feeble, unarmed efforts only served as a pretext for their own destruction. Columbus raised a force of two hundred well-mounted cavalry, equipped them with firearms and blood-hounds, and despatched them to hunt down the Indians. The dogs tracked them down and tore them, while the soldiers of Their Catholic Majesties followed the hunt like professional huntsmen. Captain Burney, an English sailor, was moved to comment :

We can certainly use dogs for protection, but a man-hunt with bloodhounds was an unheard-of atrocity before Christopher Columbus invented it. It is more barbarous than cannibalism, more horrid than the horrid feasts where man devours the flesh of man.

The use of firearms drove the Indians frantic with terror at the thunderous report and the sudden, death-dealing missile, which seemed to them to be of the devil. Ferdinando Colombo, the son of Christopher and chronicler of his father's exploits, speaks of a band of four hundred Indians routed by a single mounted arquebusier. " The timid creatures," he

adds, " fled at the first onset, and our men pursued them
with such slaughter that complete victory was a matter of
minutes."

When he returned from his second voyage Columbus,
intoxicated with his own prowess, fell a prey to an exalted
mysticism. His speech was all of God and of the divine
mysteries. His success was due to the special grace of God
and the prophet Isaiah. The next step was to be the deliverance of Jerusalem from the infidel. He wore sack-cloth, and
the rope of the Franciscan round his waist. Withal, he was
perfectly sincere, mysticism and avarice according together
in his mind.

Appearances, however, were not neglected. He appeared
at the Court of Castile attended by a train of Indians marvellously arrayed ; and at the same time sent to the slave-
market of Seville another five hundred of the poor kidnapped
wretches. When Queen Isabella heard of it her indignation
knew no bounds. Columbus had planned wholesale kid-
napping, organized as a business enterprise, to supply the
European market, but the Spanish Court forbade it.

Considered as a whole, the conduct of Columbus after his
discovery of America can only be characterized as utterly
revolting in its combination of treachery, wanton cruelty
and greed. Nevertheless there was set on foot in the seventies
of last century a movement for the canonization of this man.
Seven hundred bishops signed the requisition. Luckily a
canonical flaw was discovered in the hero's second marriage,
so that the proceedings for beatification fell to the ground
and the Church was spared much embarrassment.

When they saw the impossibility of resistance to the in-
vader, the Indians determined to take refuge in woods and
mountains, retiring before the enemy and abandoning the
cultivation which provided his food, thus, as they thought,

compelling him to leave the country. The Spaniards, however, organized the rich fisheries of the coast and drew provisions from Europe, so that it was the natives who starved. A third of the entire population of Hispaniola died in the space of a few months.

These were the events of three years of Columbus' government, immediately after the discovery of the New World.

His successor as Governor of the West Indies was one Francesco Bobadilla, who reached Hispaniola on August 23rd, 1500, when Columbus had just tortured to death seven of his own countrymen. Bobadilla was a complete ruffian. His first act was to put Columbus and his brothers in irons and ship them off to Europe. His excesses, even wilder than those of his predecessor, moved even the court of Spain. Bobadilla was succeeded by Don Nicolas Orando, who had a great reputation as an upright and just man and a capable administrator. He turned out one of the most hateful tyrants recorded in the pages of history. On his fourth voyage, Columbus made his first landfall at Hispaniola, and tried to land for repairs to his damaged ships. Orando forbade it (July 29th, 1502). These three dark profiteers in human blood and toil, Columbus, Bobadilla, Orando, held each other in mutual detestation and envy ; each desired all for himself, and Columbus had been the first with an angry protest that any but he should have the license of Their Catholic Majesties to sail the seas of the New World. Greed desired no competitors.

After all this, the latter end of the Genoese admiral is wrapt in gloom. Jakob Burckhardt, the famous historian of the Italian Renaissance, writes pityingly of his hard fate : " Some weeks before the death of Pope Alexander VI, Columbus dates from Jamaica, on July 7th, 1503, his splendid letter to Their Catholic Majesties, confounding their ingratitude. None could read this letter without indignation."

It may be that Their Catholic Majesties gave proof of base ingratitude to one who had given them a new world. One thing is certain, that they displayed, when they knew what manner of man he was, great tolerance, even indulgence. His death passed unremarked, without trace in the chronicles of the time.

The arms which Columbus assumed reveal the man : " On waves, azure, a continent and twenty-nine islands, or, on a field azure five anchors, or, below, a point, or."

Gold, gold, gold. Gold and glory. But honour is far to seek.

Turning to Copernicus, we enter another atmosphere.

The famous astronomer was born in the Polish city of Torun or Thorn, on the Vistula, on the 19th February, 1473. His family, whose name was Kopernik, were Poles, and he entered himself as a Pole on the rolls of his Italian university. His father was a well-to-do baker.

As a young man he studied at Cracow, specializing in mathematics and medicine and following assiduously the courses of a celebrated astronomer, Albert Brudzewo. At twenty he took his degree and went to Italy. He assisted Domenico-Maria Novara in his astronomical observations at Bologna. From 1499 to 1500 he was a teacher of mathematics in Rome. He became a doctor in canon law of Ferrara after a course of medical study at Padua, where he also received a grounding in the philosophy of the celebrated Arab Averrhoes, who derived from Aristotle. In 1502 he returned home, took holy orders, and became a priest and a member of the academy of Cracow. One of his uncles, a bishop, then presented him to a canonry in Frauenburg on the Frisches Haff, which is a small bay of the Baltic in the diocese of Ermeland.

Thereafter his life passed peacefully in his ecclesiastical duties. He took an active part in the administration of the diocese, and was sent by his chapter in 1522 as their delegate to the diet of Graudenz, where he distinguished himself by his advocacy of currency reform. " A sound and stable currency," he said, " is an essential of a healthy political economy."

His leisure he divided between free medical treatment of the poor and his astronomical speculations, from which latter was to spring a work which places its author in the first rank of the great scientific minds of all time.

At Frauenburg, Copernicus had built and fitted up a kind of small tower, a crude observatory to house the still cruder instruments he constructed himself for the study of parallaxes. This consisted of three pieces of wood; an upright, fixed in the earth, another fixed to the top of it like the movable leg of a compass, and a third, fastened perpendicularly to the second, on which 1,414 divisions for the calculation of angles were marked in ink.

So early as 1507, Copernicus seemed to have had clearly in his mind the bases of his " system ".

By careful observation, with the naked eye, of the phases of an eclipse, he had discovered the dual motion of the planets on their own axes and around the sun. By 1512, this system was worked out to the smallest detail. The work itself, the *Six Books on the Revolutions of the Heavenly Bodies*, was finished in 1530, but the author hesitated to publish it. His motives he explains candidly in his preface to Pope Paul III :

I can well believe that, when what I have written becomes known, there will be an uproar. I myself am not so infatuated with my own ideas as to disdain all those of others, but though a philosopher's ideas may conflict with those held by the vulgar —since the philosopher seeks only truth within the bounds set by God to human intelligence—I do not believe that they should therefore be rejected out of mere prejudice. This, and the fear of the ridicule which must needs be called forth by the novelty and apparent absurdity of my system, had determined me to abstain from publishing my work. The insistence of my friends, however, and chief among them Cardinal Nikolaus von Schomberg, Archbishop of Capua, and Tiedemann Giese, Bishop of Kulm, overcame my disinclination. Mgr. Giese, above all, insisted that I should print this book, which has been in preparation, not nine only, but thirty-six years.

Copernicus thus explains to the Pope how he was led to form his conceptions :

If one imagines a number of human limbs, taken from persons of different stature and appearance, and tries to construct from them a complete body, then their disproportion and their difference of shape would produce a monster rather than a normally constituted human form. But astronomy, as it was, appeared to me precisely such a monster. In endeavouring to explain the celestial motions, I constantly met with objections which destroyed all generally admitted theories. Hypotheses favourable to certain cases could not possibly cover certain others and, being now admitted and now rejected, they sowed confusion in practice and bewilderment in the mind instead of illuminating the path of reason.

They failed to convince because they turned the wondrous works of nature into a madman's dream. What was I to think of such an ill-built structure, shrouded in the mist of obscurity and falling to ruin under the weight of contradictions and difficulties ? I could but think that the very foundations were unsound.

He recalls those parts of the works of the ancients which favour his system, and continues :

Considering these authorities, I was myself led to meditate on the motion of the earth, and, though the idea may seem absurd, I thought—since others had already taken the liberty of supposing a multitude of circles to explain astronomical phenomena—that

I might risk an explanation of the motions of the celestial bodies based on the hypothesis that the earth itself was in motion.

After long study I have reached these conclusions : that the sun is a fixed star, surrounded by planets which revolve round it and of which it is the centre and the light : that besides the principal planets there are secondary ones revolving, as satellites, round their principals and, with them, round the sun : that the earth is a primary planet subject to a triple motion on its own axis and round the sun, by which means I explain the phenomena of diurnal and annual movement, the alternation of the seasons with all the changes of light and temperature that go with them. Further, I hold that the apparent courses of the stars are merely an optical illusion due to the actual movement of the earth and the oscillations of its axis, and finally that the motions of the planets as a whole give rise to two entirely distinct orders of phenomena, those proceeding from the movement of the earth, and those which result from the revolutions of the planets round the sun.

For Copernicus, then, the sun is the centre of the universe, with planets and their satellites revolving round it. " From his royal throne the sun rules the planets which circle round him." The sun is thus the centre of the glorious sphere contained by those stars which Copernicus held to be fixed. Mercury, according to him, revolves round the sun in eighty days (eight too many), Venus in nine months (actually 224 days) ; the earth, bearing with her the moon, takes a year ; Mars two, Jupiter twelve and Saturn thirty years. Beyond all these lie the confines of the universe, marked out by the fixed, unchanging stars. All, stars, planets and satellites alike, receive their light from the sun.

Copernicus not only established the sphericity and the triple motion of the earth, but went further. In a chapter of his book devoted to weight he foreshadows Newton's gravitational explanation of the general movement of the universe.

From the viewpoint of modern science, the truth and falsehood of Copernicus' system stands out at once. So far as the solar system is concerned, it leaves no loophole. But he could not conceive, hampered as he was by his primitive instruments, the vastness of a universe in which the light of the most distant stars takes a million years to reach us at a speed of 186,000 miles per second.

The amazing thing about the discoveries of Copernicus is that they were the products of pure reason, applied to facts known to the ancients and carefully noted by Ptolemy. The astronomer of Frauenburg, solely by the power of his own intellect, shaped these scattered observations into one harmonious whole, and did not rest till every apparent contradiction vanished, fact accorded with fact, and the perfect body—to use his own simile—was built up from its proper components.

In the absence of those aids to science which are the commonplace furniture of a modern observatory, without even a telescope, Copernicus could only adduce in confirmation of his system its perfect concordance with established facts.

His work, completed as early as 1514, was revived and amplified through the years till 1530, when he touched it for the last time. It did not appear in print till 1543, at Nuremberg. Three years earlier a letter of his disciple, the German mathematician, Georg Rheticus, had revealed the new system to the world. The famous scientist was already seventy-one when this treatise, which has been justly called "the first and most curious monument of modern science", appeared. The printing of it had been cared for by his faithful pupils, chief among them Rheticus. Copernicus was paralysed, helpless. When at last his disciples brought to him his life's great work he managed, in despite of his incapacity, to stretch out a feeble hand and touch in blessing the child of his intellect.

In the same year Vesalius published his anatomical treatise *De corporis humani fabrica*—Of the constitution of the human body. Little by little, men were learning the movement of the stars in their courses and of the blood in their veins.

Copernicus died at Frauenburg in May 1543, shortly after the appearance of his book.

It is remarkable that no clerical protest greeted so revolutionary a work. There was, however, good reason. The author's ecclesiastical dignity, the respect of his colleagues, the protection of lofty dignitaries, one of whom, a bishop, had brought about its publication and, finally, the personality of the Pope who could accept its dedication : all these combined to stay the immanent lightnings of the Inquisition. In revenge, the pontiffs of Protestantism, Luther and Melancthon, hastened to condemn with triple anathema the criminal novelty of its teachings. Only later, in 1610, when Galileo's resounding proofs of his predecessor's deductions became known, did the Inquisition rouse itself to criticize. Galileo proved Copernicus' theory first by observation of the swinging lamp in the dome of Pisa, and then with the aid of the telescope he invented, which still bears his name. For this he was summoned to the Vatican and prohibited in the future from teaching the doctrines of Copernicus, which were declared " absurd and canonically heretical, as being contrary to the Scriptures ". Finally, on March 6th, 1616, that great work *Of the Revolutions of the Celestial Bodies* was placed on the Index *donec corrigetur*—until such time as it should be corrected. By a decree which has never been repealed, the solar system, as described by Copernicus and as accepted with unanimity by the whole world to-day, remains the " Copernician heresy ".

His life was a model of modest intelligence and devoted

kindness. Poland may well be proud of such a son, the greatest she has given the world in all her history.

Tycho Brahe, the famous Swedish astronomer, piously preserved Copernicus' crude instrument, the " three sticks " shaped by his unskilled hands, which had sufficed to work out a theory which was to prove immortal.

Tycho Brahe writes of him :

> In these centuries his like has not been seen on earth. He stayed the course of the Sun in the heavens and set the unmoving Earth in motion. He made the Moon to move about her and changed the face of the Universe. And this, all this, with three poor sticks. No memento of this great man, wooden though it be, can ever perish. Gold would envy their value, could it but know it.

The ideas of Copernicus revolutionized the ideas of mankind about the universe. The earth ceased to be a disc covered by a vault so low that a child's kite could mount to it. God no longer looked down, stern but benevolent, to survey the deeds, the words and the thoughts of men. Angels no longer came and went, nor saints descended to hold familiar converse with a Joan of Arc. The earth had become infinitely small, a mere imperceptible speck lost in space. Beliefs, traditions, sentiments on which the whole of civilization was founded were shaken to the core. A vast vacancy appeared to the human mind, a vacancy shortly to be filled by a hundred new ideas.

Columbus discovers a new world and thereby opens a new field for practical and commercial enterprise. Thence flows a stream of wealth in gold and silver to sweep aside the secular contracts which had bound man to man and to falsify or destroy all established relationships.

III

BANKERS AND SPECULATORS

THE discovery of America by Columbus and the subsequent opening of the Cape route to the East Indies by Vasco da Gama in 1497 effected a revolution in economic and social conditions. The influx of gold and silver from the New World, combined with the increasing facility of exchange between different countries, imposed new conditions on international commerce.

In the reign of Louis XII, Claude de Scyssel, bishop of Marseilles and later archbishop of Turin, could write, " It is now less difficult to go to Rome, Naples, London or elsewhere abroad than it used to be to travel from Lyons to Grenoble."

The stories of the conquistadores, of distant lands beneath unknown stars, stirred imaginations to the depths. Treasure was there for the taking ; strange plants and animals ; parrots red and green ; buffaloes maned like lions. If we think of the excitement caused, even in the reign of Louis XV, by the foundation of the French East India Company, we can form an idea of what went on in the minds of the men of the sixteenth century after the voyages of Columbus. Did he not maintain that he had rediscovered Paradise ? Soon Portuguese, French and English vied with Spain in fitting out expeditions to take the seas for the new Indies. In 1501 Cabral's caravels were cast on the unknown shores of Brazil, and another country was opened up to European activity.

The flow of gold from the New World entailed devaluation and therefore a rise in prices. It was an inflation in which money retained its normal form of good, sound coin, and yet was not unlike the present inflation caused by the wholesale use of the printing-press necessitated by the war. The phenomena of inflation and price-raising first appeared in Spain, whose ports received directly the shipments of treasure from the New World. Spain was short of men as a result of incessant wars and distant expeditions, and supplied this shortage by importing highly-paid French workers. The Venetian Ambassador of the day wrote, " The Spaniard can only live through France. Hence he must import corn, textiles, paper, books, even to carpenter's work, and must himself travel to the ends of the earth for gold to pay for them."

From 1533 onwards, the fall in the value of money took on the proportions of a landslide. The economist Bodin remarks that in the following years more than one hundred millions in gold and two hundred millions in silver were imported into France ; a colossal sum for the finances of those days. After 1545, when the mines of Potosi were opened, the downward movement became a catastrophe.

This economic disturbance was to throw the whole social mechanism out of gear.

A multiplicity of contracts, for the most part centuries old, bound the landowning classes, lay or clerical, to their tenants. After the English wars they became even more numerous. Rents were immutably fixed, but the medium in which they were paid had lost three-quarters or four-fifths of its value. The peasant farmers were the gainers and the landlords proportionately losers. Thus, both lay and clerical lords, whose incomes were derived from rents or feudal dues, were wounded in their most vulnerable spot.

The minor nobility of Germany fell so low as to be reckoned hardly better than the common people.

Charitable foundations—" works of piety " as they used to be called—were ruined, almshouses and hospitals closed, landed estates were put up to auction, and the patrimony of illustrious houses passed into the hands of the middle class. Patricians and merchants by the hundred thus bought their way into the nobility. On the other hand, the sudden circulation of money, which had long lain idle, raised the spectre of pauperism. From the reign of Henry VIII dates the harsh legislation against sturdy beggars.

The final effect of this glut of money and the rapidity with which it circulated was to alter the whole aspect of international trade and thus to produce what is known as " capitalism " in banking and commerce.

Trade increased : the flow of gold continued and produced instability in the exchange system : new sea routes were opened and the number of ships using them was multiplied. New sources of ore were tapped, new industries were founded, and those which, like printing, had been a restricted " luxury " trade, expanded rapidly. Human relationships were profoundly changed and money, with its reactions and its profits, became an ever greater factor in both economic and social life. Soon there appeared for the first time the typical figures of modern life, the great financiers. Their interests and their activities recognized no frontiers ; their realm was international. We find German bankers established in Lyons, on French soil, but close to Switzerland and Italy, and midway on the road to Castile and Aragon.

Lyons was the capital of the printing world. Its first press was founded in 1473 and was followed by some fifty others in the last quarter of the fifteenth century. By the time of Henri II it possessed hundreds of printers and booksellers.

Moreover, printing by this time was not only a vehicle for the circulation of ideas, but could be used also to spread stock and share quotations, commodity prices and rates of exchange.

Certain of the German financiers of Lyons assumed French nationality, among them the notorious Kléberger, who was later to become a legendary figure as " the worthy German ". He became the faithful, though far from disinterested servant of Francis I, who ennobled him and hall-marked his " fire-new nobility " with a place as gentleman of the bedchamber —a rank to which every true-born nobleman aspired.

Other Germans settled in Antwerp, a town also famous for its printing, and there served Charles V in like capacities and with like rewards. It is obvious how the extent and diversity of Charles V's empire tended to forward the progress of international finance. Spain must be kept in touch with Austria, Flanders with Naples. In that age of unceasing warfare, it was unsafe and often dangerous to send large sums in cash from Antwerp, say, to Milan. A Flemish banker could solve the problem with a bill of exchange drawn on an Italian colleague. The armies in the field in Germany, in Flanders or in Italy must be paid, and the civil service in Spain. The Cardinal of Sion, in Rome, awaited 30,000 ducats from England. The only channel that offered was a representative of the powerful Strozzi family who happened to be in London. Even this risk was held too great, and Henry VIII finally settled the account by means of what we should call a cheque drawn on a banker of Rome. This was in 1516.

Many diverse and distant places had their fairs, among them Lyons, Leipzig, Antwerp, the well-known fairs of Champagne, even distant Nijni Novgorod in Russia. Financiers speculated in goods for them, which they paid by bills.

Exchange rates, in the absence of modern means of communication, varied from country to country to a marked degree, but the great banking houses had channels of information as rapid as the resources of the time permitted. Here we have the germ of the modern newspaper, a simple bulletin of financial and commercial news. These bulletins were withheld from all but the initiated, and thus financiers could buy and sell under the most favourable conditions goods which differed in price in different parts of Europe. A banker in Lyons, for example, might learn that silk, costing so and so much there, fetched a much higher price in Frankfurt or in Milan. He therefore buys in Lyons and sells again in Milan.

By a gradual process of evolution the financiers ceased to deal in commodities and restricted their activities to the mere buying and selling of credits from one country to another. It was an epoch of building, of pomp and luxury. Credits therefore abounded. A Genoese merchant has a credit, of long or short term, drawn on a patrician of Florence. For one reason or another, he wishes to realize quickly. A Genoese banker discounts it for him and receives his just but not inconsiderable profit when it falls due. The larger firms, who never lacked for ready cash, were thus able to make large profits in a short time.

The Church of the Middle Ages had anathematized the " hateful power " of money : it was still, at least to a Spanish preacher of the time, a hateful power, but none the less a power which steadily increased.

There was further development. By methods well known to-day, profits were hastened and increased by an artificially produced scarcity of given commodities in given places. The price of the commodity rose and accumulated stocks were sold at the higher rate. Already we glimpse the " freebooters of commerce" who are such familiar figures of contemporary life. In the sixteenth century we have Gaspare Dolci as an example.

Certain financiers now began to see that dealing in commodities only hampered their operations, and dealt exclusively in money. At once the scene becomes completely modern : we have speculation, Stock Exchange flutters, bulls and bears, sudden fortunes and equally sudden failures, in short, all the phenomena of modern finance.

Ambrose Hochstädter, an Augsburg banker, was in the recklessness of his ideas the true precursor of the financier of the nineteenth and twentieth centuries. The financier needed a constant reserve of ready money for use on the one hand in loans to nobles and kings, to the Emperor and the Free Cities, and on the other hand for his speculations in commodities and his attempts at " corners ". Hochstädter had the brilliant idea of appealing for funds to the man in the street, the ultimate source of all wealth. He therefore drew on the savings of the public, on which he paid five per cent, and which he used in his colossal speculations. Noble and simple, prince and peasant alike flocked to him, the great noble and the artisan, the prosperous merchant and the cheap-jack from the fair. In his coffers mingled the contents of the miser's iron-bound chest and the peasant's woollen stocking. In a single year he was known to pay out a million florins. It is an amazing thought that, even in the sixteenth century, one banker could pay £2,000,000 in interest to his depositors.

With the ready cash thus placed at his disposal, Hochstädter specialized in " corners " and became a monopolist of wood, corn, wine, copper, and especially of mercury. The Americans would have dubbed him the " Mercury King ". Mercury, it should be explained, had attained an

exaggerated value on account of its use in the treatment of
precious metals. In his mercury dealings, however, he found
powerful competitors in the Augsburg family of Fugger.
He failed, and thus brought about the first credit crisis in
financial history.

He had his imitators in France, in the entourage of Henri II,
but the best example of a financier of the economic revolution
is found in Augsburg. The house of Fugger was native to
the village of Graben, near Augsburg. The line begins with
Jacob, a farmer and weaver and later a cloth-dealer, whose
sons, Ulrich and Johann, migrated to Augsburg about the
end of the fourteenth century. Augsburg was then the centre
of the textile trade, and was particularly famous for a coarse
cloth of wool, hemp and flax. The two brothers imported
Levantine cotton via Venice, and added dyeing to weaving.
Johann Fugger became a citizen of Augsburg by his marriage
with a city girl, by whom he had two sons, Andreas and
Jacob. The elder, Andreas, so far advanced the industry
founded by his father as to be called by his fellow-citizens
" the rich Fugger ". His son obtained the first grant of arms
made to the family : azure, a hind or ; but that branch died
out in 1483, while his younger brother Jacob, the Master
of the Weavers' Guild, founded another, the " Lily " Fuggers,
which still survives.

This Jacob Fugger had seven sons, including Ulrich, Georg
and Jacob II, who between them raised the house to great
heights of prosperity. Ulrich was the first to engage in international finance. His factors were to be found not only in
Venice, in the famous " Fondaco dei Tedeschi ", but also in
Antwerp and Lisbon ; his business extended from the Spanish
and Portuguese coasts to the shores of the Baltic in the north
and the bay of Naples in the south. He was also the first of
his family to interest himself in the arts, though from a purely

commercial standpoint, by exporting to Italy the paintings and engravings of Albrecht Dürer.

Jacob Fugger II had taken orders and was peacefully engaged in theological study in the college of Herrieden, in the diocese of Eichstädt, when, four of his brothers having died, Ulrich recalled him to the turmoil of a business life, from which he had taken refuge in cloistered seclusion.

It was this Jacob under whom the house reached the zenith of its power and prosperity. Under his régime the trade in wool, silk and spices, on which was founded its first prosperity, was banished to the background, while its place was taken by mining enterprises (and in especial the working of the mines of Schwaz in Tyrol), and by purely financial speculations. The mines of Schwaz alone brought him a fortune, part of which he expended on the Fuggerau, a splendid mansion in the neighbourhood, in which his successors lived in royal style.

Jacob Fugger was one of the first Germans to make use of the new route to the East Indies discovered by Vasco da Gama. In 1505, in partnership with two other merchant bankers, the above-mentioned Hochstädter of Augsburg and Welser of Nuremberg, he imported direct into Germany three cargoes of Indian goods, which till then had only been obtainable by way of Venice and the old caravan route. In 1509 he made his famous loan of 170,000 ducats to the Emperor Maximilian for the Italian campaign. Both he and his brother had been ennobled by the Emperor in 1504, from which year date the lilied arms which gave his branch of the family their nickname. Maximilian and Pope Leo X both made Jacob an Aulic Councillor, to which title the Pope added that of count. Fugger's Bank was the collecting point of and source of interest in the money raised in Germany by the traffic in Indulgences. Finally, in 1519, when Charles V was a candidate for the Imperial dignity, Jacob Fugger advanced him the 310,000 florins which paved the way for his triumph over the rival candidate Francis I of France. As security for this immense loan, Charles had pledged the whole city of Antwerp and, in further recompense, had enriched the house of Fugger by the addition to its patrimony of the lordships of Kirchberg and Weissenhorn, Wullenstein, Pfaffenhoven and others.

Luther tells the following story :

The Cardinal Bishop of Brixen died, as it was thought, very rich. No money was found among his possessions, but a slip of paper was discovered in the sleeve of his habit, a credit note for 300,000 florins from the Fugger bank. The Pope summoned the bank's agent in Rome.

"Are you able to pay this amount ? "

"To-day."

A short time afterwards, Julius II asked the English and French ambassadors : " Could your rulers produce three tons of gold at an hour's notice ? "

" Certainly not, Holy Father."

" But a mere merchant of Augsburg would make no bones about it."

It was Jacob who built the famous palace at Augsburg, the Fuggerhaus, which was gorgeously decorated in fresco by Albrecht Altdorfer. He built, too, the choir of St. Anne's Church and founded the " City of the poor ", a group of some hundred houses where poor families are housed at nominal rents, still known as the " Fuggerei ".

He died in 1525, leaving no sons, and made his nephews, Raimund and Anton, his heirs. A contemporary chronicler writes of them : " The names of Jacob Fugger and his nephews are known in every land, even in those of the infidels. Emperors and Princes sent embassies to Jacob, the

Pope embraced him as a dear son, Cardinals stood in his presence."

The two brothers Raimund and Anton lived together in the Fugger mansion in the Wine-Market in Augsburg. They were typical representatives of the Renaissance. Raimund, the elder, was a fine figure of a man, jovial, sound in body and mind, very good-natured and good-hearted, specially toward the poor. He was a patron of letters, particularly of historic study, and a generous benefactor to the Arts. A true son of the Renaissance, he collected specimens of classical art which he imported at great cost from Greece, Italy and Sicily. According to Beatus Rhenanus, he spared no expense in this respect. Rhenanus, in a letter of March 6th, 1531, describes enthusiastically to the surgeon of the Archbishop of Mainz the mansion of Raimund Fugger and its surrounding gardens. Everything was magnificent but in perfect taste. There was even a menagerie of exotic beasts brought by explorers from distant lands.

The two brothers were created by Charles V Counts of the Empire, with rights of the high justice, the middle and the low. This seldom-granted privilege is dated March 1st, 1530, and in 1534 they attained the royal prerogative of coining their own money.

The House of Fugger, like some noble families of France, had its own private constitution. It was divided into junior and senior branches, and, by its own special rules, provided for the transmission of its patrimony and its commercial monopoly from eldest son to eldest son in a way that ensured the continuance of the family power till the nineteenth century.

A few generations had sufficed to raise the Fuggers from humble weavers to the rank of feudal lords, and many a prince of their day had neither their power nor their authority.

Even Charles V, on whose realm the sun never set, was compelled to rely implicitly on their devotion. Rabelais, in a letter dated 1536, calls the Fuggers " the richest merchants in Christendom ". The previous year they had made large advances to Charles V for the Algiers expedition, and when on his return Charles passed through Augsburg, Anton, to warm the royal guest, lighted a fire of cinnamon wood—cinnamon then being enormously expensive—at which he proceeded to burn the Emperor's notes of hand for the sum he had borrowed. Later, when Charles was at Paris, and was visiting the royal treasury with his host, Francis I, he told him he had in Augsburg a merchant who would give him a good price, in cash down, for all the crown jewels of France.

When Anton died he left two sons, Ulrich and Johann Jacob, both of whom carried on the family tradition of patronage of arts and letters. The Fuggers did for Augsburg precisely what the Medici were doing at the same time for Florence ; they made it one of the great art centres of Europe. Ulrich, like his great-uncle, was to have entered the Church, and became chamberlain to Paul III, but on his return to Germany he embraced the Reformed faith. He was a distinguished humanist and commissioned from Henri Estienne editions of the works of various Greek authors, and particularly of Xenophon. He assembled, at great expense, a marvellous library containing many rare Greek, Latin and Hebrew manuscripts. He also developed a taste for contemporary art, but at this point his brothers, on the ground that his liberality to men of letters and artists was dilapidating the family fortunes, took steps to have a trustee appointed for him. Their real motive in this was their fear, as zealous Catholics, that he might use his money in support of doctrines which to them were heretical. Feeling himself injured,

Ulrich fled from Augsburg and took refuge with the Elector Palatine Frederick III. The persecution to which he was subjected greatly changed his character, and he became melancholy and misanthropic. He later regained control of his fortune, as is shown by his will, in which provision was made for a fund to provide subsidies for six poor students. His library he left to the University of Heidelberg. He died in 1584, aged 58.

The Fuggers remained for some generations financiers and patrons of the arts, and afterwards produced governors of Augsburg and several famous soldiers. Count Anselm-Maria Fugger, the head of the family at the beginning of the nineteenth century, was created by the Emperor Francis II a Prince of the Empire.

The Fuggers of Augsburg were not unique in their generation. They may be taken as typical of their time and class. They had associates, the Bohemian Thurzos, for example, a family of Levatscha, who remained faithful to their native town and made of it a centre of Italian influence in art. They collected omnivorously : their buildings were Italian and their furniture Venetian, but they also possessed Burgundian triptychs and Flemish altar-pieces. The Welser of Nuremberg were a similar clan.

In France we have the famous Jean Ango, the shipowner of Dieppe. His fortune never equalled that which the Fuggers used to such artistic effect in Augsburg, but that he must have been passably rich is proved by the fact that in 1530, in revenge for the plundering of one of his ships by the Portuguese, he fitted out his own armed fleet and sent eight hundred men to blockade Lisbon and raid the Portuguese coast. He even attacked the Portuguese in the Indian Ocean. Finally, the King of Portugal was compelled to treat with him on an equal footing, and sent him a formal embassy.

Francis I made him captain and governor of Dieppe, where he went to live and built a splendid mansion, the Manoir d'Ango, at Varangeville, close by, adorning it with French sculpture and Italian paintings. Even in towns of small importance, such as Tournon and Annonay in the Ardèche, there were men of the same stamp, though naturally of more limited scope.

In Italy, we have the great banking establishment founded in Siena, in the fourteenth century, by Mariano de Agostino Chigi, whose son Agostino was the most important banker in Italy at the beginning of the fifteenth. He employed twenty thousand men in his branches at Lyons, Antwerp, London, Constantinople, and even in distant Alexandria and Cairo. Like Jacob Fugger, he made loans to sovereign states. The Chigi bank advanced money to Charles VIII of France, and Pope Julius II was so much in its debt that he authorized Agostino Chigi to add to his own name the papal family name of della Rovere, and went so far as to excommunicate people in financial trouble with the bank.

Agostino Chigi, like the Fugger and the Medici, was a great patron of the arts. Rafael and Giulio Romano did work for his villa, which later became the Farnese. He commissioned from Rafael the drawings for the mosaics he presented to Santa Maria del Popolo in Rome.

Rome possessed another fabulously rich banker in the person of the young Bindo Altoviti, also a collector of art and antiques. He maintained at his own cost a troop of three thousand men-at-arms, whom he lent to Cosimo dei Medici for the Pisan war. He was a personal friend of Michael Angelo ; Cellini made a bust of him ; Rafael painted his portrait and also painted for him the famous Madonna della Impannata now in the Pitti palace.

Florence, too, had its galaxy of art-loving merchants and

bankers, the Pazzi, Strozzi, and Peruzzi among them. "The development of this centre of patronage," says Regné, "was a powerful aid to the flowering of the Renaissance."

But there was another side to all this.

The Renaissance made money, and money, in its paper form as bills of exchange, bonds and credits, the undisputed ruler of the world. The whole framework of society as regards the distinctions between classes was profoundly modified. In this dazzling period of prosperity are already found the seeds of future revolutions. Man is hurried irresistibly onward by the march of events to an unknown destination. The people with whom we have been dealing may fairly be described as the "new rich". But their rise produced a class of "new poor", who were not in the least inclined to suffer in silence. To it belonged nobles and squires who had been ruined by the processes we have explained above, and who were thoroughly exasperated by the great physical and intellectual changes in which they had unwillingly shared. "The intellectual and economic Renaissance, springing from a too sudden dislocation of existing institutions and a ' general post' of society, was only the prelude to the political and religious crisis of the century of St. Bartholomew."

IV

THE MEDICI

THE Medici of Florence might have served for examples to the Fuggers of Augsburg. The Medici never had the capital resources of their German colleagues, but their fame in the realm of arts and letters stands infinitely higher. It is to be noted, however, that in Italy there was no central authority analogous to that of the Holy Roman Emperor in Germany, so that the Medici and their like in the various Italian cities could aspire to play a part in their own governments which was beyond the reach of the Fuggers.

The original home of the Medici family was Mugello, to the north of Florence. They were country-folk who sold their farm and migrated to the city to start in business with the proceeds. In the thirteenth century they ranked as fairly well-to-do citizens of Florence. Later, when their influence in Florence was all-powerful, a more fitting pedigree was unearthed for them. Their arms, the six rondels gules on a field or, were said to have been granted by Charlemagne to one of his paladins who vanquished the giant Mugello in single combat. Others, however, maintain that the six red balls are simply pills, in memory of the ancestral apothecary shop. One thing is certain, that the balls themselves—in Italian *palle*—gave their name to the Medici party, the " Palleschi ", when the family became leaders of the popular party—also known as " Guelphs " or " Popolosi "—in its century-long struggle against the " Ghibellines " or " Grandi ".

Towards the end of the thirteenth century there appears in Florence a certain Ardigo dei Medici as " Prior of the Arts " or leader of the guilds. In 1314 he became gonfalonier of the city. The popular party triumphed under his banner, and Dante, a Ghibelline, was exiled to spend the weary years in the production of his immortal epic.

Again in the fourteenth century the family tradition is carried on by Silvestro dei Medici, leader of a party called the " ciompi " (barefooted), chiefly wool-carders (wool being the staple industry of Florence), and again the popular party gains the power in the little republic on the Arno.

At the beginning of the fifteenth century the Medici were still of the same party, but were now infinitely richer. They were now financiers and bankers, rivalling the Fuggers themselves. Giovanni dei Medici, father of Cosimo the elder, was treasurer to John XXII, who made him his executor. In the first half of the fifteenth century the Medici bank paid 428 florins in taxes, while its nearest competitor paid only 44. About this time the banker turned politician, and rapidly organized his own party.

It was Cosimo, known as the Elder to distinguish him from his great-nephew the first Duke of Tuscany, who brought the fortunes of the Medici to their highest pitch. He was certainly one of the most striking figures in all history. Without any definite title, and solely by virtue of his personal authority, he was for thirty years as undisputed a master of Florence as were Pisistratus and Pericles in the cities of ancient Greece. Furthermore, the state of Florence was not merely the city and its immediate surroundings ; its power extended over the greater part of Tuscany, even including its ancient rival Pisa, which had at last fallen under the Florentine yoke. In the city, Cosimo was known merely as " the great merchant ", but at his death he was given the official title of " Father of his Country ". A contemporary wrote of him that without him Florence was nothing. He was Florence.

Æneas Sylvius Piccolomini, who afterwards became Pope as Pius II and was well known as an author and a classical scholar, wrote to him : " Thou art the arbiter of peace, of war, and of justice. Of royalty thou lackest nothing but the name."

Cosimo's portrait by Benozzo Gozzoli shows him wearing the long black robe and scribe's bonnet ; he might well be one of the clerks of the Uffizi. Gozzoli painted him twice in this garb, once, in 1460, in his marvellous " Visitation of the Magi ", now in the Riccardi chapel in Florence, and again, fifteen years later, in his celebrated frescoes in the Campo Santo of Pisa.

He was painted as Saint Cosmo, on the right hand of the Virgin, and by Botticelli in his " Adoration of the Magi ", where he depicts the heads of the Medici family, surrounded by their friends and retainers, at the feet of the Divine Child. Finally, there is another portrait of him, this time by Bronzino, in the Uffizi.

Botticelli gives us the likeness of Cosimo as a little old man, so bent as to seem hunchbacked, with clean-shaven, deeply wrinkled face. His nose is disproportionately large, but the features are clean-cut, and the complexion is of that olive tint inherited by his grandson Lorenzo " il Magnifico ".

His bearing and expression in slyness and false affability are strongly reminiscent of Louis XI of France. Both were of the same bourgeois cast. Cosimo's frail body owed its stoop, perhaps, to long hours spent crouching over his ledgers and peering at their spindly commercial script. He had neither beauty nor distinction ; in society he was grave and taciturn, speaking chiefly in monosyllables, accompanied by a nod, or in short pithy phrases, but sometimes breaking out into totally incomprehensible speech. Vespasiano says of him that he could read people from their faces alone. In public, he was no orator, but a skilful conversationalist, full of logical subtlety and unforeseen twists of speech, with often a spark of malice or some broad and popular witticism. He had the art of convincing without reasoned argument. In private life he was serious, taking no pleasure in play-actors or buffoons, but his delight was in chess and in his vineyard and garden. He was no warrior, and in time of need relied on the sword of Francesco Sforza, the gonfalonier of the Church. His greatest assets were his subtlety, his indefatigable patience, and his imperturbable cunning. He was as skilful a politician as he was a banker, and the fortune he amassed from banking he used for the furtherance of his political ambitions.

Cosimo's father, as leader of the popular party known as the Whites, had had a bitter struggle with the Florentine patriciate, at the head of which stood the great Albizzi family. He himself was arrested, released on the demand of Venice, and exiled, to be recalled in 1434 when an election brought his party back to power. On January 1st, 1435, he became chief of the state. He was never to lose his grasp on the power he attained on that day. He was forty-six years old, more able than scrupulous, full of common sense and experienced in business. His administration of his own private fortune was exemplary, and raised his house to heights unknown before, but always in the most practical way. He thus admonished Luca Pitti, whose ambitions he held to be too venturesome :

"You chase the infinite, I hold to the finite. You seek to prop your ladders against the sky, I see that mine are firmly set on the earth with no risk of falling."

Like the Fuggers, he extended his trading as far as the Far East, opening branches everywhere, from Bruges to Cairo. Like the Fuggers, too, he made advances to kings and princes. The Pope was forced to pledge to him, for money lent, one of his strongholds, the town of Assisi.

The King of Naples allied himself with the Venetians against Cosimo, but the banker did not even trouble to engage condottieri; he simply closed down his credit business and Neapolitans and Venetians were driven to surrender.

"What I should like," he once said, "would be to have God the Father, God the Son, and God the Holy Ghost all on my books as debtors."

He governed Florence largely by the power of public opinion. His power was a symbol of the popular reaction against the patriciate, and entailed the settlement of long overdue scores by his supporters, whose goodwill was a constant source of strength to him in his task of attaining stability in government and politics, after so many years of disorder and barren agitation had brought the State to the verge of ruin.

Cosimo tolerated not the faintest trace of opposition. He exiled a dozen of the noblest families of Florence. All public offices fell to his supporters, and he imposed a further check on the Ghibellines by his influence on the decisions of the Courts. His party numbered various officers whose duty it was to spy out treason and mark suspected persons : the shadow of Italian fascism in the dawn of the Renaissance.

In addition to these precautions, Cosimo took particular care to see that the interests of his fellow-citizens were inextricably entangled and involved with his own, so that Florentine commerce should have reason to pray for the success of the Medici, as for its own. "Cosimo," says Guicciardini, "followed only his own interests," but, as another historian observes, " His skill lies in his identification of his own with the public welfare."

Though rich and powerful, he still kept to a modest style of living. The all-powerful leader of Florence might be seen any day hurrying through the streets like the most modest citizen, and dallying in the shop of some small trader who is recounting to him his domestic worries. His will was felt everywhere, in great things as in small, in general policy and minor every-day details, but he himself never appeared. Without the trappings of authority, he was an omnipotent tyrant. He was liberal without generosity and conciliatory without ever yielding an inch which he desired to retain ; magnanimous to his friends but pitiless to his enemies, whom he never pardoned, utterly vanquished though they might be. When an enemy's period of exile drew to its close, Cosimo had it extended. The aged Palla Strozzi, respected by all his fellow-citizens, remained thirty years in exile and was not even permitted to return to die among his household gods. If any exile dared to seek foreign support for his attempts to return, Cosimo had his citizenship revoked and his property confiscated. He cared not a fig for those who spoke of toleration and of liberty. " Yes, yes," he would say ; " that is all very well—in principle—but men are not led by paternosters." And in pursuit of these aims, many a high and mighty personage, many a good old man and nobly-born woman lost rank and fortune and was reduced to beggary.

He went further. He desired the utter destruction of every family which opposed him, and, fearing that they might gain new resources by marriage, he forbade their daughters to wed. In his hands taxation became a merciless weapon. All taxes were levied according to his desires, and he used them like an axe to strike down any fortune which seemed likely to render its possessor independent, always " for the

good of the lower classes, for the good of the people ".
Many families, to escape this vindictive taxation, emigrated
to the surrounding country, but even there it found them
out and they were punished with "rustication", which
confined them rigorously to their own country-houses.

Cosimo invented even stronger measures to cope with
any default in the payment of the taxes he levied. Twice a
year his police paraded the country-side and seized the contents of certain houses, carrying away all food and ravaging
the standing crops. But nothing that was thus taken or destroyed could be deducted from the amount due to the treasury ; all was regarded simply as a fine for non-payment.

These facts display only the bad side of his administration.
It had, however, a good one. Burckhardt, in his *History of
the Renaissance*, writes :

That man is a true prince who, like Cosimo dei Medici, ranks
as head of a city, though but a simple merchant. He is indeed
a prince when he has on his side writers, thinkers, men of action,
when he is, by right of family, the first among the Florentines,
but when he shows himself, in his taste for art and letters, the
foremost man in Italy, he deserves tenfold the princely title.

Cosimo's lasting title to fame rests on the fact that he
recognized that the thought of Plato was the supreme expression of the soul of antiquity, and that he succeeded in
filling those around him with its spirit. He it was who opened
the way for a second and fairer Renaissance by turning to
Greek studies the earlier one, which in Italy had been confined to the study of Roman literature and antiques. Florence
was to be the centre from which Greek culture spread throughout Italy.

Cosimo welcomed the exiled scholars whom the Turks
had driven from their homes, men like John Lascaris and
Cardinal Bessarion. What is surprising is that Cosimo, who

brought about this scientific and literary revolution, was himself an unlearned man. He sought out everywhere manuscripts of classical authors, and on the death of the scholar Niccolo Niccoli, who had ruined himself by his prodigal expenditure on manuscripts, he paid off his creditors and thus acquired his treasures, which he deposited in his own foundation, the famous convent of San Marco. The public, learned or unlearned, were freely admitted to consult documents and manuscripts in what is now the Marcian Library. Nevertheless, Cosimo, like a good man of business, never hesitated to seize a chance of dealing in the precious manuscripts that came into his hands, at least if he saw his way to a large profit.

Himself all-powerful, Cosimo played the humble disciple to his reverend teachers : he was a modest and attentive scholar in their school. He attended Plétho's courses and read and re-read Bessarion. He sought the solitude of the cloister to drink in the learned teaching of Traversari and humbly sought, in a poor cell in San Marco, the recondite conversation of St. Antonine, later Archbishop of Florence. In this convent he devoted much time to pious meditation, in a humble retreat, adorned, at his command, with one of the finest of Angelico's frescoes.

Marsilio Ficino, the great humanist and translator of the *Phædo*, was proud to call himself the intellectual son of Cosimo. The task he had set himself was to reconcile Platonism with Christianity, a task in which he preceded Rafael, who set the " School of Athens " beside the " Triumph of the Sacrament " in his frescoes in the Vatican.

It was Cosimo's wish that Renaissance Platonism, like its great forbear, should have its gardens of Academe, where the loftiest ranges of human thought could be explored in the shade of pine and cypress, in bowers of lilies and roses.

His finest villas and most verdant gardens were thrown open to the new academy, whose chief was Ficino and whose influence on contemporary thought was immeasurably great. This academy, by its opposition to scholastic philosophy, was to hurl Aristotle from the throne on which the Middle Ages had placed him, and to crown Plato in his stead.

Only yesterday, [wrote Cosimo to Marsilio Ficino] did I arrive at my villa of Careggi, moved less by the wish to improve my lands than to improve myself. Come to see me, Marsilio, and do not forget the book of your divine Plato on the sovereign good. No effort would be too great for me in the search after true happiness. Come, and bring with you Orpheus' lyre.

Italy owed to Cosimo not only the revival of Greek studies, but also the first flights of its native Tuscan dialect, and Florence owed to him the moral and material encouragement which made its University prosperous.

Cosimo the Elder adorned Florence with fine architecture, villas and palaces, loggias and gardens, the church and cloister of San Lorenzo, the convents of San Marco and Sta. Verdiana, the Via Larga. In the Florentine country-side the slopes of the rounded hills which border the Arno were the site of many elegant buildings. Cosimo had a passion for building, which he indulged not only in Florence but in Rome, and as far afield as Paris, where he restored the Florentine College, and at Jerusalem. When one of his stewards, horrified at his prodigality, pointed out to him that 7,000 florins had been spent on the abbey of Fiesole and 5,000 on the church of St. Mark, he only said, " You were right to warn me. I see that they are idling at San Marco, but working well at Fiesole."

The greatest architects of the time designed and supervised the buildings he had erected, among them Michelozzo and Brunelleschi, who was responsible for the beautiful dome of Sta. Maria del Fiore. Niccolo Valori states that Cosimo dei

Medici spent on this building half a million florins, roughly a million pounds in our money.

"The father of his country" thought the money well spent, and toward the end of his life regretted that he had not built more. "I know my fellow-citizens," he said. "In fifty years they will only remember me by the few poor buildings I leave them."

Cosimo set Brunelleschi and Michelozzo the task of preparing competing designs for his own palace in Florence. Although Brunelleschi's reputation stood higher, Michelozzo gained the palm, for Cosimo admired the severe beauty of his simple design. The building still exists as the Palazzo Riccardi. He had commissioned from his architect a dwelling which was to place comfort before mere show, but contemporaries agree in lauding the magnificence of this, for the age, unparalleled residence. Pius II calls it a house fit for a king, and writers celebrated it in both verse and prose. One of the rooms was decorated with frescoes by Paolo Uccello. "It was a wonderful room full of fairy-like birds in full flight and lions in combat. One lion," says Vasari, "fought with a serpent whose eyes and jaws dripped black venom." The very courtyard was a museum. The Riccardi of the seventeenth century were only carrying on the tradition of their predecessors when they adorned it with ancient works of art. There were to be seen the eight marble medallions of Donatello, linked by festoons in black and white, which have just been rediscovered under a thick coat of whitewash.

Cosimo likewise employed the Della Robbia. His sculptor in ordinary, Donatello, ranked next to Michael Angelo as the greatest of modern times, and it was under his dispensation that Ghiberti cast those gates of the baptistry of Our Lady of the Flower which Michael Angelo declared worthy to be the gates of Paradise. His painters were Andrea Castagno,

Fra Angelico, Benozzo Gozzoli, Paolo Uccello, Botticelli, Baldovinetti, Ghirlandaio, and Lippo Lippi.

Lippi was a Dominican monk. In 1456, when he was thirty, he was working on the decoration of the monastery of Santa Margarita in Florence. His frescoes, however, were violently interrupted by his sudden elopement with a young nun, Lucrezia Buti, who was sitting to him as a model for the Virgin. The mildest punishment he could expect for this crime was to drag out his life on the bread of sorrow and water of affliction in some papal dungeon, but " the father of his country " intervened in his favour with Pius II, who, at his request, absolved the pair from their vows and married them, to their complete satisfaction. From this union sprang another artist hardly less famous than his father, Filippino Lippi.

Cosimo treated handsomely the writers and artists whom he admired, paying them largely and at the same time giving ample proofs of delicacy of feeling in his simple intercourse with them. He was the first in the State and unrivalled in fortune as in prestige, but he was sincere in his treatment of artists, poets and scholars of renown as his equals. His anger and his implacable malice were disarmed by the sight of a talented author.

The learned poet Filelfo attacked him bitterly with both sword and pen, but Cosimo permitted him to return to Florence, there to live out his life in peace in pursuit of his studies and his commentaries on the *Divina Commedia* of Dante. This familiarity was the most charming feature of the relations of the Medici with their artists.

The great banker was greatly given to charity and assisted all poor citizens who did not happen to belong to the opposition, which they rarely did, since his own party was that of the poor, and it was his constant care to see that their civil rights did not lapse through mere destitution. He lavished splendid entertainments on the people, but if any patrician should be suspected of any attempt against his power, he was hanged by the heels from the façade of the Signoria, a punishment which was to become traditional in the Medici family. After this fashion were executed first the Ghibelline leaders Rinaldo and Ormanno Albizzi, and later Ludovico dei Rossi, Stefano Peruzzi and many others. Nor did their punishment end with their death, for they were painted in life-size as they appeared in death on the very spot that had seen their ends, the front of the Podesta's palace. These grim portraits were at least painted by a master's hand, that of Andrea del Castagno, for which reason his name underwent a gruesome change. His original name, translated, means Andrew of the Chestnut-tree, but he was soon generally known as " Andrea degli Impicati "—Andrew of the Hanged.

When Cosimo was reproached with depopulating Florence he replied, " I had sooner depopulate than lose it." He was not content with hanging and painting those whom he disliked ; he employed poets to libel them. It was a custom of the time, and Pietro Aretino made a fortune by it.

The sage and thoughtful Commines, in face of all this, could yet appreciate the government of Florence in these words :

" Authority wielded in gentleness, well suited to a free city."

The last years of the great tyrant were gloomy. He suffered terribly from gout and a disease of the stomach. He grows visibly thinner, from the frescoes of Gozzoli to the Botticelli portrait. At last he was reduced to giving audiences in bed or else in the room of his son Pietro, who was likewise bed-ridden. This son, Pietro the Gouty, was all his life a wretched invalid, but his room was the meeting-place of the Florentine Signoria, or, as we should say, the Cabinet.

Cosimo first lost his brother, Lorenzo, and then his younger son Giovanni, who was the hope of the family, seeing that Pietro was incapacitated by his gout. This second loss was a great blow to the old man, but his character was unshaken by it. A certain Nicodemo, one of his intimates, writes to Giovanni Sforza on November 4th, 1463 :

He is never seen to shed a tear, his voice does not tremble, and he never utters a word unworthy of a saint and a philosopher. He consoled those who sought to console him, saying : " Only two kinds of men need consolation, those who have no memory and those who have displeased the Lord."

On the first of August 1464 died this great one of the earth in the loneliness which is the usual penalty of greatness. His people feared that his illness was infectious, and though in life he had showered gifts and favours on his intimates, their memory faded like a mist in spring.

A little before his death he had asked that he might be buried simply, without unnecessary pomp.

His son, Pietro the Gouty, though devoid alike of mental and physical health, was recognized without much opposition as his heir. He continued both the policy and the task of his father. The same patronage was extended to scholars, painters and sculptors, but on a meaner scale. Pietro used his bad health as a pretext for not going to inspect the finished works of art he had ordered, so that he might delay payment for them. None the less, he had in his turn his Academy in the gardens of the Villa Careggi. It was in his reign that Louis XI, as a mark of signal favour, granted to the Medici the right to quarter with their own arms the lilies of France.

Pietro the Gouty dragged on a feeble existence for five years after the death of his father, and then died, leaving two sons, Lorenzo and Giuliano.

Lorenzo, the elder, was then twenty-one, and Giuliano sixteen. Two days after their father's death, a great multitude of Florentines flocked to them to beg them to assume power. Lorenzo replied that he was " resigned " to doing so. Thereafter, says Macchiavelli, he spoke with such gravity as to give rise to the highest hopes for the future, hopes which were to be more than realized.

Lorenzo thoroughly deserved the title which posterity has given him, that of " the Magnificent ". He is the most complete and most brilliant type of the great tyrants of the Renaissance, who could combine the practice of government with humanism and patronage of the arts.

" Under his rule," says Guicciardini, " the city enjoyed profound peace." The Florentines had never felt so united or so strong. Necessities and luxuries alike abounded ; festival followed festival of unexampled beauty and splendour ; arts, letters and sciences found in Lorenzo an intelligent patron ; the external power of Florence rose under his wise direction to heights beyond the imaginings of the most ambitious patriot. Lorenzo succeeded in establishing an equilibrium among the states of Italy, but it was in the hands of Florence that the balance rested. Lorenzo was the focal point of the politics of his day : the Duke of Ferrara was his debtor and the King of Naples, the Pope and the Duke of Milan his declared allies.

In 1488, he married his daughter Maddalena to the son of Pope Innocent VIII, and his son Giovanni, who was later to wear the triple tiara as Leo X, received at the tender age of fourteen the promise of a cardinal's hat, which promise was duly carried out as soon as he was seventeen.

Lorenzo, according to Lebey,

was tall and strong and of very dark complexion. His disproportionately large forehead drew all attention, crowding out, as it were, the rest of his features. He had a large mouth and was short-sighted, and his twisted nose had no sense of smell. His voice was unpleasant but convincing in argument. He loved hunting, horse racing, tournaments and carnivals. He bred dogs. He was interested in philosophy and art. He was easily first in any subject which could rivet his attention. He was conscious of his own worth.

According to Ficino, " he possessed the three graces sung by Orpheus : bodily vigour, mental clarity, and delight in the power of the will ". Like his grandfather Cosimo the Elder, Lorenzo disdained a title to cover his authority. Also, like his grandfather, he dressed simply, wearing in winter a violet cloak and in summer the " lucco ", the long Florentine robe which was afterwards to become the judicial costume. His son-in-law Cibo, the Pope's son, who was used to the luxury of the Roman court, was astonished at the simple life and frugal table of his father-in-law. Lorenzo would not even permit his daughters to dress in rich fabrics.

Lorenzo, like Cosimo, went in for Platonic philosophy under the guidance of Ficino. He maintained that without Plato he could be neither a good citizen nor a good Christian. He lived in a learned society which he himself had chosen and which met in his house. Pico della Mirandola declared that he was only really happy in Lorenzo's presence.

But he was not only a patron, he was himself an artist, and designed the porch for the church of the Madonna del Fiore. It seems amazing that such a man as he should be the son of a feeble creature like Pietro the Gouty. But his strength came from the side of his mother, Lucrezia Tornabuoni, who was a striking figure possessed of a literary talent which she transmitted to her son. She was only forty-five when her eldest son assumed the reins of government, in the prime of life, and exceptionally gifted in a variety of ways. She had good taste in literature and art, and skill in household management : she could compose a hymn or turn a sonnet as well as she could draw up the family budget, oversee the kitchen or feed her pigeons. She was well worthy of a place among the lofty spirits who collected round her son.

But there was more than the mere physical resemblance shown in Bronzino's portraits between Cosimo and Lorenzo, and there was soon to be proof of it. The new government was immediately faced with a conspiracy, if such a name is not too dignified for the half-hearted efforts of Bardo Nazi, who tried to raise the people of Prato to the cry of "Long live the people" and "Long live Liberty". The good people of Florence had had enough of Ghibelline "Liberty" and stayed at home. The unfortunate agitator paid the usual penalty, and dangled edifyingly from the Signoria, with eighteen of his accomplices to keep him company. Even Guicciardini considers Lorenzo a little high-handed. "He arrogated to himself so unmeasured an authority that the city was no longer free," an authority which would only have been upset by violence.

The Albizzi were no longer leaders of the Florentine patriciate, their place being taken by the Pazzi, a family famous in the annals of the Republic, and acknowledged chiefs of the "Black" faction. One of them took an honourable part in the first crusade and was the first to plant the Christian banner on the walls of Jerusalem, whence he brought home stones from the Holy Sepulchre. In memory of his feat, the Pazzi had instituted a holiday which is still held. Last but not least, the Pazzi had suffered as bankers from Medici competition.

The Pazzi determined on the murder of the Medici brothers. Salviati, Archbishop of Pisa, whose family had been exiled by the Medici, joined the plot. Pope Sixtus IV favoured the conspirators and his eighteen-year-old nephew, Cardinal Rafael Riario, was also involved in it.

On April 26th, 1478, there was a solemn service in the church of Our Lady of the Flower. At the very moment of the elevation of the Host, to the accompaniment of clouds of incense and the tinkling of bells, a strangled cry was heard : Bernardo Bandini had fallen on Giuliano and buried a dagger in his breast. Giuliano staggered and fell. Another conspirator, Franceschino, bent over him and continued to stab him in frenzied rage till at last he wounded himself in the thigh.

Two priests threw themselves on Lorenzo where he stood in the choir, but their aim was not so good as Bandini's. He parried the first blows, and then, wrapping his cloak round his arm and drawing his own dagger, defended himself valiantly. His friends had time to rally. Some of the congregation rushed wildly from the church. Women shrieked and fainted, men swore ferociously. Lorenzo and his friends shut themselves in the sacristy. The plot had failed, for the people were solidly for the tyrant and the " ciompi " rushed into the church to the battle-cry of the Medici, " Palle ! Palle ! "

Salviati, his brother, his cousin and Jacopo Bracciolini were soon hanging from the windows of the Palazzo Vecchio. Bandini escaped. Another conspirator found a hiding-place beneath a heap of faggots and was pardoned on being discovered four days later " because of the time he had spent in so undignified a position ".

The people, after their wont on such occasions, went mad with rage and lust for blood. All who were suspected of friendship for the Pazzi were slaughtered. Franceschino was dragged to the Signoria, taken to a window and displayed to the mob. Beneath him dangled a corpse, head downwards in a violet robe which had fallen back and left it naked to the thigh. Its trappings showed it to be a priest—it was Salviati. Franceschino's other friends hung in a row from the other windows. The rope was placed round his neck and he was thrust forth. He dangled, swung a few times against the dead bishop, struggled, opened his eyes for the last time, and died, deaf to the obscene clamour of the mob.

Another conspirator, the aged Jacopo Pazzi, was caught by the mountaineers on his way over the Apennines. Knowing the fate that awaited him, he tried in vain to bribe them with all he possessed to kill him. He was carried to Florence and there hanged. Some friendly hand cut him down and gave him decent burial in his family vault, but the mob dug out the corpse and dragged it through the streets, hooting with mirth as the skull bumped over the paving-stones and splashed through the miry kennels. Finally, tiring of the game, they flung it into the Arno to the tune of a street ballad composed for the occasion.

Bandini escaped to Constantinople, but the long arm of Lorenzo's hatred followed him even there. His extradition was asked of and granted by the Sultan, who was " shocked by this murder in a church ", and he was hanged from a window of the Bargello. There is still extant a sketch by Leonardo da Vinci, who was desired by Lorenzo to paint him hanging.

The Pazzi arms on buildings were blotted out and their place taken by the Florentine lily. A square named after them had to take a fresh name, as had also the surviving members of the family. Any person marrying a Pazzi became *ipso facto* illegitimate and his children likewise illegitimate and incapable of inheritance or of possessing civil rights. Botticelli's divine brush was degraded to depict the row of corpses where they themselves had once dangled. It was accounted a masterpiece, but some thick-headed magistrate had it scratched out. Antonio Pollaiuolo engraved a commemorative medal and Orsino made waxen effigies of Lorenzo and Giuliano, to wear the clothes they had worn on the day of the crime.

The Pazzi were utterly destroyed.

Later, Lorenzo had many others slaughtered on the pretext that, since the Pazzi had once plotted, those he condemned to death might have done likewise. Like his ancestor Cosimo, it seemed quite normal to him to go direct from pronouncing sentence of confiscation, exile or death on a fellow-citizen to the noble academy of his Villa Careggi, where, with heart at ease and mind composed, he breathed in the lofty morality of Socrates, the philosophy of Plato.

Lorenzo's fame is stained by varied cruelties. He cast innocent children into prison, and forbade the daughters of his opponents to marry. According to Guicciardini the weakest point in his character was his restless suspicion, which was not so much inborn as acquired through its necessity in governing a city which had known freedom, and in which affairs still needed to be handled by the magistrates at least with the outward forms of legality and liberty. For this reason he commenced at the very beginning of his reign to undermine the position of any citizen of any consideration in the city, whether through birth, wealth or deeds. It was the policy of the tyrant of Miletus, a lesson learnt by Lorenzo from the classics.

Through this same suspicion, [says Guicciardini] Lorenzo prevented the alliance of prominent families by marriage, and displayed much ingenuity in marrying off young people to others whom they would never themselves have chosen, but who were unobjectionable to him. He went so far that no marriage of any importance could be arranged without his consent. He went even further : he confiscated the girls' dowries.

Lorenzo, throughout his reign, always went about surrounded by armed men who never left his side. Cambi, in his *Delights of the Learned Tuscans*, says : "Lorenzo has always with him cloaked footmen wearing swords, and one of them, a certain Savaglio, precedes him sword in hand." He lavished money freely on this pretorian guard, even giving them the income of hospitals and other pious foundations.

These were the petty sides of a great man, for even Guicciardini admits that none of his opponents denied his intelligence—"An intelligence which allowed him to govern twenty-three years with ever-increasing power and glory." The highest princes of the world respected him ; Innocent VIII, the Kings of France and Spain, and even the Sultan who sent him presents of a giraffe, lions and rams. The glory of Florence at this time was beyond compare. Artists seemed to spring up all about him ; Brunelleschi, Ghiberti, Lucca della Robbia, Ghirlandaio, Castagno, Botticelli, Luca Signorelli, and last but not least the divine Leonardo and the sublime Michael Angelo. He was passionately fond of engraved stones and cameos, of which he possessed a fine collection of antique specimens. He had rare and curious manuscripts copied wherever they were to be found, whether in Greece or in the East, spending 30,000 ducats a year on this alone. He founded the famous Laurentine Library and the University of Pisa, which soon outrivalled the earlier foundations of Pavia and Padua in teaching, if not in number of students. The villa of Lorenzo at Careggi became one of the most marvellous centres of artistic and literary culture the world has ever known. He himself was one of the foremost orators and best writers of his day. His speech, both in public and in private, was, according to Guicciardini, so artful and penetrating as to be irresistible : his letters are full of wit and adorned by eloquence as much as by elegance of style. He wrote rustic ditties in peasant dialect, long and dull narrative poems, carnival songs, philosophic poetry, lauds and canticles, satires, a dramatic poem, *canzoni* and sonnets which are not far inferior to those of Petrarch. He wrote, for the wedding of his daughter and the Pope's son, a mystery, *John and Paul, Martyrs under Constantine*, and took one of the principal parts in its performance in a church in Florence.

He could handle the beautiful Tuscan dialect with consummate delicacy. His verse is at times licentious, but often reaches ideal heights. " Break, O my soul, the shameful chains that bind thee. Banish all vain desire, and restore the mastery to thy nobler, purer part." As a poet, he loved imagery and metaphor, but his colour is a little crude for his over-refined verse, rather like the painting of his contemporary Botticelli. In one of his *canzoni* he compares the tears on a maiden's cheek to a stream flowing through flowery meads : the thoughts which pass rapidly from his heart to his lady's are compared with a swarm of ants hastening from one ant-hill to another ; the rays of his beloved's eyes are like sunshine lighting up the dark interior of a bee-hive. Lorenzo was particularly fond of violets.

O violets [he writes] so fresh and fair of hue, violets plucked by the hand of innocence, what play of rain and sun hath nourished you, flowers that nature cannot excel !

And again,

Venus, mourning for Adonis, passed through a wood. A thorn pierced her naked foot, and the amorous white violets eagerly gathered the blood of her fair body. Since that day they are purple. Their colour comes not from the freshness of wind or rain, but from the sighs and tears of Love.

In his later years, Lorenzo fell under the influence of a Florentine lady, older than himself, Bartolomea dei Nasi, wife of Donato Benci. She had neither grace nor beauty, but Lorenzo loved her ardently. When she went to spend the hot days of summer in her country house, and the cares of state kept him in Florence, he would post out to her every evening, returning to Florence in the early morning. Friends and faithful servants who displeased this capricious woman were ruthlessly sacrificed. " It was madness," says Guicciardini, " that a man so highly placed and esteemed so wise should at the age of forty fall a victim to a woman neither young nor fair, and that he should do for her things that would be accounted folly even in a young man."

At the beginning of the year 1491 Lorenzo contracted an illness which his physicians at first thought a trifle, but which nevertheless carried him off on April 8th, 1492, at the age of forty-four.

Lorenzo's death, according to Guicciardini, was a fatal blow to the peace of Italy.

His prudence, his authority, the rare genius which guided him so well had given the republic wealth, abundance and all the other benefits of enduring peace. All Italy felt his loss, for, besides his care for the safety of his own dominion, he was often a peace-maker between Milan and Naples. He used to smoothe over the jealousies and suspicions of the two rulers, whose power and whose ambition were nearly equal.

Lebey concludes his work on Lorenzo dei Medici with the words :

Lorenzo the Magnificent seemed a new kind of magician. The ancient keep, where bats and skeletons were neighbours, was razed to the ground, and on its site arose a wondrous palace, where the meditative owl sits on the helm of Pallas Athene, while in the surrounding park the flute of Apollo sounds among the reeds of a lake in whose clear waters are mirrored the columns of a temple.

We should not grieve at the hangings and quarterings and ghastly tortures. Before that day Florence was a place of bats and skeletons in antique dungeons; now it had become the home of Apollo, whose flute beneath the laurels filled the air with melody, under the serene eye of Pallas.

V

THE HUMANISTS

IT has rightly been said that humanism was the source of the Italian, and especially of the Florentine Renaissance. Florence remained the soul and inspiration of the Renaissance until her part was assumed by Rome, and we have already seen the two men, Cosimo and Lorenzo dei Medici, who were in turn the inspiration of Florentine humanism.

To-day we should answer the question, " What is Humanism ? " with some such definition as " The study of the humanities, that is, of literature, and particularly Greek and Latin literature ". At its birth toward the end of the fifteenth century, it was essentially the study of those sciences which advanced the happiness and perfection of the human race, in contradistinction to theology (now become scholastic) which turned away from man to God. Humanism owes its name to this contrast with scholasticism. It received a decisive impulse from the Italian fourteenth-century cult of antiquity, which cult was in its turn advanced by humanism.

The humanists professed a deep and attractive faith, clearly enounced by Pico della Mirandola. Nothing which in the past has stirred and inspired the soul of man should or can perish, whether it be faith or language, customs, arts and letters, science or philosophy. All are products of human toil, faith and love. The labour of man is always admirable and must needs have left fertile seed for the future. The relics of the Romans, and of the Greeks who were the source of Roman civilization, naturally took first place among the sacred memorials of the past which the present piously collected and preserved.

Humanism, deeply influenced by classical culture, spread from the Italy of Rome and Florence over all the neighbouring lands.

The Middle Ages were certainly far from ignorant or contemptuous of the Ancients. Many of the Fathers of the Church, as St. Jerome, St. John Chrysostom and St. Gregory of Nazianza, had a good grounding in Greek. St. Ambrose set the Pandects beside the Gospel and Cicero beside St. Paul. Gregory the Great held the study of ancient philosophy and literature to be of great value for the understanding of the Scriptures. Plato's *Phædo* had been translated into Latin in the thirteenth century. It may even be maintained that Aristotle was better understood in the Middle Ages than since : does not Dante call him " the master of those who know " ? At the same time the " subtle doctor ", Duns Scotus, was subjecting the logic and metaphysics of the Peripateticians to his minute and thought-provoking analysis.

The Middle Ages wanted to make Virgil a saint, and Dante makes him his laurel-crowned companion on his travels to the nether world. But besides Virgil, the Middle Ages studied Ovid and Lucan, though except for Cicero, most of whose works they knew, they made little account of Latin prose.

As a matter of fact, when we draw up a list of the Latin authors known and appreciated in the Middle Ages, we find that only Tacitus and Lucretius, Quintilian and a part of Cicero are lacking of those we know to-day.

The Middle Ages, too, made constant use of their classics. The first support a thirteenth- or fourteenth-century writer seeks for an opinion he wishes to maintain is its agreement with the opinion of some classical author. The Latin of Frenchmen of the twelfth century was perhaps more vigorous and less slavishly Ciceronian than that of the Florentine author of the quattrocento, so that it served better to express their thought.

The monasteries, too, in the days of " Gothic barbarism " were the pious preservers of the philosophical and literary treasures of Antiquity. From the tenth century onwards the convent of Bobbio prided itself on its Greek and Latin manuscripts. The monks plumed themselves on possessing Demosthenes and Aristotle, but they had also most of the Latin poets and even the grammarians Adamantius, Papirius, Priscian and Flavian.

Passing to the thirteenth century, Petrarch and Boccaccio were both enthusiastic Latinists. Petrarch ransacked first Italy, then France, Germany, Spain and even Greece for manuscripts. Thus he brought to light the Institutions of Quintilian and some letters and a few distiches of Cicero. Certain Latin works, now lost, were known to him, among them a collection of letters and epigrams of Augustus.

Petrarch is the illustrious precursor of the Renaissance, as Erasmus was to be its Pontifex Maximus. He eschewed the conversation of the living, to talk with Cicero and Virgil. Antiquity, to him was a temple of beatific meditation. " The mere sight of the men of to-day offends me," he wrote, " but the memory, the shadow of the great deeds, even the names of the ancients fill me with delight." Even his beloved Laura existed only in his imagination.

His library, dearly bought in money and toil, was his greatest treasure. Through it he could converse with Virgil. Homer he had too, but knew no Greek. " My Homer," he says sorrowfully, " lies dumb beside me. I am deaf to his voice, but at least I can see and often embrace him." If he had occasion to visit a convent, he went into raptures at the thought of the classical texts there might be in its library. He valued his own *Africa* and *De Viris Illustribus*, which celebrate the heroes of Rome, far more highly than the *Canzoniere*, which contains his love poetry in the vulgar tongue. It was to him only " the follies of youth, which he desired might remain forever unknown to others as to himself". The letters, both in prose and in verse, which he wrote to his friends, were all in Latin, and it was as their writer, and as the singer of Laura, that he attained the proud position as an intellectual leader of Europe that Erasmus was to obtain two centuries later by the same method.

Petrarch became the familiar of Popes, and Princes begged him to act as godfather to their children. In 1360 the Duke of Milan sent him as his ambassador to Paris to congratulate King John on his return from exile. The Roman Senate crowned him with rose and myrtle on the Capitoline hill. The Venetian Republic put at his disposal the splendid palace on the Riva dei Schiavoni, where he lived from 1362 to 1368. Even in his lifetime his birthplace at Arezzo was a place of pilgrimage.

He had entered the Church in 1326, so that we can say that the three greatest of the humanists of the Renaissance, whose most marked characteristic is the cult of pagan antiquity, were churchmen : Petrarch, Ficino and Erasmus.

Boccaccio, like Petrarch, ransacked the monasteries, especially that of Monte Cassino. Like Petrarch, too, he was ashamed to be known as the author of the *Decameron*, and held only his Latin writings of any worth.

Petrarch, who loved the ruins as well as the literature of classical antiquity, travelled all through Italy, Greece, the Islands, and part of the Asiatic and African coasts in his search for inscriptions and coins and to make drawings. He was once asked why he took such trouble, and replied, "To bring the dead to life."

This was the Renaissance.

Gradually it spread with the spread of Latin and Greek, and in the most diverse quarters. We have seen, in the persons of the Medici and the Fuggers, how classical thought and classical languages conquered the minds of the great financiers, and it is interesting to note that this great movement in literature and philosophy began in the merchant class. It was only later that the great ones of the earth became converts.

There was more than a mere æsthetic curiosity behind this desire to recall antiquity to life. Men were weary of the dry and barren scholastic wrangles which had engulfed alike the thought of Gerbert and the science of the precursor of Descartes and Spinoza, Duns Scotus, the touching faith of St. Francis of Assisi, and the wholesome, living doctrines of Thomas Aquinas.

Erasmus took up the cudgels against the scholastic theologians :

Their whole energy is given up to questioning, dividing, distinguishing, defining : the first part is split into three, the first of these three into four, and each of the four again into three. What could be further from the style of the prophets, of Christ and of the Apostles ?

All this was true, but all the same, their thought must be assimilated as far as possible. At least it was not surrounded with that vague halo of mysticism which has formed round the scientific discoveries made since their day. Copernicus' disturbing revelation of a world rolling through space was yet to come. Everything was still fixed and definite, on earth and in the heavens as in the minds of men. They had the Scriptures, and the Scriptures had themselves been fixed and defined by the Fathers of the Church, by Popes and Councils.

The Scriptures were Truth made absolute, an unshakable Truth which could neither be broken nor bent.

The processes of theology were like the processes of algebra or geometry to us. "The three angles of a triangle are together equal to two right angles" is a definite proposition, on which a man can find firm foothold. The truths of religion were at that time equally definite, and as a mathematician, starting from irrefutable axioms, proceeds by deduction to discover and demonstrate further truths, so did the scholiasts, by processes which seemed to them equally scientific, go forward to discover theological truths till then unknown.

To-day, when thought has been overlaid by a hundred new extravagances, such efforts do not seem utterly ridiculous, but in the dawn of the Renaissance, when Aristotle, Socrates and Plato burst anew on man's sight, they seemed dull and frigid, and the discovery, translation and circulation of each new masterpiece of classical literature seemed to the eager minds of that day the dawn of liberty, new life to a world in which life was almost extinct.

To this, quite apart from purely æsthetic and literary reasons, humanism mainly owed its triumph. There were, it is true, complementary causes, and among them the new order of society which arose when the leaders of the Middle Ages, feudal lords and patricians of the towns, had accomplished their appointed task and could find no place in the new order of things. In this new order there was a gulf fixed between aristocracy and commonalty, a gulf widened by the flow of wealth from the New World, by the spread of commerce and the fortunes that accrued therefrom. Though a Cosimo dei Medici might be leader of a " popular " party, though he might dress as a peasant and hold familiar converse with workmen, yet he was far removed from the people in the high place to which money had raised him.

High finance was outside the orbit of the common people ; they could only stare and marvel at its results.

The new class distinctions naturally produced a change in the ideas and tasks of the ruling class. " Humanism," says Imbart de la Tour, " rebelled against scholasticism and against the people." The vulgar tongue, the language of the Chansons de Geste, of popular lays and ballads, the language of Commines, of Gringoire and of Villon, was despised and rejected ; anathema was the tongue in which Dante, Petrarch and Boccaccio wrote, the tongue which had sung the Nibelungs and Gudrun.

The humanists thus wrote only for a small and select public. As Erasmus, the best of them, puts it, " A good prince should admire nothing which the mob extols. He should disregard the opinions of the common herd. It would be unworthy of him to feel as do the people."

The same tendencies appeared in religious matters. Religion must be freed from the vulgar accretions of popular observance which had overlaid it for many ages. Away with the processional dancing round saintly relics, away with their motley bearers. Away with the candles lighted before the Virgin of the Via Larga, while her neighbour Virgin of the next quarter is not honoured with the raising of a hat. Away with the crowd of Saint Sebastians who ward off epidemics, and the still greater crowd of Christophers who shield their devotees from accident, so that even the troops paint them on their tents and pray to them as to God. Away with Saint Roch who vies with St. Sebastian as a protector against plague, and St. Apollina who cures toothache. St. Anthony of Thebes, his faithful pig by his side, can deal effectively with skin diseases, except that which affects Job, as he sits melancholy on his dunghill. St. Anthony of Padua finds that which is lost. Away with all these vulgar superstitions.

All this provided plentiful material for the Ciceronian jests of the humanists. This religion of charcoal-burners and old women seemed to them pitiable and nothing else. Religion should be based on the knowledge of man as an individual and of mankind as a whole.

Unmeasured was the zeal of the converts to this new faith. One would go hungry to buy his favourite author, Cicero or Plato, Virgil or Epictetus. Another would do menial tasks for a teacher whose fees he could not hope to pay. The classics were their life as the religion of Christ was life to the early Christians.

Marsilio Ficino, a priest, wrote to a mother grieving for her dead son a letter which might have come from some Athenian rhetorician. Not one word does it contain of Christian comfort. Ficino preached on Plato from the pulpit of San Lorenzo in Florence, and tried to reconcile his teaching with that of the Gospel.

Ficino, whose father was physician to Cosimo the Elder, was born on October 19th, 1433. He was a small, meagre man, gentle and melancholy, a great dreamer. His enthusiasm for the philosophy of Plato and the knowledge and talent he devoted to its propagation made him the centre of the intellectual life of Florence under the Medici. He was famed alike in France and Germany, in England and in Hungary. He was in touch with the greatest men of his time, with kings and princes, prelates and men of letters. He adorned his house with mottoes from the classics. His chief work, *De Religione Christiana*, is an attempt to reconcile religious and scientific truths, and in his commentaries on Plato's *Symposium* he stresses the points of contact between religion and philosophy. "Wise men are believers and believers are wise men." In his mind Platonism becomes a theology and Christ himself a Platonist. According to Ficino, Plato had made it clear that his teaching would only prevail at the coming of One from whom all truth should flow, and the ancient gods had foretold the coming of Christ, immortal like themselves and filled with religion and piety. " They spoke of him very kindly," he says.

University teaching stresses the Christian tendencies of the Aeneid, and the beauties of classical poetry in general, both Greek and Latin, are explained as allegories of divine truth. Pius II summarizes the general tendency in a letter to the Sultan. " Christianity is only a modern version of the ' supreme good ' of the ancients."

Tyrannicide after the antique manner became a fashion. Boscoli, who tried to kill Giuliano dei Medici, believed himself possessed by the soul of Brutus, and Lorenzaccio boasted that when he murdered his cousin Alessandro his hand was guided by the spirit of antiquity.

Erasmus tells of a conversation on the immortality of the soul which he once had with an Italian priest. The priest could only allege in support of the Christian doctrine the testimony of Pliny the Elder. Filelfo, in his funeral oration on Francesco Sforza, proves this same immortality by reference to the Greek philosophers, adding that " the Old and New Testaments afforded additional evidence ". Cardinal Pallavicini roundly declared that Christianity would be an untenable hypothesis were it not for Aristotle.

Preachers edified their flocks with tags from Homer or Horace. Savonarola says of them that " they know nothing of the Scriptures, and can do nothing but quote Aristotle and Plato ". During his stay in Rome Erasmus went one Good Friday to hear a sermon on the Passion. Julius II was present, so that most of the sermon was directed at him, and in it he was called " good, great, and all-powerful Jupiter ".

Cardinal Bembo, private secretary to Leo X and one of

the best poets of his day, discouraged one of his friends from
reading St. Paul's Epistles, saying that the Latin of them was
indifferent and might spoil his style. The same Cardinal,
speaking of a papal election, states that the Pope was raised
to the throne of St. Peter " by favour of the immortal gods ",
and refers to the Virgin as *dea*—goddess. In another place,
Christ becomes Jupiter, Paradise the Elysian fields. On
tombstones in the churches themselves are inscriptions re-
cording that the dead have been raised to Olympus. Michael
Angelo banishes the Devil from his painting in the Sistine
Chapel, and the damned are cast into Hell by a boatman
named Charon, son of Erebus and Night. And Paolo Cortese,
in his *Dogmatics* of 1502, makes Styx and Cocytus rivers of
Hell. Sculptors like Antonio Riccio, who carved the famous
Pascal candlestick for the church of St. Anthony in Venice,
mixed Jupiter slaying sea-monsters with the Adoration of
the Magi as decorative *motifs*. To artists such as these, Easter
itself became a pagan feast with sacrifices, garlands and troops
of young men and maidens.

The personages of Scripture were treated like heroes of
Olympus, and in return, the great figures of antiquity became
Christian saints. Virgil, as we have seen, became a precursor
of the true faith, Aristotle and Plato were nearly canonized.
A translator of Ovid takes pains to make clear his point of
view by invoking the aid of the Trinity in his first line, a
proceeding which would probably have caused some surprise
to the author of the Metamorphoses and the Art of Love,
whose copyist, a Parisian monk, would have amazed him
more by dedicating it " to the honour and glory of the
Virgin Mary ".

Between 1433 and 1445 Antonio Averlino executed the
carvings of the entrance to St. Peter's in Rome, the focal
point of every Christian eye. But Averlino called himself

" Philaretes "—lover of virtue—and his typically humanistic treatment of his task may be seen from the subjects he used. There were the Fables of Æsop, " which I have read in the Greek ", as he proudly says, Mars, the Roman wolf with Romulus and Remus, and finally, a masterpiece of incongruity at the threshold of a Christian church, the sculptured fable of Leda and her amorous swan.

The Renaissance received a new impulse from the discovery of ancient statuary, which was recognized as the finest so far known. The soil of the Eternal City and the Roman Campagna, and even the bed of the Tiber, were meticulously searched for further examples.

In 1430 the sculptor Donatello and the architect Brunelleschi came to Rome in search of antique treasure-trove. They dressed like labourers, says Vasari, and took pick and shovel in hand. They were called the " treasure seekers ", but it was no common treasure that they sought. Their money was soon spent, and with so little result that in order to live the precious pair had to work as journeymen in a goldsmith's workshop.

The city of Rome had been invaded by the desert of the Campagna to such a degree that it was itself almost a desert. Only a third of it was inhabited, the remainder being fields and gardens studded with the ruins of former buildings. Shepherds pastured their flocks in the city fields, and the Florentines scorned the Romans as " cowherds ". The people of the inhabited part of the city had their villas—their " vines " as they called them—in the deserted parts. " They were real country houses," says Montaigne, " with large gardens and pleasaunces of singular beauty where I learnt for the first time what profit art could draw from a rough and irregular site." These houses were open to all and sundry, for their owners seldom visited them. Sermons and discussions on theological points took place there, and less innocent diversions with the notorious courtesans of the city, who, Montaigne goes on to say, " sold mere conversation dearly, the thing I sought for the sake of their subtlety, and are as grasping in that respect as in the rest of their trade ".

Girolamo Rorario, afterwards a Papal Nuncio, thus describes a visit to the country-house of Blosio Palladio in the time of Leo X. This particular villa stood behind St. Peter's.

I took certain German noblemen to the gardens of Blosio. I showed them the fountain surrounded by marble benches set in the shade of laurels. I led them by the broad path through the closely-planted vine to the terraced orchard on the hillside, and thence beneath the scented lemon-trees to the double bath. There, where the murmuring stream flows by stalactites like those of Tivoli, Blosio Palladio loves to take his meals. Near by is a theatre crowned with vines, and runs for fowls.

In this charming spot met famous authors like Bembo and Sadoleto, one of whom lauds its delights in Latin : " Blosii villula ter quaterque felix "—O thrice and four times blest villa of Blosio—while Ariosto celebrates in a satire the learned assemblies held there.

In Rome itself, the streets were grass-grown, filthy, tortuous. Ferdinand, King of Naples, confessed to the Pope his surprise at the state of the Eternal City, with its foul alleys, the lurking place of footpads. The paving of the squares was broken, shrubs sprouted from the cracks, heaps of garbage defiled them, for they served as common refuse-heaps. There was no street-planning and buildings jutted out haphazard into the streets. A visitor had to worm his way among vast dilapidated piles, often turned into fortresses, among the madly magnificent ruins, scattered by time with wayward hand, and covered with plants which at once adorned and destroyed them.

Even the churches were crumbling into ruin. Rome had too many of them for the Pope to maintain all.

Statues [writes Michelet] were seldom seen. They lay beneath the earth ; but huge baths, eleven temples now, alas, no more, colossal foundations and monumental sewers through which a Cæsar's triumph might have ridden, all these are to be seen. Deep below ground one might come upon the summit of a temple still erect. To discover Rome, one must follow the goats to the summit of tottering cornices, or, torch in hand, dare the gloom of subterranean labyrinths.

In Rome, life was lived in the open. Family history was enacted in the street. On the first of May, young lovers decorated the dwelling of their beloved, gilded its door, hung garlands and wreaths upon it and suspended from them a variety of gifts : bright fabrics, cages of singing birds. They fixed to it sonnets of their own making or purchased from poets, describing in mottoes their loves and their hopes. Every quarter of the city was alive with people going about to look, to criticize and to admire this lovers' exhibition.

At every wedding the streets must have the chance to admire the bride's trousseau ; so she is marched through the streets and put on show in the squares. Even the chests —" cassone "—in which the wedding-gifts were arranged are works of art now much sought after by museums. Funerals vie with bridals as an occasion for display, and criers were sent about the streets to announce them to the populace.

This publicity in daily life extended to matters which the opinion of to-day banishes to decent obscurity.

Joachim Du Bellay, a canon of Notre-Dame, accompanied his uncle, the Cardinal Jean du Bellay, to Rome as steward.

He spent five years there, and gave vent to his impression in a series of sonnets, the " Regrets ".

> Celui qui, par la rue, a vu publiquement
> La courtisane en coche ou qui pompeusement
> L'a pu voir à cheval en accoutrement d'homme
> Superbe se montrer ; celui qui, de plein jour,
> Aux cardinaux en cappe a vu faire l'amour,
>   C'est celui seul qui peut juger de Rome.

The Apollo Belvedere was discovered in 1450 on an estate of Cardinal della Rovere. The Laocoon group mentioned by Pliny was brought to light in a Roman estate near Sta. Maria Maggiore. Michael Angelo himself had directed the excavations. It would be no exaggeration to say that it was the most sensational event of the time. The group was first of all drawn to the Capitol on a triumphal car and thence to the Belvedere, where Bramante, at the Pope's expense, had prepared a fitting site for it. On its passage through the streets houses were beflagged and garlanded as for a triumph. Church bells pealed, the cannon of the castle of St. Angelo thundered salutes. When it reached its destined place the marble was hidden by the flowers thrown by frenzied admirers. No victorious general of Rome could have had a more splendid triumph.

Early in the sixteenth century the Apollo and the Laocoon were joined by the Vatican Torso, the Tiber group, the Cleopatra and the Medici Venus. We must not forget, either, the so-called " grotesques ", the light and gracious Roman mural decorations which had so strong an influence on the decorative art of the Renaissance.

From Rhodes arrived whole ship-loads of antiques, and the taste for collections, in which the Medici had so triumphantly led the fashion, attained vast proportions. " American " prices were paid for the smallest fragment of Greek or Roman art. Eight or ten ducats—twenty or thirty pounds in our money—were paid for a single corroded coin. Ancient mosaics were especially in demand for the adornment of the inner court or the halls of a palace.

Ideas of honesty changed greatly under the impact of this collector's zeal. "Theft became honest and robbery honourable," as Castiglione said in 1507. Isabella d'Este, Duchess of Urbino, obtained from Cæsar Borgia an antique figurine which he had stolen from one of her friends, but the charming Duchess of Leonardo da Vinci's famous portrait would not hear of restoring it to its rightful owner.

Hand in hand with the discovery of works of art went on the search for lost works of classical authors. Gian-Francesco Bracciolini, called Poggio, deserves honourable mention among the searchers. He discovered in the monastery of St. Gall manuscripts of the *Institutions* of Quintilian, of a part of the *Argonautica* of Valerius Flaccus, and certain unknown speeches of Cicero. Later were discovered the *De Rerum Natura* of Lucretius, some *Odes* of Horace, the *De Re Rustica* of Columella and many more.

When but a simple monk, Pope Nicholas V had already run into debt in his search for copies of Greek and Roman authors. His elevation to the papacy was his opportunity to indulge his taste still further. The manuscripts he collected form the basis of the Vatican Library.

Niccolo Niccoli, a friend of Cosimo the Elder, carried on the same work with his own and with Medici money. He it was who first brought to light the complete works of Ammianus Marcellinus, Cicero's *De Oratore*, and the basic text of Lucretius, which, as we have said, was discovered by Poggio, as were the works of Pliny, bought from a monastery in Lübeck. There were in Venice and Florence days of rejoicing, comparable with the day of Laocoon in

Rome, when Giovanni Aurispa or Filelfo or Guarino da Verona, home from Byzantium, laid before the eyes of the humanists some new fragment of Greek literature. And with reason, since these fragments contained Plato, Xenophon, Strabo and Dio Cassius. The first five books of the *Annals* of Tacitus were disinterred from a Westphalian monastery and presented to the astonished eyes of Leo X.

Antonio Urceo, nicknamed Codro, wrote in his *Discourse on the Liberal Arts* :

Rejoice and be glad, for I speak of Greek literature and in especial of Homer the divine, who, as Ovid says, purifies the verses of poets with his eternal flow. From Homer thou mayst learn grammar, from Homer rhetoric, from Homer medicine, from Homer astrology, from Homer fables, history, morals, philosophy, from Homer the art military and the art culinary, from Homer architecture and the government of states. In short, all that is good and worthy may be found in Homer.

Urceo held an interesting position among Italian humanists, so that a sketch of his life may not be out of place.

He was born in August 1446, at Herberia, in the province of Reggio. His great-grandfather had been a potter, his grandfather Bartolomeo Urceo a fisherman. The latter, while digging a field, unearthed a pot full of coins which enabled him to set up as a perfumer. He had two sons, one of whom, Cortese, was the father of Antonio the scholar. Cortese gave his son a good education, ending in the University of Ferrara, where he distinguished himself in teaching the young. In 1469 he was called to lecture on the humanities at Forli, where he became tutor to Sinibaldo Ordelafo, son of the lord of that city. He was a little man, thin and always ailing, pale-faced, sickly and prematurely bald. His deepset, pale eyes had a strained look, so that at first sight he appeared dissipated, though his life was always most modest. A contemporary shows him to us reading the Iliad, open on his knee, while with one hand he skims milk and with the other turns a spit before the fire.

In virtue of his position as tutor to the young prince, Urceo had a room in the palace, but it was so dark that even in the daytime he was compelled to work by the light of a lamp on which he had engraved " Studia lucernam olentia optime olent "—Studies are best which smell of oil.

One day he went out leaving his lamp burning. It fell over and set on fire not only his own manuscripts but a costly book which he had borrowed. Flames shot from the windows, and Urceo hastened home. Reaching the threshold, he exclaimed, " O Christ, what crime have I committed against the faithful that this should be my punishment ? " And then, turning to an image of the Virgin : " If, in the hour of death, I come to you in prayer, heed not my supplication, for I wish to spend eternity in hell."

Immediately afterwards he left Forli and settled himself up for six months in the house of a miller. When the lord of Forli died, Urceo was called to Bologna to teach in the university there. In spite of his outbursts of rage and his fantastic humour he was greatly loved by his pupils. All bowed before his vast knowledge of the classics. Politian submitted to him his Greek epigrams, Aldus Manutius dedicated to him a collection of letters, also in Greek, scholars concurred in praise of his Latin writings after his death. His works went through four editions between 1502 and 1540.

He occasionally shocked his contemporaries by his doubts as to the immortality of the soul and by denying the existence of Hell, but on his death-bed he returned to the faith of his childhood and prayed the Virgin to pardon his blasphemous wish when his manuscripts were burnt.

His pupils, gathered round him, asked for some last word worthy of their dying teacher. He made them a fine set speech, rather academic in tone if the version we have of it is to be trusted. He also said, however, " Pray to God to make you like me," and " How much good will be buried with me ! " He died in the monastery of San Salvatore in Bologna, aged eighty-four, and was buried in the cloisters, with his own chosen inscription on his tombstone.

" Codrus eram "—I was Codros.

The numerous makers of fashionable verse, epigrams and epigraphs, madrigals, distiches and tercets, took Catullus for their model. Sannazaro and Pontano, the founder of the Neapolitan academy, were famous in this genre. For six Latin verses in praise of Venice, the Senate gave Sannazaro six hundred ducats in gold (about £1,200). Catullus was imitated in various ways to suit various occasions : to praise or slander the great, to sing the beauty of a loved one, or the death of a lap-dog or parrot. He was, indeed, so well and truly imitated that many verses known definitely to be of the fifteenth and sixteenth might well pass for those of the first century B.C.

The idol of the humanists was Cicero, that prolix, pre-tentious, empty windbag. On him modelled themselves a host of slavish imitators and a few writers of worth. Bembo advised his friends to spend whole years on reading Cicero and nothing but Cicero and to eschew all words, both in writing and in conversation, which were not to be found in him. Some of them even followed his advice. Cicero's contemporaries shared his fame. " Cicero's century, immortal, half divine." He became a cult which had its own theo-logians. When Erasmus dared to write that, though Cicero was worthy of all praise, there were other sound writers and that some words and expressions were permissible beyond those found in his works, he was shouted down and told that none but a drunkard could advance such extravagant views.

Latin thus came to be the only language for the thinker and the scholar, and even for most ordinary writers. Niccolo Niccoli asks whether it is possible for a man to be a poet if he does not write in Latin. Poggio declares that the man who has no works in Latin to his credit has never lived, and laments that the Divine Comedy was not composed in Latin. It is stated that Dante had considered it, and had even begun to write in Virgilian Alexandrines. Fortunately he reverted to his native tongue. It must none the less be recognized that Latin was for the humanists at least a kind of Esperanto, understood all over Europe in countries which did not study merely " foreign " tongues. Filelfo said that Italian was only used in matters not destined for posterity, but even in Italy the diversity of dialects hampered the formation of a written language, before the sweet Tuscan dialect of Florence attained pre-eminence. Till that time, Latin was the language not only of the scholar and the philosopher, but of good society and of all with any pretensions to gentility. A gentleman used only Latin in his correspondence, and welcomed his guests in Latin. Even ladies delivered set speeches in that tongue. Latin epigrams, such as those of Pontano or Sannazaro, were more likely to wound their object than if they were in Italian. To all but her intimate friends Lucrezia Borgia's reputation was irretrievably destroyed by a single such epigram. Pius II demanded from his abbreviators and protonotaries a Ciceronian elegance in their writing. Latin too was used for an endless variety of purposes ; lullabies, mottoes for wedding presents, and epitaphs on tombs. A Latin inscription may record the erection of a new fountain by a country squire or the dedication

of a street-corner shrine by a pious townsman. The incisive-
ness of the Latin, so meet to be carved in stone, naturally
made it more acceptable in practice. In this everyday use
the idiom of Cicero, of Horace and of Virgil gained a supple-
ness and grace which it had lost in the Middle Ages. It was
reborn.

In our day [writes Aldus Manutius, the famous Venetian
printer] we see a great many Catos, and by Catos I mean old men
who have taken to the study of Greek, for the number of old
and young who are endeavouring to learn it is nearly as great
as that of the students of Latin.

Politian confirms this when he writes that the sons of the
Florentine patricians spoke from their earliest years the purest
Latin dialect. Alessandro della Scala, whose father was chancellor of the Signoria of Florence, used to go about reciting the
great speeches from Sophocles and Euripides. It is true that
the fall of Constantinople to the Turks in 1453 assisted this
spread of Greek studies by driving many scholars westwards,
but before this time there were renowned Latinists in Italy,
as Plethon, Argyropoulos, and Chalcondylas.

This wide and sudden diffusion of ancient Greek literature
is the more surprising when we consider the poor material
at the disposal of the men of that time. There were no lexicons,
and manuscripts were often so worn as to be almost un-
decipherable. Matters, however, soon improved with the
beneficent aid of the great printer Aldus Manutius. Venice
was particularly well placed as regards Greek culture, through
its commercial relations with the East. Not only was Aldus
devoted to the cause of spreading the knowledge of Greek
through his press, but he was also himself a great scholar,
who produced both a grammar and dictionary of Greek.
When Cardinal Bessarion presented his library to the
Venetian Republic, Aldus seized the chance offered by the

invention of printing, and published one after the other his famous Aldine editions of Aristotle, Euripides and Thucydides. Another benefit which he conferred on scholars was the publishing of volumes in octavo, easy to handle and to produce in quantity, which held the market till the printers of Lyons brought out still smaller editions.

From the time of Petrarch and Boccaccio onward the Italians held themselves to be Latins, direct heirs of the grandeur that was Rome. Pius II, a Piccolomini of Siena by birth, declared to the people of Verona, " I am as much a Roman as a Sienese, for in ancient days the Piccolomini migrated from Rome to Siena, as witness the names of Æneas and Sylvius which are traditional in the family." A later Pope, Paul II, claimed descent from the consular family of Ahenobarbus, one of whom was the husband of Agrippina, mother of Nero. Ahenobarbus, translated, means " redbeard ", and the Pope's brilliant genealogy rested solely on the fact of his own worldly name being Pietro Barbo. In spite of this a lecturer on Nero, the Pope being present, took care not to criticize that Emperor, " lest the Pope's family feelings be hurt ". It also became the fashion to Latinize family and even Christian names.

As Burckhardt has pointed out, while in the rest of Europe Latin and Roman literature remained of necessity the province of scholars and writers, one element only of an all-round education, in Italy they were part of the national life. Italy relived its own proud past in the tradition deeply implanted in the national consciousness and amid the imposing remains of its historic greatness. Life was lived in the classical manner. Christmas certainly remained Christmas, the anniversary of the birth of Christ, but the Romans honoured as highly the anniversary of the foundation of Rome.

A merchant like Niccolo Niccoli could live among his statues, his medallions and his cameos, having antique vases for his table service. Vespasiano has painted him thus, in a long toga-like robe, the very pattern of a Roman patrician of Cato's day. Pietro Pazzi, son of a colleague of Niccoli and an idle, pleasure-seeking youth, chanced one day to pass by the Podesta's palace. Niccoli hailed him :

" What does thou with thy life ? " " I take it as it comes." " Listen, and be ashamed that thou, the son of such a father, shouldst yet lack knowledge of the Latin tongue to grace thee. If thou hast no Latin, thy life will be as nothing, and, youth once past, thou wilt be but a poor miserable creature."

The young Pazzi took the hint, the more readily since Niccoli promised he should lack for nothing if he followed his sage counsels. Niccoli found teachers for him, and he developed a taste for study, going so far as to learn the whole Æneid by heart, and the speeches of Livy's heroes which he declaimed aloud all the way from his villa at Trebbio to Florence and back again.

A reverend teacher, reproached by Aretino for his too frequent visits to the tavern, replied : " The Ancients drank no water."

Alfonso of Aragon, King of Naples, possessed a bone of Livy, which he revered as a relic. The reading of Quintus Curtius is said to have cured him of a violent quartan fever.

As in life, so the Renaissance would be classic even in death. When Duke Guidobaldo of Urbino—he who sent Rafael to study in Rome—lay dying, he consoled his wife, gave sage advice to his successor, confessed himself, and then passed away murmuring Virgil's lines,

> Circum me limus niger et deformis arundo
> Cocyti——

Humanism had many and important results. The first and

most obvious was the tendency towards the abandonment of purely national tradition in letters and arts, and especially in architecture. The change in taste it produced had the effect of condemning the Gothic style as the futile refuge of a barbarous world. The second result was the accentuated gulf between the two classes of society, the " greater " and the " lesser ", " majores et minores ".

Humanism, like finance, was international. Pico della Mirandola corresponded with Reuchlin in Germany, Budé in Paris with Aldus in Venice, and Erasmus with all Europe, but always within their own class, never with the people. Great and small are no longer separated merely by wealth or social position, but by taste, that taste which is the prerogative of the leisured class.

The humanist shuts himself away in his study to pore over his manuscripts, his whole mind and soul taken up with the striving to assimilate the thought of Plato, the eloquence of Cicero, the dreams of Homer and Virgil. The people, on the other hand, living in the open, whether they follow the plough or work in the towns, sing their own songs, full of life, love, beauty and faith ; they still gather round the strolling singers to hear the stories of Merlin, of the Four Sons of Aymon or of Fair Melusine. Two " ciompi " were known to come to blows in front of the Signoria in Florence, over the question of the relative merits of Roland and Renaud de Montauban, two heroes of their puppet plays.

Meanwhile, the humanists were deep in their Greek and Latin. The people clung to ancient beliefs and practices, old wives' tales, perhaps, but nevertheless penetrated with the beauty and strength of the past. The humanist had no longer lot or part in the ideas and feelings of the people ; he wilfully shut himself off from communion with the vulgar, toiling mob, the " vulgum pecus ".

The final result of humanism was the introduction of new ideas into religion itself. Ficino kept a lamp burning day and night before his bust of Plato, as if it were an image, and yet remained a good Catholic. Another equally good Catholic, Erasmus, once gave vent to the heartfelt murmur, " Saint Socrates, pray for us ".

But time was to have its revenges on a society which exalted pagan wisdom above all others and foreign thought above that of its own ancestors, which preferred an ancient beauty far removed from Christian faith to all other forms of beauty, which gave to a civilization " where four thousand gods found not one unbeliever " an admiration it withheld from that of the One God. The studious humanist thought more of the loves of Jupiter, of wise Minerva and beauteous Venus, of fair Helen and the Siege of Troy, than of the preaching of John the Baptist, of the miracle of the Incarnation, and the faith of the martyrs. Mythology seemed to them vastly more attractive and interesting than the Gospel story.

It is not easy to envisage the enormous shock to the thought of mankind given first by the discoveries of Copernicus, who left the world unstable and far from the watchful eye of an imminent God, and then by the sudden dazzling view of the genius and thought of the ancients. Some historians take the view that the humanists were themselves the involuntary precursors of the Reformation. Erasmus and Ficino made the bed ; it was Luther and Calvin who were to lie in it.

VI

ERASMUS

IN the first rank of the humanists of the Renaissance we find the name of Desiderius Erasmus. His original name, in Dutch, was Geert Geerts, and he was illegitimate. The first part of his nom-de-plume, Desiderius, is Latin, the second, Erasmus, Greek. In later life, like a true humanist he regretted that it was not " Erasmius ", a closer approach to the Greek ἐράδμιος (amiable).

He was born in Rotterdam on October 28th, 1467. His father Geert Praet, being a cleric, could not acknowledge him, and being banished to Italy, abandoned mother and child. Soon after his return, Erasmus's mother died, and a little later Geert Praet himself. The boy was then thirteen. He started life as a choir-boy in the church of Utrecht and was then sent by his guardians to the college of Deventer, where he distinguished himself in classics.

When he was of age to choose a profession, his guardians, who do not appear to have been anxious to give him an account of their stewardship, pressed him to enter the Church, and willy-nilly he donned the Augustine habit in the convent of Steyn, near Gonda in Holland. He was, however, far too independent by nature to feel any vocation for a monkish life, and was soon disgusted with both the life and thought of the cloister.

From his later remarks on the subject of monks, his sojourn in the convent of Steyn must have been a horrible experience. He writes, for example, in his *The Praise of Folly* :

The names " religious " and " monk " are both assumed, since most of them are far removed from religion and I know none less solitary. I know no more pitiable class of men than these. So greatly are they hated that to meet one is esteemed unlucky, and yet they have a great conceit of themselves. Their greatest devotion is their ignorance of letters and inability to read. They cannot understand the psalms, which they recognize only by the metre, and bray them out like asses in the choir in the pious belief that they are producing a divine harmony. Many of them trade profitably on their own dirt and misery, begging their bread with groans at the church-doors and taking the food of the poor by their clamour around every inn, every carriage, and every ship.

Literature and a little painting were the young monk's only consolation. There is preserved in Delft a picture of the crucified Christ bearing the inscription " Do not despise this, for it was painted by Erasmus when he was cloistered in Steyn ". When he was only twenty some of his published writings attracted the attention of Henry of Berck, Bishop of Cambrai, who called the young man from his convent, ordained him priest on February 25th, 1492, and took him into his own service. Erasmus was now free to pursue his Greek and Latin studies. He worked at Delft under the direction of two famous humanists, Hezius and Rudolf Agricola, who, however, were not particularly satisfied with him. In 1496 the Bishop of Cambrai sent him to complete his studies in Paris, obtaining for him a scholarship in the Collège Montagu. He was now twenty-nine.

The reputation of the college was based on that of the theologians who taught there. " Even the walls," says Erasmus, " were theological." In other respects, if we may believe contemporary testimony, it was a grim place enough.

Rabelais refers to it through the mouth of Ponocrates speaking to Grandgousier, father of Gargantua.

Think not, my lord, that I have put him in that beggarly college called Montagu. I would rather put him in St. Innocent's gang, for I myself have known the cruelty and villainy of the place.

(St. Innocent's gang were the poor who found free lodging in Paris in the burial-ground and cloister of the Holy Innocents.)

The Moors and Tartars treat their criminals better, the murderers in prison, even your dogs, live better than the poor devils in this college. If I were King of Paris, the devil fly away with me if I wouldn't set fire to it and burn along with it the principal and ushers who suffer this inhumanity to be practised.

Students of the college are said to have fallen ill, to have gone out of their minds and even to have died as a result of their ill-treatment.

For Erasmus it had yet another disadvantage. The principal food of the students was fish, of which, owing to a constitutional weakness, he could not bear even the smell. At that time fish was an important article of diet, the Parisians eating as much as or more herring than they did bread. Finally the students were compelled to dress as monks, so that altogether it is no wonder that when Erasmus returned to Cambrai he had added to his distaste for monks an equal dislike for the dogmatic teaching and barren theology of his masters in the Collège Montagu.

He went back from Cambrai to Holland, where a young English nobleman, Lord William Mountjoy, whom he had met in Paris, persuaded him to visit England in his company. He spent rather more than a year studying at Oxford and Cambridge, where he perfected his knowledge of the classical tongues, and became intimate with the great and noble

Thomas More, Chancellor of Henry VIII. The first time he called on the great Chancellor, then at the highest point of his career, he was not known to him by sight. After a few moments of Latin conversation, Sir Thomas More, charmed by his wit and graceful airs, embraced him heartily, saying in mock consternation : " If you are not Erasmus, you must be the devil ! "

Erasmus was a little man, thin, frail, withered and nervous. His health was always poor, his digestion was bad, and in later years he was a martyr to the stone. Several portraits of him exist, the best being Holbein's masterpiece in the Louvre. Erasmus is there seen in profile, with meditative air, a black clerical bonnet on his head. He wears the dress of a secular priest and over it a tippet of rich fur. He is writing with the classical reed pen. His mouth alone, large, thin-lipped, with lines of thought about it, is enough to give character to his face. Beneath this half-length picture the celebrated Calvinist theologian Theodore Beza wrote the following inscription in Latin verse : " This picture contains the half of the great Erasmus. And why not all of him ? Wonder not, O reader, the whole earth would not suffice for all of him." Another portrait, also by Holbein, is to be found among the illustrations to *The Praise of Folly*.

The moral character of Erasmus made him a most attrac-tive person, even in his faults. He was both kind and intelli-gent, and his life as a whole was dignified, in spite of his incessant quest for money from the rich and powerful. Tolerance was an admirable feature of his character. He was a great peace-maker, and if he did not succeed in still-ing conflicts, reconciling hostile opinions and avoiding excess, brutality, burnings and armed conflict, it was only because a single human voice, however great its authority, could not but be lost in the howling tempest of human passions.

His knowledge was vast, his labour unceasing. No one can ever have worked harder than Erasmus did. He wished well to all, and always sought out in the teaching of an adversary all that was just and true, and begged him, for Christian charity, to abandon that part which contained the seeds of discord. This naturally enraged both sides. After being the hope of both Catholics and Protestants he ended as the butt of their united hatreds. Renan has said that there are few doctrines without a kernel of truth, and this kernel was the object of Erasmus's constant and disinterested search. When his clear mind led him to the hidden flame he rejoiced to let it burn in the open, only to see it extinguished by the tempest of human hatreds.

One is still amazed at the European power of this subtle and rather timid writer, who could express himself so well in Latin that under his pen it became once more a living language. Popes, Emperors and Kings, patricians and nobles, the universities and even the iron condottieri sought the honour of his correspondence. The most famous craved a written word from him. Princes sent embassies to him, towns were gay with bunting and flowers on his arrival at their gates, crowds thronged to meet him. City Corporations sought ingenious pretexts to keep him in their midst. Basle and Besançon were rivals for the honour of housing him. Henry VIII wished him to teach at Oxford and Cambridge, Charles V made him his Counsellor in Flanders, Francis I offered him the headship of the Collège de France. The German humanists made him the goal of a pilgrimage. " We go," wrote one of them, " through forests and plague-stricken lands to find one pearl of price."

The part played by Erasmus in the Europe of the Renaissance has often been compared with that of Voltaire in the Europe of Louis XV and Frederick the Great.

The great humanist finally settled at Basle (1521). There he lived, as peacefully as his fame allowed, with two other great men, Hans Froben the publisher and Hans Holbein the painter. He clung to this retired life partly from inclination, since nothing pleased him more than his work, but partly, as he slyly said, from calculation, since "writers, like pictures in a tapestry, look better from a distance".

His greatest delight was in his studies and the incessant stream of editions of authors sacred and profane, that flowed from his pen ; Cato, Cicero, Eutropius and many others. He was the first to publish the Greek text of Ptolemy, the first to provide a complete Aristotle. He produced learned editions of Demosthenes, of Josephus, the historian of the Jews, a Greek text with Latin translation of the New Testament. He published Latin translations of Euripides, Isocrates and Xenophon ; nor did he neglect the Fathers of the Church —Hilary, Jerome, Cyprian, Ambrose and Augustine.

In addition to these were the numerous original works in which his keen mind is displayed ; moral and philosophical tracts, pamphlets and satires. He published grammars and dictionaries, a treatise on Greek and Latin pronunciation and another on the *Art of Letter-Writing*. In date as in worth he takes first place in the history of teaching and of children's education. He drew up courses of study and composed manifestoes " on the education of children in virtue and literature from their birth ", in which latter he appears as precursor of modern theory and practice on this subject. His small treatise on " Civility in the manners of children " is as full of charm as of good sense. As with Voltaire, it is hard to see how Erasmus managed to write so much in one lifetime.

The *Adages* appeared in 1500. It was the dawn of a new century, and here " dawn " is used advisedly, for the whole century was enlightened by the *Adages*.

The book itself is a collection of ancient thoughts and proverbial sayings and witticisms, with a pertinent commentary drawn from Erasmus's own knowledge and experience. No other humanist, however great his eagerness to bring Antiquity closer to modern life, has ever produced so cogent an argument as this. The celebrated Hellenist Guillaume Budé, speaking of the *Adages*, said, "It is the storehouse of Minerva and we open it as we might the Sibylline Books." They had an immediate and overwhelming success.

In England, in 1509, Erasmus composed the most popular of his works, which even to-day is still edited, translated and read, *The Praise of Folly*. He had gone to England by invitation of Henry VIII, who liked and admired him and had entrusted him with the teaching of Greek at Cambridge. *The Praise of Folly* was as successful as the *Adages* had been ; it passed through seven editions in a few months and twenty-seven in a few years. It was immediately translated from the original Latin into most European languages. It is a satire on the society of the Renaissance, and in it the ecclesiastical hierarchy is singled out for particularly drastic treatment. It contains a picture of the heavily-armoured German prelates of the day, who drew rich profits from their votes in the Imperial elections :

They are satraps, caring nothing for religion, its blessings and its ceremonies, and holding it cowardly and shameful for a bishop to die otherwise than in battle. Their clergy valiantly follow their example, and fight like warriors for their tithes. They lack no kind of weapon, sword, stone or javelin. Their eyes are wide open to seek texts from Holy Writ wherewith to frighten their flocks into paying more than their lawful tithe, but they never think to read what is written of their duties toward these same flocks. The tonsure alone does not convince them that a priest should be free of worldly desires and intent on the blessings of Paradise.

They are sensual brutes, who think their duty well done when they have mumbled over their breviaries. And how they mumble ! That none can hear or understand. Perhaps they do not understand themselves what it is that they are mouthing. One thing at least they have in common with the laity : their eyes are wide open for money and they forgive no man his debt. Any distasteful duty they bandy like a shuttlecock from one to another. As lay princes delegate their administration in part to commissioners, who in turn pass it on to lower officials, so do our prelates delegate their pious duties to the regular clergy, who pass them on to the monks, the less strict of whom pass them to the stricter, and from them to the begging friars, and from them to the Carthusians, among whom piety is so piously buried as to be almost undiscoverable. So too the Popes, intent on their golden harvests, leave their apostolic labours to the Bishops, these to their curates, these to their vicars, these to the begging friars, and the friars themselves to those whose piety is to shear the lambs closely.

The *Colloquies* appeared at Basle in 1516. In a few months twenty-four thousand copies were sold, a fabulous figure for a period without modern publicity and with few means of distribution. The book is full of keen observation, humour and good humour, vigorous sarcasm and incisive criticism, the whole in an elegant and limpid Latin. The philosophic scope of the book is wider and deeper than that of its predecessors. It may be said that it cleared the way for the liberty of thought—not the " free-thinking "—of the sixteenth century.

All these works were in Latin, in which Erasmus not only wrote, but felt, thought, loved and hated. He declared that he knew neither French, German nor English, nor even Dutch, and if he ever brought himself to utter a sentence in the last-named tongue it was only to give an order to some servant who knew not the divine tongue of Virgil and Quintilian.

THE RENAISSANCE

He handled Latin more skilfully than any since classical times, but if he made it a religion, it was a religion without superstition. He admired Cicero, but did not idolize him. Some humanists objected to the use of any Latin word or construction not to be found in Cicero, and therefore were often driven to the most absurd lengths of periphrasis, especially if their subject were theology, modern politics, mechanics, or even cooking. Cicero had no occasion to mention Transubstantiation, nor Guelph and Ghibelline, nor arquebuses nor stuffed peacocks. Erasmus proudly avowed himself the faithful follower of Cicero, but not his ape. This point of view he defended in a charming little book, *The Ciceronian Dialogue*. In it he gives a humorous picture of the " Ciceromaniac ", huddled in his study and shutting his ears to all that might possibly disturb his communion with his deity. He hardly takes food, so great is his devotion. His lunch is a few grapes, his supper a few grains of coriander seed. His friend Tatius has borrowed manuscripts and not returned them, so that a letter must be written to Tatius, and in it must be no word, no syllable, no jot or tittle that is not in Cicero. Our humanist seizes his hero's works, which lie piled on his table, searches every page, weighs minutely every expression, measures the periods, counts the tropes and tricks of speech, in short, spends a whole night on one short sentence, and, as Erasmus carefully points out, a winter's night at that. An endless time such a letter must take, and meanwhile Tatius keeps the manuscripts ; but epistolary literature has at least been spared one imperfectly Ciceronian letter.

It is all very good fun, and to-day would only amuse the most ardent student of Cicero, but then it roused the assembled humanists of Italy to wild fury. The sacrilegious author was lucky to be out of their reach. Giulio-Cesare Scaliger, in his

Orations in defence of Roman eloquence against Desiderius Erasmus, pours a hail of insults on his head ; insults taken from the speeches against Catiline. He ends, " Did you not profit by your time spent correcting proofs at Aldus's ? Were your errors there due to printer's ink or to the wine in your head ? " There was worse to come. At Scaliger's request the Sorbonne launched its thunders at the head of the reckless author of the *Ciceronianus.* Poor Erasmus ! First the pope-haters and the pope-lovers, and then the humanists turn on him. In the eyes of all these he had one unpardonable fault : he was right.

Through all the noise and confusion Erasmus proceeded with the even tenor of his studies. He was not indifferent to the epigrams of his critics ; on the contrary, they pained him deeply, for he was sensitive to the least pinprick.

One of his friends took the part of a printer in trouble for publishing a libellous pamphlet, and was severely blamed by Erasmus.

But [said the friend] his wife and children must be fed.

Let him go and beg, then [said Erasmus], or send his wife on the streets : that would be better than ruining his neighbour's reputation. You say he has a wife and children ? Would that be an excuse if he robbed my house ? In any case his offence is worse, unless you esteem gold more highly than honour.

Bayle, who tells this story, is careful to add that Erasmus was the soul of gentleness and modesty.

His modesty itself was not left untouched by slander. He had taken for his device the god of boundaries, with the motto *Nulli cedo,* which his friend Bonifacius Auerbach afterwards had carved on his tombstone. This has been mis-translated " I am inferior to none " : the actual meaning was certainly " I yield to none ". And, in fact, Erasmus never yielded to threats when the truth was in question.

He is admirable as a scholar, thinker, and writer, and as a representative of what he called " Christian philosophy ", but still more as the apostle of concord and tolerance amidst the strife of the sixteenth century. He was indefatigable in his efforts to conciliate and appease, efforts which only drew down redoubled hatreds on himself.

For Erasmus the watchword of ancient as of modern philosophy was " Liberty " ; in religion the watchword was " Charity ". " Charity," he writes, " is the greatest of God's commandments." He did his utmost to prevent the struggle between Catholics and Reformers. When Luther wrote him an affectionate letter in 1519, he replied, " Your letter breathes a Christian spirit. It seems to me that one can go further by gentle moderation than by importunity. Was it not thus that Christ brought the world under his sway ? " He tried to show his Protestant friends that the libels and caricatures they spread broadcast over Europe were only harmful to their own cause. " Is it thus that you would make a way for the Gospel ? I fear rather that stupid malice and malicious stupidity will destroy good literature, even, if it can, the Gospel itself, and will bring you your-selves into discredit."

Then, turning to the Roman Court, he besought Adrian VI to abstain from persecution. " The evil is too deep-seated to be cured by fire and sword. Concessions are necessary on both sides, so that doctrine, the basis of faith, may remain intact." Erasmus, a priest, had the courage to add to the Pope himself : " Besides this, the world must be given the hope of seeing a change in certain matters which give just cause for complaint. All hearts will open to that sweet word, Liberty."

Violence could not be restrained and men were burnt on both sides, in Paris and in Geneva, but Erasmus persisted

in his task of appeasement. Why should not conflicting doctrines, instead of charging each other like angry bulls, seek
mutual understanding under the shadow of the Gospel which
to both of them represented the whole truth ? The conflict
was one of form, concerning only irrelevant man-made
details and arbitrary rulings on unimportant points. According to Erasmus, the remedy was simple and practicable :
the men of mark on both sides should meet on the basis of
the Scriptures, without regard for the useless lumber that
the centuries had piled around them. If that were done, no
doubt but that, given good will, an understanding could be
reached.

The Catholic priest was valiant in defence of the great
Reformer.

In Luther's heart [he writes] is the spark of the true apostolic
doctrine, but theologians who do not understand and have often
not even read him denounce him furiously to the mob instead
of gently reproving him and showing him the truth. They wound
him by their attacks, and find no words for him but heresiarch,
schismatic and Antichrist, condemning in him as heresy the
orthodoxy of St. Bernard and St. Augustine.

More daring still, he continues : " Many of those who
curse Luther do not themselves believe in the immortality
of the soul."

To the Archbishop of Mainz he writes : "Theologians,
who should most fittingly show meekness, seem to breathe
human blood in their desire for Luther's arrest and destruction."

He even attacked the Bull which condemned Luther.
" This Bull which displays rather cruelty than the benevolent
thought of Leo XI."

Luther, on his side, wrote on March 28th, 1518, " In what
corner of the earth is Erasmus's name unknown, and who

does not hail him as his master ? " Yet some years later he
was writing : " Erasmus of Rotterdam is the greatest rascal
who ever lived." The old Erasmus, for whom he had nothing but admiration and affection, is now become a venom-
ous serpent, the declared enemy of Christ, the Judas of
Christendom, an epicurean swine, a mere buffoon. No words
are bad enough for him.

The reason is not far to seek. Erasmus had written, with
studied moderation, in his *Discussions on Free-will*, that he
did not share Luther's view on predestination.

The unfortunate humanist received no better treatment
at the hands of the Catholics. When he passed through
Louvain the students raised a riot against him. Monks who
had never read him and boasted that they could not understand him called him clown and fool, ox and ass. The leader
of the chorus of condemnation started by the Sorbonne was
Noel Beda, head of the Collège Montagu, the scene of
Erasmus's early sufferings. " In my view," he said, " the fire
is the only way to deal with these gentry." And indeed it
was by his efforts that Erasmus's friend and translator Louis
de Berquin was publicly burnt in Paris.

Erasmus was almost exclusively a thinker ; his thought
elegant and distinguished, logical and full of common-sense
and accurate deduction, sometimes a little over-subtle. He
was not, however, by any means an ascetic. He had decidedly
no taste for martyrdom. Rabelais said of him that he defended
his convictions " as far as this side of burning " : in truth
he would hardly have gone so far, as he himself roundly
admits. He loved good cheer and the " magnificent " wines
of Burgundy (the adjective is his own). He could not conceive of a good meal in the absence of women, among whom
he most admired the English for their complexions. One
English custom he found admirable, the kissing which took

place when one paid a visit. " Sweetly perfumed embraces," he calls them. From England he wrote to his friend, the Latin poet Fausto Andrelini, an Italian in the service of Louis XII : " Here are fair and facile nymphs whom you might well prefer to your Muses."

In science, humanism and philosophy he was an Epicurean, but a well-bred delicate one, slightly self-centred. He is sometimes reproached with importunity in his endless begging to achieve what was necessary to his creature comforts. In the *Adages* he makes great play with the saying of Anaxagoras to Pericles : " Those who wish to use a lamp fill it with oil," meaning thereby that if the great ones of the earth wished to draw profit and pleasure from his fame, his writings and his wisdom, it was their duty at least to feed him. His needs, however, sometimes led him into unpleasant paths of hypocrisy, as when he sings the " chaste and harmonious " loves of Henry VIII.

These are blots on his memory, but it must be remembered, as at least a partial justification, that if modern copyright had then been in existence he would have been a rich man solely by the sale of his books, which far surpassed that of any of his rivals. As it was, they brought him in little but the generous friendship of Froben. The " mendicity " with which he has been reproached was almost a necessity for any writer without private means. Erasmus, at least, never descended to the level of Aretino.

He openly avows that his trunks are full of presents and his cellar full of the good Burgundy that has been given to him. His contemporaries found nothing to condemn in all this, even those who attacked him the most vigorously with opprobrious names. Certain modern historians have asked why he did not find some well-paid post instead of going begging. The reproach is unjustified. Erasmus was a professional editor. Besides, a profession which brought in more money would have taken up his time. What would then have become of his works ? What of *The Praise of Folly* ? Those who eased the laborious life of the Dutch humanist with their ducats had in return a century of remembrance and the gratitude of posterity. Was it too dearly bought ?

Erasmus's last years were one long agony from the stone, which he endeavoured to cure by a course of carefully selected Burgundies. An even more saddening influence was the increasing bitterness of the religious conflicts which it was his dearest hope to still.

In 1529, when the Reformation finally triumphed, amid scenes of violence, in Basle, Erasmus retired to Freiburg, where he went so far as to buy a house, but life in Basle had become, from habit, a necessity, so that he was forced to return there. Aged and sickly, he worked on in the unceasing hope that somehow the Reformers and the Catholic Church would be reconciled. He had never broken with the Church of Rome. He had frankly criticized its abuses, but had always respected the fundamental dogmas of Catholicism.

At long last his lofty intellect and thought were fitly recognized. In the midst of all the clamour loosed against him, Paul III offered him a cardinal's hat, the highest dignity it was in his power to bestow, and the aim even of the most ambitious. Erasmus refused without false modesty, preferring to live out his life as he was.

He had already taken to his bed for the last time. A few faithful friends, Froben, Auerbach and others, were at his side. They asked his last wishes, which should be piously fulfilled. " Order my coffin," was all he said.

Desiderius Erasmus of Rotterdam died at Basle on the night of the 11th-12th July 1536, aged sixty-nine. He died without asking for a priest. It was neither carelessness nor scorn, but the calm consciousness that he had lived his life and acted according to his conscience. From his couch he raised his eyes to Heaven, confident in its justice. He left his large fortune of seven thousand ducats (about £25,000) wholly to charity, to the "aged and infirm", to young orphans, and for a special foundation in favour of young persons of promise.

Professors and Students of the University of Basle, magistrates and citizens, all followed to its grave in the cathedral the body of the great humanist, whose greatest commendation was that he was the apostle of toleration.

VII

THE ART OF LETTERS IN FRANCE

FRENCH humanism arrived simultaneously from the North, with the books of Erasmus, and from the South, with the Italians. At first Erasmus's influence was the stronger, but after the first-comer Gregorio Tifernato, there came flocking from Italy a crowd of others : Beroaldo the Elder, Andrelini the poet, and the young Girolamo Aleandro, who arrived in Paris in 1508 and taught Greek with such success that he had two thousand students in the Collège de la Marque. In 1513, he became head of the University.

Paris, which till the end of the fifteenth century clung stolidly to the traditions of scholasticism and prided itself on remaining the living centre of mediæval dialectic, broke with tradition and went with the current of the new idea.

Guillaume Budé, of Francis I's foundation, the Collège de France, was the first Greek scholar of Europe, as Erasmus was the first Latinist. A throng of students, among them the sons of princes, flocked from all parts of Europe to Paris, greedy for knowledge. Foreign towns like Soleure in Switzerland raised funds to send their young men to Paris, which had become the centre of humanism, from which the taste for classical literature spread throughout France. The rich bankers and merchants of Lyons, like the Medici of Florence, protected and patronized the humanists of that city.

Rabelais, in *Pantagruel*, has vividly drawn the changed

aspect of literary studies. Gargantua is writing a letter of encouragement to his son at the University of Paris, and speaking of his own student days :

Those days were not so well suited to study as these, and I had no such teachers as you. The age was still full of darkness and the sorrow and calamity of the Goths, who had destroyed all good literature. Now, by God's mercy, light and dignity have returned to letters, and I behold such improvement that I could hardly hope to enter the first class among the little school-boys, I who in my day was rightly reputed the wisest of my century. Now discipline is restored and languages are in the curriculum ; Greek without which none can honestly call him-self a scholar, Hebrew, Chaldaean and Latin. Books, inventions of God as artillery is an invention of the devil, are well and correctly printed. The world is full of scholars, learned teachers, and ample libraries, so that I am persuaded that study was not so easy even in the days of Plato, Cicero or Papinian. Nay more, women and girls aspire to the heavenly manna of good learning. Thus it is that I, at my age, have been forced to learn Greek which like Cato I had condemned, since I had not time in youth to understand it.

Rabelais was speaking of what he had actually seen. Elderly men, in France as in Italy, were infected by the enthusiasm of their juniors and devoted their last years to the study of Latin and Greek.

Latin poets, too, began to appear—Virgilians to balance the Ciceronian prose writers. They celebrated their loves and hates, the small-beer events of their lowly lives or the Italian wars, all in the forms and metres devised by Horace, Catullus or Virgil. Their imitations were slavish and parrot-like. Erasmus mocked them. " The only originality they seek is lack of all originality." Their model among living poets was Fausto Andrelini, who had settled in France as the favourite of Anne of Brittany, whose virtues he trumpets

forth in heroic verse. In her honour he used every trope in
the classics : the grace of the nine Muses, the song of Orpheus,
Amphion's golden lyre, Penelope's constancy and Cornelia's
lofty soul, all are laid under contribution in his pæon of
adulation. When Anne died he seized the opportunity to
surpass himself. " Hear ! All ye people. Anne was beloved of
the Sun, but like a true Penelope, a true Cornelia, she was
cold to his fiery love-making. She ascends to the skies where
Jupiter gives her a splendid burial with her rejected lover."

The same state of mind and methods of thought are common to France and Italy. We no longer find Christians writing
of Christianity but Greeks of the time of Alcibiades, Romans
of that of Cato. Paradise is once more Olympus, the saints
are deities. When a poet describes a storm and the following
calm, he summons Neptune and Æolus, who calls the winds
to heel and locks them securely in their kennel. Mars is the
arbiter of battles, and the King of France fights like a Hercules.
All the rest is in the same vein.

Among these poets—who cannot be called rhymesters,
since their works were only to be distinguished from prose
by the alternation of long and short syllables—there is, however, one worthy of the name. This *rara avis*, as the Latinists
would have styled him, is Julien-Pierre de Mazières.

He relates in clear and simple verse his own thoughts and actions,
incidents of his daily life. He sends a cockerel to a friend or receives
a gift of flowers. He watches a candle burn down and is reminded
of the shortness of his own existence. He admires youth and solitude,
he loves to open his window to the green of woods and fields,
and to drink in the scent of the roses of May. He at least has a
soul.

But the average would-be Pindar of the age did not understand the classical poets he so zealously imitated. He is always

talking of " epic " and " epic song ", but without the faintest idea of the real nature of the epic. He thinks of Homer as a poet peacefully writing in his study a well-thought-out and harmonious poem. He could easily imagine him a member of the Valois academy. The vast mythology which swarms through Homer's epic is to him the creation of a single genius. The learned Scaliger, whose profession was the study of the classical texts, was no better in this respect than Ronsard ; he rates the Æneid as an epic above the Iliad and the Odyssey. The humanist repeats to infinity that the Middle Ages did not understand the classics. It seems that the Renaissance, for all its scholarship, understood them even less.

It should be remembered that these " Latinizers ", as Ronsard called them, thought themselves the equals of the great writers they plagiarized. Since their own works consisted only of the best elements of their predecessors, must they not naturally be as good, or even better ? Petit de Julleville has an ingenious explanation for this strange conception of poetry. The Renaissance began with humanism, that is to say scholarship, and from this scholarship sprang the poets, who therefore prefer to say what they know rather than what they feel. The worst result was that not only Latin but French poetry became infected. Rabelais calls the whole school the " Pindarizers ". Their most famous representatives are the group known as the " Pléiade "—the seven sisters who are enthroned among the stars. Their names were Ronsard, Du Bellay, Baïf, Belleau, Jodelle, Jean Dorat and Pontus de Thiard ; and among them Du Bellay ranks as a talented and Ronsard as an inspired poet.

Du Bellay calls Ronsard " the Pindar of France, whose brow touches the stars ". Ronsard was born at the Château de la Possonière in the Vendômois on September 11th, 1522. On both the father's and the mother's side his family was

of high rank. His father, Louis de Ronsard, was *maître d'hôtel*
to Francis I, who sent him to Spain with his two sons François Duke of Brittany and Henri, afterwards Henri II, who
were handed over to Charles V as hostages for their father.
His mother was a cousin of Bayard. According to Bayle,
Ronsard was through his mother a cousin seventeen times
removed of Elizabeth of England.

By his own confession the dæmon of poetry tormented
him from his earliest youth.

> Je n'avais pas douze ans, qu'au profond des vallées
> Dans les hautes forêts des hommes reculées,
> Dans les antres secrets de frayeur tout couverts,
> Sans avoir soin de rien, je composais des vers.

His father put him to school in Paris with Jean Dorat, professor of Greek at the Collège de Coqueret, and author of
celebrated anagrams derived from Lycophron, the friend of
Theocritus and a member of the "Pléiädes" of Ptolemy
Philadelphus. Dorat was the teacher of both Baïf and Ronsard, and became their associate in the new Pléiädes where
they met as equals and friends. This fact is noteworthy for
the development of Ronsard's poetic thought.

His apprenticeship over, Ronsard's destiny was to have
been the profession of arms, as befitted a gentleman of good
family. Besides, he was tall and good-looking, a good horseman, who excelled at fencing, at tennis and wrestling, and
was admired by the women for his noble bearing and beauty
of feature. All this was to count for nothing. He became
deaf. This deafness explains to a great extent his reserve with
all but his intimate friends, a reserve which has often been
attributed to pride. Since he could no longer follow the
career most suited to his birth and inclination, he took orders
and received the tonsure, but did not become an ordained
priest lest he should lose his independence of life and thought.

His round clerk's cap was found no obstacle to his discharging his duties of squire and courtier. His luxuriant chestnut hair early turned grey, which gave his rivals, who did not know his age, an excellent chance to mock him as an infatuated greybeard writing love poetry. The gout from which he suffered in his later years was attributed by these same rivals to a life of debauchery.

His most violent opponents were the Protestant ministers. He had aroused their hatred by raising a band of partisans to chastise their co-religionists, who had broken images and destroyed pictures in the churches of his province, and had gone so far as to violate the tombs of the princely family of Vendôme.

Lampoons such as the " Metamorphosis of Ronsard into a priest " and " The Temple of Ronsard " make capital of the fact that the author of so much amorous verse was the holder of various benefices, among them of that of Saint Côme-en-l'Ile near Tours. These he owed to Charles IX, who admired his poetic talent and treated him as a friend, but at the same time said in jest, " I am afraid to lose my Ronsard. I fear too great possessions may lead him to neglect his Muse. A good poet, like a good horse, should not be too well fattened. Both must be kept, but not too well kept."

Age brought with it infirmity, which came even before its due season.

> La goutte, jà vieillard, me bourrela les veines,
> Les muscles et les nerfs, exécrable douleur !
> Montrant en cent façons, par cent diverses peines,
> Que l'homme n'est sinon le sujet de malheur.

His last years were spent in melancholy retirement in the peace of one or other of his priories in that fair Loire country which had seen the growth of his genius.

> Je n'ai plus que mes os, un squelette je semble,
> Décharné, dénervé, démuscle, dépeuplé,
> Que le trait de la mort sans pardon a frappé :
> Je n'ose voir mes bras que de peur je ne tremble.

He died on December 27th at his priory of St. Côme, in his sixty-second year.

His literary fame was equalled among his contemporaries only by Erasmus. Even in his lifetime he took rank as a classic. His works were studied and commentaries written on them in the universities of Flanders, England and Poland as well as in France. Mary Stuart used his poems as a bedside book in the long and dreary years of her imprisonment. Condemned men declaimed them as a farewell gesture from the scaffold. The enthusiastic Italians placed him above their own poet Tasso, even above Petrarch. The young students of Paris fought to touch his garments as he passed as if he were a king or a saint.

From the beginning Ronsard had written " under the Ægis of the Greek and Latin Muses ", that is to say, he studied Greek and Latin poets " so that his lyre might have the soft and singing subtlety, the variety of tone and the splendid amplitude of the poets of Italy ". He imitated Pindar, Theocritus, Anacreon—

> " Anacreon pleases me, sweet Anacreon."

He imitated Horace and Virgil—

> Les François qui mes vers liront,
> S'ils ne sont Grees et Romains,
> Au lieu de ce livre, ils n'auront
> Qu'un pesant poids entre les mains.

Unfortunately the French were neither Greeks nor Romans, but Frenchmen, and so they needed a special lexicon to understand his poetry at all. As soon as each new " pindaric " work appeared, a host of commentators hastened to the task of interpreting it to the public. Minet wrote a commentary on the *Amours de Cassandre* and Belleau on the *Amours de Marie*. Jean Besli took charge of the *Sonnets pour Hélène*, and Pierre de Marcassus undertook the thankless task of reducing the hieroglyphics of the *Franciade* to some degree of intelligibility.

Contemporary opinion was not unanimous in admiration of this extraordinary conception of what French poetry should be. The authors of the *Parnassus Reformed*, for example, disliked " this obscurity, impenetrable without the aid of a commentary ", and pointed to the sonnets to Cassandre as a ground for their objections. They put to the poet the pointed question whether it was likely that his heroine would be familiar with the " Dolope soudart ", the " Myrmidon ", the " Corèbe insensé " and the rest, and whether a mere girl could possibly guess all these riddles.

Ronsard was acting as a squire of the Royal household at the château of Blois when, at a festival on the 28th April 1545, he saw Cassandra Salviati, daughter of a Florentine nobleman. She played the lute and sang the accompaniment to a Burgundian dance, and charmed the eyes, if not the ears, of the deaf poet. She was sixteen, black-eyed and black-haired, with shining white teeth and ruby lips. Even after eight years, the poet could recall the wonder of her appearance.

> Toutes beautés a mes yeux ne sont rien
> Au prix du sein qui, soupirant, secoue
> Son gorgeron sous qui, doucement, joue
> Le branle égal d'un flot cythéréen.
>
> En la façon que Jupiter est aise
> Quand de son chant une Muse l'apaise,
> Ainsi je suis de ses charmes épris,
> Lorsqu'en ses doigts son luth elle embesogne
> Et qu'elle dit le branle de Bourgogne
> Qu'elle disait le jour que je fus pris.

This poem [says Mathias Tresch] would be charming but for the totally superfluous introduction of Jupiter, and of a Jupiter in whom the poet obviously did not believe. All he can think of as a comparison bringing out the charm of his lady is Jupiter listening to the song of one of the Muses. The whole thing is grotesque.

There were moments, however, when Ronsard fell out of love with his classical bag of tricks, as when he very well says in the preface to his deplorable *Franciade*, "It is lèse-majesté to desert one's own living tongue to dig up the mouldering relics of antiquity."

The attraction of old French forms and traditions became more marked in his later years, but he was the victim of his own past, and fettered by the taste of his contemporaries, whose favourite model he had been for so long.

His sonnet to his friend and colleague in the Pléiade, Pontus de Thiard, throws light on his anomalous position and his hesitation as to how to deal with it :

Mon Tyard, on disait, à mon commencement,
Que j'étais trop obscur au simple populaire ;
Mais, aujourd'hui, on dit que je suis au contraire
Et que je me démens, parlant trop bassement.

Toi, de qui le labeur enfante doctement
Des livres immortels, dis-moi, que dois-je faire ?
Dis-moi, car tu sais tout, comment dois-je complaire
A ce monstre têtu, divers en jugement ?

Quand j'écris hautement, il ne veut pas me lire,
Quand j'écris bassement, il ne fait que médire.
De quels liens serrés ou de quel rang de clous.

Tiendrai-je ce Protée que se change à tous coups ?
Tyard, je t'entends bien : il le faut laisser dire,
Et nous rire de lui comme il se rit de nous.

His greatest mistake was the *Franciade*, which sprang from a false conception of the nature of the epic, a misjudgment of the author, or rather authors, of the Iliad, and a desire to outrival Virgil, whom, like most humanists, he admired more than Homer. Virgil had left the Trojans led by Æneas on the banks of the Tiber : Ronsard, to bring his Trojans to the Seine, invented one Francus, son of Hector and nephew of Æneas, an ancestor of Pharamond and of Clovis.

It would have been better if he had confined himself to sonnets such as the famous one for Hélène.

> Quand vous serez bien vieille, au soir, à la chandelle,
> Assise auprès du feu, dévidant et filant,
> Direz, chantant mes vers et vous émerveillant :
> " Ronsard me célébrait du temps que j'étais belle."
>
> Lors vous n'aurez servante oyant telle nouvelle,
> Déjà sous le labeur à demi sommeillant
> Qui, au bruit de mon nom, ne s'aille réveillant
> Bénissant votre nom de louange immortelle.
>
> Je serai sous la terre un fantôme sans os,
> Par les ombres myrteux je prendrai mon repos,
> Vous serez au foyer une vieille accroupie,
>
> Regrettant mon amour et votre fier dédain :
> Vivez, si m'en croyez, n'attendez à demain,
> Cueillez dès aujourd'hui les roses de la vie.

Of the protests evoked by the slavish imitation of classical and foreign literature to which the Pléiade was prone, the best is the curiously named *Quintil Horatien*, whose author, Charles Fontaines, hits the nail on the head when he accuses the " Pindarizers " of breaking with French tradition and alienating the people by their high-flown style.

The Italians, as descendants of the ancient Romans, had some excuse for looking backwards. Besides, they had at that time practically no popular tradition of their own, the sources of their poets being mainly French. Dante drew his inspiration from various French " Divine Comedies ", among them that of Raoul de Houdan who, however, only visited

Heaven and Hell, since in the tenth century when he wrote Purgatory had no canonical existence. (It was only declared part of Catholic dogma by the Council of Florence in 1439.)

Boccaccio, born in Paris of a Parisian mother, drew much upon the French "fabliaux". Petrarch, who studied at Montpellier and lived at Avignon, chose a Frenchwoman for his heroine. Pulci's *Morgante Maggiore* only retells the tale of the Chanson de Roland, which he himself had from a wandering singer, who had received it in his turn from a French "jongleur". The French epic was the source of both Boiardo's *Orlando Innamorato* and Ariosto's *Orlando Furioso*, while Ariosto's comedies are founded on French popular tales. Tasso had started a "Rinaldo" on one of the heroes of the French epic, and in his *Jerusalem Delivered* the French heroes Godfrey of Bouillon and Renaud himself play the principal parts.

It is a curious paradox that at the beginning of the Renaissance the really popular literature of Italy, whose figures were universally loved by the people, was French. From this sprang a curious language, a mixture of French and Italian, whose vigorous expressions were generally favoured. Roland became Orlando, Renaud de Montauban Rinaldo di Montalbano, Ogier l'Ardennois was mis-translated Ugieri il Danese (Ogier the Dane) and so on. The mob knew every one of them by heart. We have already noticed an argument between two Italians of the people regarding the respective merits of Roland and Renaud. This was repeated on a more polished note by Galeazzo Visconti and Isabella d'Este Marchioness of Mantua, on the occasion of an excursion by water.

The Italians went even further. Though Roland was supposed to have been Lord of the Marches of Brittany, Sutri and Fiesole claimed to be his birthplace and a score of Italian towns remember him in their coats of arms, on their church doors and at their street-corners.

If all this is true of Italy, how much greater is the pity that Ronsard and his friends, who had a living tradition ready to hand, did not use it instead of straying into byways of pedantic rhyme on subjects that are now dust and ashes.

The second objection raised by the *Quintil Horatien* is as serious and as well-deserved as the first. The " Pindarists " had effectively cut themselves off from the only possible source of new life in literature, the mind of the populace. The old French epic had reached every class in France, from the highest to the lowest. The new school, however, wrote only for the Court, for the rich and for a few initiates. The wildflower of poetry had become a hot-house bloom, needing constant shelter and unwearied care.

The new poetry, however, did not entirely drive out the old. There remained the " mysteries " of the Middle Ages, the Nativities and " Adorations of the Shepherds " and suchlike, which were continued, especially by the " Confrérie de la Passion " of Paris, till Protestant puritanism forbade them in 1548.

There also remained the popular farces, such as the famous *Pathelin* which, overleaping the Renaissance, formed the connecting link between the Middle Ages and the genius of Molière.

Rabelais and Ronsard were known to one another, having met at Meudon in the château of the Guises, built by the Cardinal of Lorraine. One of its towers was named after Ronsard, who had his rooms in it. The two great writers were hardly capable of mutual understanding. " They fought like two cocks," says a seventeenth-century biographer. Ronsard, the nobleman and courtier, with his refined haughtiness accentuated by his deafness, could not be other than repelled by the outspoken, hard-living curé of Meudon.

Ronsard himself did not disdain good wine, such as Chambertin or Montlouis, the latter for preference, since it came from his own province of Touraine, but the gargantuan drinking-bouts of Rabelais could not but sicken and repel him. The memory of Rabelais the drinker is enshrined in Ronsard's epitaph on him. If the poet is to be believed, he was one of the most insatiable topers the globe has ever known.

> Jamais le soleil ne l'a vu
> Tant fût-il matin, qu'il n'eut bu
> Et jamais au soir la nuit noire,
> Tant fût tard, ne l'a vu sans boire ;
> Car altéré, sans nul séjour,
> Le galant buvait nuit et jour.
>
> Mais quand l'ardente canicule
> Ramenait la saison qui brûle,
> Demi-nu, se troussait les bras
> Et se couchait tout plat à bas
> Sur la jonchée entre les tasses,
> Et, parmi des écuelles grasses
> Sans nulle honte se touillant,
> Allait dans le vin barbouillant,
> Comme une grenouille en la fange . . .

There are striking likenesses between the lives of the two great men, Rabelais and Erasmus, who dominated their century, though in temperament they were totally dissimilar. Rabelais knew no measure or proportion : Erasmus is so nicely proportioned as to seem almost narrow. Rabelais stands for the triumph of unbounded imagination, Erasmus for reason and reflection ; but both judged contemporary events and society in the same way, with the same understanding and in the same spirit of broad tolerance ; both had the same conception of divinity, of nature, of human life, and of the conditions necessary to human happiness. They are a case in point of the proverb that " Great minds think alike ".

It is uncertain whether Rabelais was born in 1483, 1490, or 1495. He was the son of a respectable citizen of Chinon, who combined the trade of vine-grower with that of publican or, as some say, apothecary. Like Erasmus, he was early pressed into monastic orders. He spent some years with the Franciscans of Fontenay-le-Comte, who, as Colletet said, " professed ignorance rather than religion ".

Again like Erasmus, he devoted himself to classical study in surroundings that militated against it. He learnt Latin, Greek and Hebrew and corresponded with all the great scholars of his time, with Budé, with the celebrated lawyer Tiraqueau and with Erasmus himself. He was ordained priest, and, yet again like Erasmus, abandoned the priesthood. He was harried by the authorities and protected by the Bishop of Maillezais, Geoffroi d'Estissac, as Erasmus had been by the Bishop of Cambrai. Neither Erasmus nor Rabelais was fond of monks, who, indeed, confiscated Rabelais' works and flung their writer into prison. Rabelais, in a passage that might have been taken from *The Praise of Folly*, describes them " muttering endless legends and psalms, none of which they understand, and punctuating their paternosters with long-drawn-out Ave Marias, devoid of all thought or understanding ".

Erasmus attacked the monks directly in biting pamphlets ; Rabelais in quite a different way. Rabelais' satire took the form of depicting a monk as little like his old associates as possible, the least monkish of monks that ever monked in a monkery, the worthy Friar, Jean des Entommeures, who was as devoted a worker for the good of his convent as he was a good trencherman at the blessed hour of meals. A

stout tippler and a good companion, a good monk without
trace of bigotry, he is good-hearted and pitiful, and helps
whomsoever is in need or trouble. He is sound of heart as
of head.

Rabelais was ordained priest in 1511, afterwards obtaining
leave to study medicine at Montpellier, where he won the
admiration of his teachers. *Pantagruel* appeared in 1532, and
was immediately condemned by the Sorbonne. The author,
however, was protected by the Bishop of Paris, Jean du
Bellay, a striking figure, a high dignitary of the Church,
a skilful diplomat and a great scholar. His religion was tempered with a philosophy very like that of Erasmus and
Rabelais, and his ordinary discourse was well seasoned with
Rabelaisian salt. Like Rabelais himself, he had no mean
reputation as a toper.

When he was appointed Ambassador to the Pope he took
Rabelais with him as his physician. This first stay in Italy
lasted three months, from January to March 1534, but Rabelais paid a second visit which lasted from July 1535 till March
of the next year. There we find a good instance of the diversity of his interests. He had noticed the plants in the Pope's
privy garden in the Belvedere, and contrived to obtain seed
from them. These he sent to his friend the Bishop of Maillezais, and thus introduced into France the carnation, the
lettuce which is still called "Roman", the artichoke and
the melon.

On May 22nd, 1537, Rabelais attained the degree of
Doctor of Medicine at Montpellier, where he taught success-
fully for some time. It is said that he introduced dissection
there before Vesalius. He then went to Lyons, where he was
appointed head of the great hospital of Pont-du-Rhône and
professor of anatomy.

His writings, however, brought down trouble on his

head. The Cardinal de Tournon, a great diplomat and one of the most intelligent men of his time, had branded him at Rome as an evil-liver, and said that he would like to clap him into gaol as an example to " those new-fangled writers ". Du Bellay offered Rabelais the refuge of a canonry in the abbey of Saint-Maur-des-Fossés, which the latter describes, in a letter to Cardinal de Chatillon, as " a place, or more properly a paradise, of salubrity, amenity, security, convenience and every righteous pleasure and delight there is in agriculture and a rustic life ".

In 1551, much to the indignation of the Sorbonne, Rabelais was given the care of souls of the parish of St. Martin at Meudon, which, after eleven months, he resigned in order to pursue his own labours. In spite of the slight connection of his life with the place, it has become a tradition to refer to him as the " Curé of Meudon ". The main business of his life was and continued to be the study and practice of medicine and the study of literature and science. Nothing is known of his later years, but he died in Paris on April 9th, 1553, and is believed to have been buried in the graveyard of St. Paul.

His great work appeared in 1542 under the pseudonym of Alcofribas Nasier, an anagram on François Rabelais. It was called *The Horrific and Astounding Deeds and Prowesses of the renowned Pantagruel, King of the Dipsodes and son of the great giant Gargantua.*

The character and scope of this work have been the objects of much argument. Some see in it only light relief from its author's scientific and medical studies and his daily tasks. Others take the contrary view that it is full of deep ideas, of philosophic vision, of flattering or critical portraits of thinly disguised figures of the time ; a book full to the brim of social, religious and political teaching hidden under the cloak of burlesque to escape the persecuting zeal of Sorbonne and Parlement.

The truth is probably somewhere between the two extremes. Both Gargantua and Pantagruel give the impression that their author is seeking relaxation from an overwhelming burden of serious work. The whole work, as Faguet says, is only five hundred pages long, and took twenty years to write. It can therefore have only occupied a very modest place among its author's occupations. Nevertheless, Rabelais could not help pouring into it his abounding thought and the impressions made on it by his varied life among men, ideas and events.

Within the frame of a book which must have amused the author as much as the reader, swarms a splendid host of ideas and reflections on men and things. These ideas show a penetration the more remarkable in that they are the spontaneous products of a single gigantic imagination ; one of the greatest that has ever existed.

Erasmus had reached the same conclusions as Rabelais on almost every subject of general interest, whether moral, social, religious or political. He, however, had reached them by reflection and arduous thought, by logical deduction after long and critical application, while Rabelais' confused picture of truth springs direct from a vivid imagination tempered by sovereign common sense.

Every page of Rabelais displays his essential soundness and generosity, and principally because the elements of his work are essentially of the people. His earliest works were almanacs, a literary form destined solely for popular consumption, but in 1532 there appeared a popular work, *The Great and Inestimable Chronicles of the Great and Enormous Giant, Gargantua*, which has been attributed, apparently in error, to Rabelais.

This first *Gargantua* was a direct descendant of the old romances of chivalry, and in it are found stock figures such as King Arthur and the wizard Merlin. It had a great success. More copies of it were sold in three months than Bibles in nine years. Rabelais was enchanted with it and resolved to take up the tale.

In Rabelais' work, which alone of the works of the Renaissance is in the direct line of tradition with those of the Middle Ages, the style is subject to astonishing variations from one passage to another. In the more serious parts the author, for decorum's sake, makes use of a Latin syntax, in others he uses the speech of the porter and the bargee.

As Léon Daudet has shown, his language has a large element of slang, and that a particular variety of slang, the " trimard ", which was the jargon of the birds of passage who at that time thronged the highways of Europe. It was then the custom for journeymen just out of their apprenticeship to go the rounds of France, and they, with ballad-singers and strolling-players and musicians and vagabond scholars, made up a specialized class, which later engulfed François Villon. It was a floating population with its own manners and customs and its own language. It lived from hand to mouth on a stock-in-trade of knavery on which Rabelais drew for his description of Pantagruel's " sixty-three ways to raise the wind ". Their thieves' cant was full of racy phrases, of unknown origin, but thoroughly and picturesquely appropriate to their meanings, such as one finds in Molière and even in the common speech of to-day. Léon Daudet catalogued the words peculiar to Rabelais and divided them into five groups. Of these, the first consists of words taken from the " langue d'oc " or southern French dialect. The second contains words of Rabelais' own coinage. The other three groups are taken from Latin, Greek, and the " trimard " respectively.

Rabelais, like Erasmus, abhorred and detested theology, which he called, in a Greek invention of his own, " nothing-ology ". He believed that toleration should be extended to all men of sincere belief and good behaviour. Toleration is the guiding principle of Rabelais' teaching as of that of Erasmus, and it was for that reason that it was condemned by the orthodoxy of the Sorbonne, in spite of the privilege accorded by François I to guard against that very danger. In 1543 the faculty of theology denounced *Gargantua* and *Pantagruel* to the Parlement. The author was in grave danger, for Dolet had just been arrested. He was protected by the favour of Francis I, but the king died and Rabelais was compelled to leave for Metz so hurriedly that he had no time to collect any money.

In 1549 the Benedictine monk Gabriel de Puits Herbaut published a most virulent attack on him, while at the same time Calvin was demanding that he should be burnt as " one of those dogs who . . . insinuate themselves by their tricks, as though they only sought to divert those who listen ", but whose aim is to destroy all reverence for the Deity.

Like Erasmus, Rabelais was at one time inclined toward the Reformers, as witness the words of an imp in *Pantagruel* :

Lucifer was wont to dine on scholars, but of late years, un-happily, they have added the Bible to their other studies, and now we cannot drag a single one of them to the devil. I verily believe that if the rascally clergy do not help us by tearing their St. Paul from their hands with threats, abuse, force, violence and burnings, we shall never have another down here to eat.

He was indignant at the way the decretals were used to " draw subtly from France to Rome every year 400,000 ducats and more, seeing that the 'most Christian country' of France is the only supporter of the Roman court ". Later, however, the intolerance and violence of the Huguenots repelled him. He attacks indiscriminately the "papefigues" (those who fear the Pope), and their opponents the "papimanes". "Papimania," he declares, "is nothing but idolatry."

Like Erasmus, he ended his days in the bosom of the Church.

Rabelais and Erasmus alike longed for peace between the factions and the concord of all men of good will. Alike they held the highest wisdom to be a reasoned conformity to the laws and wishes of nature, "a certain lightness of heart confirmed by contempt of chance misfortunes", or, as Erasmus more briefly put it, "reason".

The ultimate residue of Rabelais' beliefs extracted from his whole work would probably prove to be a kind of moral pantheism, not unlike that of his contemporary Michel Servet : "A great, kind and pitiful God, who ordained not only Lent, but salads and all kinds of fish to eat in it, and also good wine." This god, as may be seen, was very different from that of Calvin.

"I am ready," added Rabelais, "to maintain my opinions up to the fire, exclusively."

His morality might have been taken from the Gospel.

"Set not thine heart on vanity, for life is transitory, help thy neighbour and love him as thyself."

Rabelais, whose fame has only increased as time has passed and his teaching been better understood, is without doubt the greatest figure of the French Renaissance.

Joachim Du Bellay, who died at thirty-five, was together with Ronsard the glory of the Pléiade. His was the purer fame and his the charm. Of all the poets of his time he is the one whose work retains the most freshness and who can still move the reader by his colour, by the sincerity of his sentiments and the simple and natural grace of their expression.

> Oh, qu' heureux est celui qui peut passer son âge
> Entre pareils à soi ! et qui, sans friction,
> Sans crainte, sans envie et sans ambition
> Règne paisiblement en son pauvre ménage !
>
> Le misérable soin d'acquérir davantage
> Ne tyrannize point sa libre affection
> Et son plus grand désir, désir sans passion,
> Ne s'étend plus avant que son propre héritage.
>
> Il ne s'empêche point des affaires d'autrui,
> Son principal espoir ne dépend que de lui,
> Il est sa cour, son roi, sa faveur et son maître.
>
> Il ne mange son bien en pays étranger,
> Il ne met pour autrui sa personne en danger,
> Et plus riche qu'il n'est ne voudrait jamais être.

In 1551 Joachim followed his uncle, the Cardinal of Ostia, to Rome as steward. Even among the splendid monuments of Rome he was a prey to home-sickness, and thus it was that he came to write his modest volume of " Regrets ".

> Quand reverrai-je, hélas ! de mon petit village
> Fumer la cheminée et en quelle saison
> Reverrai-je le clos de ma pauvre maison
> Qui m'est une province et beaucoup davantage ?
>
> Plus me plaît le séjour qu'ont bâti mes aieux
> Que des palais romains le front audacieux,
> Plus que le marbre dur ne plaît l'ardoise fine.
>
> Plus mon Loire gaulois que le Tibre latin,
> Plus mon petit Liré que le mont Palatin,
> Et plus que l'air marin la douceur angevine.

He was born at the Château de la Turmelière, on the borders of Brittany and Anjou, in 1525, year of the battle of Pavia and the captivity of Francis I. There were in the family three famous brothers, the Cardinal, the protector of

Rabelais, as much the diplomat and more the soldier than the churchman ; Guillaume, Lord of Langey, a renowned captain and viceroy in Piedmont for Francis I ; and Martin, also a soldier and a diplomat, who completed the memoirs begun by his brother Guillaume.

Ronsard and Du Bellay met by chance in an inn in Poitiers and became fast friends. They had tastes in common, especially as regards poetry, and both shared a common infirmity, deafness, which had held them back from their hereditary profession of arms. The education of Du Bellay, who was early left an orphan, had been sadly neglected. " My youth was lost like a flower deprived of rain, without a hand to tend it."

Thus, when by his own volition he took up the study of Greek and Latin, it was too late for him to master it sufficiently to find a means of self-expression in the tongue of Pindar or that of Horace, and he was willy-nilly reduced to writing in French. It was therefore almost in spite of himself, but also prompted by Ronsard, whose ideas he presented to the world, that he wrote and published his celebrated *Defence and Illustration of the French Tongue*, which appeared in February 1550 and marks an important epoch in French literature. Written when Du Bellay was only twenty-four, this little work has all the freshness, the colour and the enthusiasm of youth.

The Latinized and Græcized writers considered their mother-tongue nothing but an archaic " gothic " dialect incapable of expressing a scientific idea or of giving to thought that grace and distinction of expression which alone made expression worth while. The *Defence* consists of two parts. In the first the author takes upon himself the defence of his native tongue ; in the second he puts forward an ideal to which poetry, according to him, should aspire.

I cannot blame enough the fatuous arrogance of certain of my countrymen who, themselves being far removed from Greeks and Romans, spurn and reject with more than stoic scorn all that is written in French. I cannot marvel enough at the strange opinions of certain scholars who think the vulgar tongue incapable of any work of art or learning.

If French is not as rich as Greek and Latin, it is because it is as yet undeveloped. It must be allowed to mature and fructify. It can be enriched with neologisms, by borrowings from other tongues and by drawing on the treasure-house of the past. In old French would be found hundreds of picturesque and expressive words and phrases now neglected. Frenchmen should write in French : the only surviving works of Dante, Petrarch and the great poets of Italy are those composed in their own language.

But, while Du Bellay's treatise is a good defence of the French language, it is far from being a defence of a literature whose basic thought had been misshapen by humanism. It is a violent attack on the older school of poetry, of which Clément Marot was the standard-bearer. Down with Gothic ! Away with rondeaux, ballades, virelais and all the other trash ! Antiquity is to be restored, even if it entails the wholesale imitation of Greeks and Romans.

The Ancients can only be surpassed if we imitate them [is one of La Bruyère's less inspired aphorisms, but Du Bellay had preceded him in it]. Frenchmen ! March boldly on this proud city and—as you have done more than once—use its spoils to adorn your temples and your altars. Heed not the cackling geese, nor proud Manlius, nor treacherous Camillus, should they find you naked counting the ransom of the Capitol. Spare not to pillage the sacred treasury of the Delphic temple.

These are sentiments which completely destroy the effect of the first part, as is pointed out by the defender of the old school in The *Quintil Horatien*.

Eustache du Bellay, Bishop of Paris, who had succeeded Jean when he went on his embassy to Rome, appointed his cousin Joachim, on his return from Rome, to a canonry of Notre-Dame, and the poet was about to be made Archbishop of Bordeaux when he died in Paris on January 1st, 1560. As we have already seen, he went with his cousin Jean du Bellay on his embassy to Rome. He there took part in the splendid life of the Roman court, though always hampered by lack of funds. His duties left him ample time to saunter in the beautiful gardens of the Porto, " where there are no shadows to annoy save those of laurel and of myrtle, where are deer and pheasants and fish for all three sports ".

In the ambassador's train he lived first in the Palace of Sant' Antonio, and then in the new Farnese palace of Borgo San Pietro, both princely dwellings with gardens where Jean Du Bellay set his antique statuary amid the green of lemon and cypress groves.

Amongst all this pomp and luxury and beauty the poet's mind was shrouded in melancholy, as can be seen from the whole atmosphere of the " Regrets ". His duties in his cousin's service held him captive, far from the even tenor of life which he desired. He confides his discontent to his friend, the Parisian printer Frédéric Morel, later the publisher of the " Regrets ".

Flatter un créditeur pour son terme allonger,
Courtiser un banquier, donner bonne espérance,
Ne suivre en son parler la liberté de France,
Et, pour respondre un mot, un quart d'heure y songer ;

Ne gaster sa santé par trop boire et manger,
Ne faire sans propos une folle despense,
Ne dire à tous venans tout cela que l'on pense,
Et d'un maigre discours gouverner l'estranger ;

Cognoistre les humeurs, cognoistre qui demande,
Et d'autant que l'on a la liberté plus grande,
D'autant plus se garder que l'on ne soit repris ;

Vivre aveques chacun, de chacun faire compte ;
Voilà, mon cher Morel—dont je rougis de honte—
Tout le bien qu'en trois ans à Rome j'ai appris.

As a consequence of his employment in the diplomacy
of his cousin, who followed Montmorency's peace policy,
he was painfully undeceived to find the Rome of the war-
like Julius III filled with the unceasing clash of arms. He
writes to his friend Robertet, in allusion to the sack of Rome
by the troops of Charles V in May 1527 :

Ne pense, Robertet, que ceste Rome-cy
Soit ceste Rome-là qui te souloit tant plaire.
On n'y fait plus crédit, comme l'on souloit faire,
On n'y fait plus l'amour, comme on souloit aussi.

La paix et le bon temps ne règnent plus icy,
La musique et le bal sont contraints de s'y taire,
L'air y est corrompu, Mars y est ordinaire,
Ordinaires la faim, la peine et le soucy.

L'artisan débauché y ferme sa boutique,
L'officieux avocat y laisse sa pratique
Et le pauvre marchand y porte le bissac ;

On ne voit que soldats et morrions en teste,
On n'oït que tabourins et semblable tempeste . . .
Et Rome tous les jours attend un autre sac . . .

VIII

THE POPES

Si je monte au Palais je n'y trouve qu'orgueil,
Que vice déguisé, qu'une cérémonie,
Qu'un bruit de tabourins, qu'une estrange harmonie
Et de rouges habits un superbe appareil ;

Si je descends en banque un amas et recueil
De nouvelles je treuve, une usure infinie,
De riches Florentins une troupe bannie
Et de pauvres Siennois un lamentable deuil ;

Si je vais plus avant, quelque part que j'arrive,
Je treuve de Vénus la grand' bande lascive
Dressant de tous côtés mille appas amoureux ;

Si je passe plus oultre et, de la Rome neuve
Entre en la vieille Rome, adonques je ne treuve
Que de vieux monumens un grand monceau pierreux.

THESE lines are also by Du Bellay, who twice took
part in a conclave as secretary to his cousin : first
at the election of Marcellus II and secondly at that
of Paul IV. His opinions were confirmed, if confirmation
were needed, by a letter of Jean Du Bellay to Cardinal Farnese,
dated March 21st, 1535, in which he says that at the election
of Paul IV the votes of all but a few pious Cardinals were
for sale. There are many witnesses to the shameless trickery
which pervaded the papal elections of the time of the Renaissance. Henri II provided his Cardinals with supplies of the
Flemish tapestries, then so much in demand, for distribution

I

to the electors as bribes to further the interests of the French candidate. The most striking examples of barefaced corruption were the elections of Sixtus IV, Innocent VIII, Alexander VI and Julius II. One cardinal received a country-house, another a post as Legate, a third hard cash, a fourth the gift of a bishopric : it was accounted to the new Pope for righteousness if by chance he kept his promises. If the letter and spirit of the canon law, which declares any papal election tainted with simony null and void, be taken into account, there was not a single Pope from Sixtus IV (1471) to Paul IV (1555) who had any right to the throne of St. Peter.

To understand the true nature of the papal office at the time of the Renaissance, the ideas of the period and the peculiar situation of the Papacy itself must be reckoned with. In the sixteenth century the most pressing claims on any given individual were those of family. This was even more true of Italy than of France and Germany. The individual was dominated by the family. Even in the eighteenth century a younger brother of the Marquis de Mirabeau could write to his brother that the only true feeling was that which aimed at the honour and profit of the family. This was exactly the doctrine of the contemporaries of Alexander VI and Julius II. The first act of every new Pope was to provide for the aggrandizement of his own kin. They were not actuated in this by motives of favouritism only, but of policy, as a means of fortifying their own authority and facilitating their government by a concentration of power in the hands of their own circle.

The nepotism of a sixteenth-century Pope was practically a necessity. Almost all the Renaissance Popes had children of their own, whom they married into noble and powerful and even royal families. Their aim was to provide these children with well-defended possessions and instal them as

" tyrants ", whenever possible on the frontiers of the Papal states, to form outposts against Venice, Naples and Milan or in the Marches or the Romagna. They entrusted their relations with key positions both in the States of the Church and in the papal government. The prime necessity of a Pope was a subservient Sacred College, and the best means to that end was to " pack " it with relations.

Contemporaries were far from raising objections. They saw nothing wrong in a Pope having sons to support him against neighbouring tyrants. They held a Pope perfectly justified in favouring his own family as far as possible : indeed, they criticized one who did not. Lorenzo the Magnificent, one of the most intelligent men of his day and a great statesman, writes to Innocent VIII in 1489 :

Others have not waited so long as Your Holiness to play the Pope : they wasted no time on nice points of honesty. Your Holiness is not only free before God and man to act as you will, but your very restraint may be misinterpreted and used against you. Devotion and duty combine to compel me to warn Your Holiness that as man is immortal and a Pope is only what he makes himself, his personal dignity cannot be bequeathed : his only patrimony is the honours and gifts he can bestow in his lifetime.

Lorenzo, it is true, had married his daughter to a son of the Pope, but his letter is none the less typical of the time.

The States of the Church were in utter disunion, studded with petty lordships, still feudal in character, even in Rome. These lordships, with their bristling independence, were a constant threat to any kind of papal authority. When Martin V became Pope the Colonna had their day, under Eugenius IV the Condolmeri. Pius II squandered all that the Church had to give on the Piccolomini, Calixtus III and Alexander VI on the Borgia, Sixtus IV and Julius II on the della Rovere,

Leo X and Clement VII on the Medici, Julius III on the del Monte, Paul IV on the Caraffa. Paul IV went so far as to excommunicate the Colonna solely in order to seize their property and hand it over to the head of his own family, the Conte de Montorio, who became Duke of Paliano by papal bull of May 10th, 1556.

His predecessors had gone even further. Calixtus III despoiled the finest bindings of the Vatican library of their precious stones and distributed them to the Borgia. Sixtus IV granted his son the huge income of 6,000 ducats, secured on the papal revenue ; Innocent VIII had the Lord of Forli murdered to obtain his lordship for his son. Alexander Borgia's efforts for his children, Lucrezia, Cesare and the Duke of Gandia, have become a legend. The important offices of State and seats in the Sacred College went the same way. Both Innocent VIII and Alexander VI made their sons cardinals, Cesare Borgia at fourteen. Julius II incontinently clapped the red hat on four of his cousins, and Gregory VIII made his son, Jacopo Buoncompagni, governor of the Castel Sant' Angelo, the fortress which dominates Rome. Nepotism was the first aim of the Pontiff on his accession : his second, the consolidation and aggrandizement of the temporal domain of the Church, was closely allied to it.

The three great political and military powers of fifteenth-century Italy were the Republic of Venice, the Kingdom of Naples and the Papacy. The aim of the great Popes of the Renaissance, such as Julius II, was to create in Central Italy a State ruled by the Pope, whose preponderance should ensure the unification of the whole peninsula under the Papal authority. This ambition was only to be realized three hundred years later by the house of Savoy.

The ambition of the more secularly minded Popes aimed even higher. In the thirteenth century the dreams of Boniface

VIII had been shattered by Philippe le Bel of France. The Renaissance Popes had still a lingering feeling that they were the heirs of the Roman emperors. They dreamed of being, as a Venetian " orator " says of the policy of Julius II, " lords and masters of the world's movements ". Thus we find Alexander VI calmly dividing America between Spain and Portugal, while Julius II in 1510, equally calmly, offered the throne of France to Henry VIII of England.

The Papacy was endowed with a dual power ; the spiritual, symbolized by the keys of St. Peter, and the temporal, of which the sign was " the sword of the Church ". The temporal soon ousted the spiritual from first consideration.

It would be pleasant to imagine the Papacy in that troubled time as an ideal, almost abstract authority, based on a lofty morality drawn only from the Gospel, neglectful of temporal possessions in its task of guidance and counsel to warring States and turbulent men. But, as Gebhardt says :

The dream of a free Church divested of temporal dominion, in a prince-ridden Italy, was impossible of realization. The Papacy would have fallen a prey to the Spanish dynasty of Naples or the Medici of Florence, as it had in the tenth century to the barons of Tusculum or to the Emperor. The only resource of the Popes was to play the " tyrant " like their neighbours. As soon as they felt themselves secure from attack within the Church by the ending of the Great Schism, the closure of the Councils (of Constance and Basle) and the suppression of the heresies of Wycliffe and John Huss, they turned to the task of building up a temporal realm.

A speaker at the Council of Constance declared :

I used to think that it would be well to separate completely religious authority from temporal power, but now I see that virtue without power is only ridiculous. The Pope of Rome, without the papal realm, would only be the lackey of kings and princes.

For this reason [says Imbart de la Tour] the creation of the states of the Church became an obsession with the Popes. Their self-imposed task reduced them to the common level of the Italian princes of their day, but the safety of the Papacy depended on their immediate success therein.

Not all the Popes took kindly to this policy. Among them were gentle, pious men, whose aims and aspirations were wholly Christian. One of them, Gabriel Condolmero, whose name as Pope was Eugenius IV (1431–47), murmured on his death-bed :

" O Gabriel, how much better for thy soul would it have been hadst thou never been Cardinal or Pope, but hadst died a monk."

Cardinal Tomaso Parentucelli spoke the funeral oration of Eugenius IV and by so doing secured his own election as his successor. "This, with his other virtues," writes Vespasiano, "induced the others to make him Pope." He took the name of Nicholas V (1447–55).

Nicholas V was the first and the best of the Renaissance Popes. He was born at Pisa in 1398. His father was a surgeon, and he himself started life as a schoolmaster and then became a librarian. Afterwards he was secretary to Cardinal Albergati, who took him to Florence, where he was admitted to the society of the Medici. There he imbibed so thoroughly the Florentine humanism and love of the arts that when he ascended the papal throne in 1447 it was as if the very spirit of the Renaissance were enthroned with him. He impressed the new spirit so firmly on the papal government that it was never effaced by his successors ; to him is due the credit for opening up the ways which they followed with such distinction.

He resolved from his earliest days to work for the restoration and beautification of the Eternal City. The results, from the point of view of the preservation of the relics of Roman art, were both beneficial and harmful ; beneficial, since they drew general attention to the value of beautiful things which till then had been despised ; harmful, because, when any work was undertaken for the adornment of modern Rome, since marble produced the finest lime, ancient ruins and fine statuary went pell-mell to the furnace.

Nicholas V began the enlargement, improvement and decoration of the Vatican. His principal adviser in this work was the Florentine Alberti, who, with Brunelleschi and Michelozzo, was one of the three pre-eminent architects of the city of the Medici. Alberti was not only well versed in his own art, but was also a man of rare intelligence and varied knowledge, comparable in this respect with Leonardo da Vinci. He was almost as skilful with the pen as with the instruments of his own profession, so that his influence on his contemporaries was nearly as great in the sphere of theory as in the practical illustrations of it afforded by his buildings.

For the decoration of the Vatican, Nicholas called in painters such as Fra Angelico, Gozzoli and Piero della Francesca. Fra Angelico painted the lives of St. Stephen and St. Laurence in the Vatican Chapel, but Piero della Francesca's frescoes were unhappily destroyed by the intolerance of Rafael when he in his turn was commissioned by Leo X to redecorate the Vatican.

Apart from his pontifical functions, Nicholas's principal interest was the foundation and development of the Vatican Library, but he is also distinguished as the founder of the Capitoline Museum. He was an enlightened collector of all kinds of works of art, tapestries, goldsmiths' work, and majolica, which he bought from all parts of Italy. He employed Rosselino to build him palaces at Orvieto and Spoleto and baths at Viterbo.

The inspiration was less authentic which made him under-take to build a new basilica in place of the old one, which dated from the earliest centuries of the Christian era, and might be considered the cradle of the Church. Alberti was charged with the demolition of the old and the design and construction of the new church. It is impossible to think without regret of the little Church which had witnessed the faith of the earliest converts and martyrs. Had it survived it would to-day have stirred the minds of men in quite another manner than the existing huge building bearing the name of St. Peter. Alberti's plans were, in fact, never carried out. After some years of vigorous work, building was stopped. The rear of the old basilica was demolished and the founda-tions were laid of the new, and there the empty shell remained for half a century. Rabelais speaks of a little chapel on the Island of the Papefigues " near the harbour, ruined and desolate, like the temple of St. Peter in Rome ". When work was finally resumed under Pius II, Alberti's plans were super-seded by Bramante's, which in their turn were modified by Rafael, who was assisted in his task by Giovanni da San Gallo and by Fra Giocondo, the architect-monk who built the old bridge of Notre Dame in Paris.

Nicholas V was to Rome what the Medici were to Flor-ence, the founder of the artistic greatness of the Rome of the sixteenth century, both by the quality of the artists he summoned from various Italian cities, and by the importance of the works he entrusted to them. As a Pope, he was broad-minded and tolerant. His fame rests as much on his protec-tion of the persecuted Lorenzo Valla as on his patronage of the arts and on his learning.

Valla was one of the greatest humanists of his time. Born in 1415, he passed from the study of Latin to that of history, in which his researches led him to cast doubt on the authenticity of the famous Donation of Constantine. The faithful were at once up in arms. Nicholas V was not yet Pope, and Valla had to flee, taking refuge at the court of Alfonso the Magnanimous, King of Naples and a great protector of the talents.

Valla was naturally of a bellicose humour. Bayle calls him "the greatest duellist in the Republic of letters", and compares his life with that of a gladiator. No sooner was he in Naples than he attacked various prominent humanists and their Latinity. After this he fell foul of the ecclesiastical hierarchy and made violent onslaughts, not only on the accuracy of their dogma, but also on their private lives. He was soon involved in a storm even greater than that which had driven him from Rome. He was accused of heresy and misinterpretations of the mystery of the Trinity and the doctrine of free-will, and condemned by the Inquisition to the stake, from which he was only saved by the intervention of Alfonso. As it was, he was publicly whipped round the Jacobin convent. He thereupon left Naples for Rome, where he was lucky to find in the person of Nicholas V a protector even more powerful than Alfonso. The Pope not only put a stop to his persecution, but gave him a salary and a license to teach.

Nicholas thus gave proof of tolerance, intelligence and kindness of heart. He opened all possible gates to the Renaissance and marked out the ways in which it should go. When he died, Filelfo, the humanist and enemy of Cosimo dei Medici, spoke his funeral oration, in which it was said that Apollo and the Muses were desolate at the death of the Holy Father of Christendom. The combination would probably have called forth a tolerant smile from the dead Pope.

Calixtus III (1455–8) was the first of the Borgia Popes. He was born in 1377 at Valencia in Spain, and was thus almost eighty when he was elected Pope. At that time the Turks had just taken Constantinople and were spreading over Europe. They held the Morea, Albania, Serbia and the Danube. It was a moment of great and imminent danger for Christendom. Calixtus sent a most pressing appeal for aid to all the Princes of Europe, but was answered only by indifference or the demand for a Council. The Pope, thrown on his own resources, managed to man and equip a dozen galleys, but they returned to port with only minor successes to their credit. His chief interest may lie in the fact that it was he who reversed the judgment passed on Joan of Arc.

He was succeeded by Æneas Sylvius Piccolomini, who took the name of Pius II on his accession in 1458. Pius was humanism personified. He was born at Corsignano near Siena in 1400, as one of the seventeen children of a ruined nobleman. The classics attracted him from his earliest youth and he hesitated for long to take orders for fear that they might interfere with his studies. He composed light verse in Latin and wrote, also in Latin, the story of *Euryalus and Lucretia*, a pleasant tale of the poetic (though not platonic) loves of a young bachelor and a married woman. He also wrote a Latin comedy, *Cynthia*, which is even lighter than his verse or his novel. As a Latinist, only Erasmus was his superior : indeed, his novel has a grace and colour which are often lacking in the writings of the great philosopher. Other fruits of his labours are a history of the Council of Basle, a history of Bohemia, a geography of Asia, and a description of Europe, and, finally, an unfinished life of the Emperor Frederick, whom the author predeceased.

He was a man of a lively intelligence and charming manners, with an appreciation of nature in advance of that of most of his contemporaries. It would be hard to find a fuller and more diversified life than his. He travelled in almost every country of Europe, from England to Hungary and from Norway to Savoy. His occupations were no less varied. He was secretary to the Cardinal of Capranica and to the Council of Basle, where he earned a reputation for eloquence. His speeches are notable for grace and subtlety combined with firmness and precision, a pleasant contrast to the didactic dryness of the contemporary Sorbonne or the stentorian dullness of the German theologians of his day.

While still a young man he was attached to the Emperor's court, and later to the Pope's. His views were apt to vary, in all sincerity, with his rapid changes of climate and position, but he was always most vigorous in support of them while held. Like Rabelais, Æneas Sylvius was fond of good cheer and the society of pretty women. With the carriage and destination of a true nobleman, he was equally at home among the people and at court. When he was in Scotland he delighted in the conversation of the women who carded flax, and when he was Pope he could be found seated on the grass by some brook in friendly converse with the peasants who had flocked to do him homage.

His bulls and encyclicals all bear traces of the obvious pleasure he took in the refinement of their Latin texts. He was conscientious, sometimes even passionate, in the exercise of his pontifical functions, fulminating against the Turk and all his works, and later against the " Pragmatic " of the King of France.

In January 1460, Pius II promulgated the Bull " Execrabilis ", which threatened with all the thunders of the Church any who should appeal to a General Council against a decision of the Holy See. In spite of this, Charles VII of France did appeal forthwith against the Pope's attempted curtailment of the liberties of the Gallican Church.

In the midst of his varied occupations and pre-occupations,

the new opinions in Germany, the Turkish menace, the opposition of the French king, and his own efforts to restore the moral and material power of the Papacy, Pius II yet found time for a constant devotion to the classics and to building ; the Piccolomini palace in Siena and the whole of the little town of Pienza are his work. He was broad-minded enough to appreciate, almost alone of his time, the works of art of the Middle Ages, the best of which he esteemed almost as highly as classical art. He did not share the common belief that Gothic art was the degraded product of a barbarian-ridden humanity. He was, however, not so generous a patron of the arts as Nicholas V had been. He was economical, almost miserly, lavish with words of praise and acute criti-cisms to the writers whose works he admired, but his liber-ality went no further. He took pleasure in works of art, but without falling to the temptation of acquiring them for himself. It is said of him that he could provide for the two hundred and seventy odd members of the Papal court on seven ducats a day, say £20 for that number. It must have needed some thought.

The end of the life of Pius II was not devoid of a certain grandeur. He finally saw the futility of his efforts to galvanize the princes and prelates of Europe into a combined effort against the Turk. Realizing that they considered their tem-porary interests and rivalries of more importance than the saving of Christendom, he determined himself to lead the fleet which, like his predecessor, he had equipped. The fleet was to sail with the Pope as admiral on June 18th, 1464. He reached Ancona to embark, but, utterly worn out with his own efforts, died there, in view of the fleet about to sail against the Turks, during the night of the 15th–16th August 1464.

Paul II (1464–71) was an accentuated version of his predecessors. He was a nobleman, even-tempered and good-mannered, but naturally frivolous. He loved art and pleasure, ancient vases and statues and the pleasures of the carnival, but he was no humanist and cared little for Virgil or Cicero. He suppressed Pius II's College of Abbreviators, which had become a European centre of learning, but in return he accelerated the task of adorning Rome, undertook the restoration of the more important of its ancient monuments, and was as zealous a collector as Nicholas V. In his dual capacity as Pope and " tyrant ", he embarked with the aid of Venice on an unsuccessful struggle with the King of Naples, who refused to acknowledge the Holy See as his feudal suzerain.

We now come to one of the most striking figures among the Popes of the Renaissance in the person of Sixtus IV (1471–84). He was a Franciscan monk, the son of one Rovere, a lighterman of Savona. He was a learned man, but with a brutal manner, an armoured Pope like his nephew Julius II, but never lacking a certain greatness in spite of his brutality and treachery. He was from the first much more the Prince than the Pope, much more the Italian tyrant than the Father of Christendom ; his rule in Rome was as much a reign of terror as that of the Visconti in Milan or the Malatesta in Rimini. His chief care was the re-establishment of the feudal authority of the Papacy over its vassal barons, who at that time were almost independent, and its extension beyond existing limits. His second object was the enrichment of his nephews, of whom Girolamo Riario became Captain-General of the Church, another, Leonardo, was made Prefect of Rome, and yet another, Giovanni della Rovere, was granted the fiefs of Sinigaglia and Mondovi ; the nephew most deserving of note, however, was Giuliano, who was made Cardinal by his uncle and later attained the papal throne, where he energetically continued the policy of that uncle with an equal disregard for all scruples.

It was Sixtus' dream to establish Girolamo Riario in the possession of rich lordships on the Romagna, and he accordingly engaged the Papacy in a tortuous maze of alliances and counter-alliances, battle, murder and sudden death. Naples and Milan, Florence, the Venetian Republic, Ferrara, Urbino and Rimini were all drawn by the Head of the Church into this medley of plots and counter-plots, oaths sworn and betrayed and all the customary politics of the day.

In the war with Ferrara the Venetians joined the Pope at his request. As soon as he had gained his own ends, he left them in the lurch by making a separate peace, and when they endeavoured to recoup themselves by continuing the war alone, he incontinently threatened them with excommunication. This policy was only a slight foretaste of that of his nephew, the future Julius II.

The best-beloved of the Pope's family, however, was Pietro Riario, on whom he lavished all his tenderness. It was said in Rome that Pietro was his own son. At his uncle's accession he was a simple Franciscan monk, but in a trice he found himself Patriarch of Constantinople, Archbishop of Florence, Archbishop of Seville, and Bishop of Mende, all benefices producing large revenues which he found no difficulty in spending. He kept horses, actresses and poets, all in equal luxury, enjoying his short life to the full, but not dying before he had attempted to repay the Pope's kindness by a plot to dethrone him and take his place.

Sixtus mourned his nephew in happy ignorance of his base ingratitude and turned his affections on Girolamo Riario, a clerk in the customs-house of Savona. He bought for him from Taddeo Manfredi the lordship of Imola, and finally, to satisfy his greedy nephews, cast his eyes on Florence and Tuscany. But there he found two insurmountable obstacles, Lorenzo and Giuliano dei Medici. He had a finger in the conspiracy of the Pazzi against them, his representative, the Archbishop of Pisa, being the prime mover in the plot. One of the Pope's nephews, Rafael Riario, was actually present in the church when Giuliano dei Medici was murdered at the foot of the altar. Having failed to murder Lorenzo, the Pope proceeded to excommunicate him and then allied himself with Naples and Urbino against the Florentines, whom he compelled to sue for peace. The patricians of Florence were forced to come to the door of St. Peter's to implore the Pope's pardon. To the mournful notes of a Miserere he struck them with a wand on the shoulders as they knelt, in token that they were pardoned for his attack on them.

After the relative failure of his Florentine war, the Pope turned furiously on the barons of the Church and in particular on the allied and powerful families of the Colonna and Savelli. His aim was the seizure of their possessions for the benefit of his nephew. The protonotary Cardinal Colonna and Cardinal Savelli were cast into the dungeons of Sant' Angelo. The quarter surrounding the fortress-dwelling of the Colonna, where lived their numerous retainers, was completely sacked by the papal soldiery and that of the Orsini, who as leaders of the Guelfs had a tradition of enmity to the Colonna. The whole quarter was ravaged with fire and sword, and then the process repeated, under the direction of Girolamo Riario, throughout the territories of the Colonna in Latium. Meanwhile the head of the Colonna family had agreed with the Pope for the release of his brother Lorenzo from Sant' Angelo in return for the surrender of the fortress of Marino. The fortress was duly delivered up, but next day

the unhappy Lorenzo Colonna was beheaded in the courtyard of the papal castle in Rome. The body was borne to
the Church of the Apostles. The mother followed in deep
mourning, and, seizing the severed head by the hair and
brandishing it on high, delivered herself of the following
words : " Behold the head of my son and the good faith
of the Pope ! He promised to free my son if we gave him
Marino. We gave him Marino, and he gives us in return
my murdered son. Thus does a Pope keep his word ! "

Girolamo Riario finally obtained the lordships of Imola
and Forli. Sixtus had achieved his object.

This war-like Pope died on August 13th, 1484, aged seventy.
Burchard, the keeper of a celebrated diary, paints a vivid
picture of his death. Hardly were his eyes closed—it was
five o'clock in the morning—than pillage reigned unchecked.
Servant and squire, man of law and cleric outvied one another in filling their pockets. The Pope's body was rolled
in a tapestry torn from the door of the death-chamber and
left naked on a table. When it was to be washed not a single
utensil was to be found, and in the end a cook had to bring
in the cauldron in which dishes were cleaned. There was no
shift to shroud the corpse, the one the Pope had been wearing having been torn up to dry the body after washing,
and the body was therefore put naked on the bier. No sooner
was the funeral over than the people stormed the palaces
of the " nephews ", burning and robbing. Colonna attacked
the Orsini, seeking vengeance for past persecution. The
cardinals barred their doors and barricaded their windows
and retired behind them with what men-at-arms they could
muster. The events at the Pope's death were an epitome of
those of his life.

Nevertheless, it is to Sixtus IV that we owe the Sistine
Chapel, famous for its choir and for Michael Angelo's paint-

ings. He built Santa Maria del Popolo, Santa Maria della Pace and the hospice of San Spirito. He aided the progress of literature and made the celebrated humanist Bartholomeo Platina, who had been persecuted by Paul II, head of the Vatican Library. This scene was painted in fresco by Melozzo da Forli. Platina, in a black gown, kneels at the feet of the Pope, who sits in his chair wearing the red cap with white cord. The Pope, seen in profile, has a fierce and arbitrary expression. Close by stands Giuliano della Rovere, the future Julius II.

Sixtus IV added considerably to the Vatican Library and threw it open to the public. He arranged the papal archives, and patronized printing, gathering round him the greatest painters of the age ; Perugino, whose frescoes in the Sistine Chapel were obliterated by those of Michael Angelo, but whose work is the most modern in spirit of any artist of the quattrocento, Signorelli, Botticelli and Lippo Lippi. He can certainly be classed among the " great " Popes.

His successor was a Genoese, Cardinal Cibo, who took the name of Innocent VIII (1484–92). His election was managed by Cardinal Borgia, nephew of Calixtus III, who himself aspired to the Papal throne, but who, having reckoned up his chances and found them less favourable than those of his rival, very prudently sold his own vote and those of his party to the other candidate.

Rafaël Maffei Volateran speaks of Innocent VIII as follows in his commentaries : " He was the first Pope to throw over the ancient discipline and publicly to acknowledge his children and shower gifts upon them." The number of his children is unknown. It was estimated by the satirists of the time at sixteen, eight boys and eight girls. This, however, was probably poetic exaggeration, though it has been too closely followed by historians hostile to the Papacy. Only two are definitely known, Franceschetto Cibo, who married the daughter of Lorenzo dei Medici, and Theodorica, who became the wife of a rich Genoese. Lorenzo dei Medici's letter we have quoted above is the best answer to the charge that the Pope squandered his treasure on them.

It is nevertheless true that the feeble and vacillating Pope was entirely under the influence of Franceschetto, who induced him to have Girolamo Riario murdered so as to obtain possession of his tyranny of Forli. The plot failed through the vigorous resistance of Girolamo's widow, Catarina Sforza, who cast her husband's naked corpse out of a window and proceeded to defend her castle so energetically that help from Bologna arrived in time to beat off the attackers. Franceschetto was granted the lordships of Fervetri and Anguillara as compensation.

In addition to his son, Innocent had a mob of nephews who combined the characteristics of the mercenary soldier and the bandit with those of the money-lender. They formed with Franceschetto a sort of insurance company against any ill-effects of murder (to the murderer). For a consideration of 150 ducats (£500), most of which went to Franceschetto, a single murder could be committed with impunity.

In 1490 the Pope fell ill and his life was thought to be in danger. A few faithful friends gathered round him, while his son carefully removed the papal treasure, with which, however, he was caught when well on the way to Tuscany.

Innocent VIII thought it his duty to continue Sixtus' designs on Naples and to that end supported the Neapolitan lords in their revolt against Ferdinand. The Orsini-Colonna strife now broke out anew, this time with the Colonna under the Papal banner. The Pope, terrified lest the superior military power of the Orsini should permit them to break into Rome, brought back the troops of banditti which his predecessors had finally expelled. Ferdinand was advancing victoriously on Rome, when the Pope sued for peace and abandoned the rebellious barons to the vengeance of their king.

Having thus learnt by bitter experience that he was no soldier, Innocent determined to devote himself to the tasks of peace. His administration certainly brought prosperity and some degree of law and order to Rome and the Papal States. His endeavours to deal with the eternal problem of the cost of living gained the affection of his subjects, some of whom even boasted of his impartial justice. Others, however, were loud in criticism. As Bayle says :

He is an example of the difficulties of the Papal office : the Pope is blamed for meddling in European politics, and if he refrains from meddling is taunted with doing nothing for his state. This last is Guicciardini's view of Innocent VIII.

He was a man of good presence and affable ; too affable, said some, in his manner. For his period he was unlearned and unready of speech. His ruling passion was the collection of jewels, which he preferred both to pictures and to statuary. There was more than a little of the miser in the pleasure he took in counting over his caskets of gold and precious stones. His avarice led him into questionable dealings with the Sultan Bayazid. The Sultan's brother Djem was his rival for the throne. Djem was taken by the Knights of Rhodes, whose Grand Master, Pierre d'Aubusson, handed him over to the Pope. The Pope came to an agreement with the Sultan by which this dangerous rival was kept under lock and key for an annual payment of 40,000 ducats. To bind the bargain, the Sultan made a most precious gift to the Pope, no less than the head of the spear which pierced the side of Christ, and which had been found by the Turks in the treasury when they took Constantinople. Innocent presented the precious relic to the Romans, with great pomp and ceremony, from the loggia of the Vatican. It was unfortunately true that France in the Sainte Chapelle and Germany in Nuremberg possessed the same spear-head. A fourth had been found during the first Crusade, but had since been lost.

In 1492 Lorenzo the Magnificent despatched his son, Cardinal Giovanni (afterwards Leo X), to Rome with these parting words : " You are going to a sink of vice and you will find it hard to conduct yourself decently."

Both Infessura and Burckhardt have left vivid descriptions of this " sink of vice ".

" The life of the priests and others of the Roman court was such that few of them but kept a concubine or at least a harlot to the glory of God and the Christian faith " (Infessura).

" Neither human nor divine law commanded respect. Rape and incest ran riot. Men and women alike were shameless. The palace of St. Peter was the dwelling-place of pimps and harlots ; a brothel would be more decent " (Burckhardt).

Burckhardt says further that most convents were merely disorderly houses. And yet all this excited no protest. Churches were as rowdy as a fair-ground. Bernardino of Siena attacked his audience in a sermon : " O woman, what clamour is here ! When I say the morning mass you cackle like so many geese. The one cries ' Joan ', the other ' Kate ! ' and so on. This is not the devotion you owe to the mass, but a farce."

Innocent VIII sought to revive the forgotten edict of Pius II against priests who kept taverns or gaming-houses, or who frequented low women, but he was helpless against the trend of public morality.

He died in Rome on July 25th, 1492. Like most of the Popes of the age, his doctor was a Jew. This man thought to prolong the Pope's life at the price of the blood of three male children. The children died under the operation, the Jew took to flight, and finally the Pope himself died.

Of the political events of Innocent's reign, which are usually dismissed as of little importance, at least one is significant ; his call to Charles VIII of France to make good the claims of the house of Anjou to the throne of Naples, claims which the Pope had recognized as a weapon in his struggle with Ferdinand of Aragon.

IX

POMPS AND VANITIES OF ITALY

THE Kingdom of Naples—to the Italian *the* Kingdom —was the great rival and traditional foe of the temporal power of the Holy See. Each envisaged a hegemony of the whole peninsula, and thence sprang their rivalry. In addition, the Pope claimed suzerain rights over the Kingdom and tribute from it. Lastly, they had a common frontier.

The Papacy was thus impelled to a fatal rivalry with whatever dynasty ruled in Naples. At this time it was the Aragonese ; hence the Pope was the ally of France. Giuliano della Rovere was the chief supporter of this alliance in the Papal court, and so far succeeded that in March 1486 he set out for France at the Pope's behest to bring back with him the French claimant to the throne of Naples. It was thus the Pope who gave direction to the nascent ambitions in the breast of the young Charles VIII.

René d'Anjou, the "good King René", exiled King of Naples, had died in 1480, leaving his rights to his nephew, Charles Count of Maine, with reversion to the King of France. In 1481, the Count himself died. The source of these rights was that tough old warrior, Charles d'Anjou, brother of St. Louis, who had carved out for himself the Kingdom of the two Sicilies (Naples and Sicily), and had been formally invested with the royal title by Clement IV in 1265. He had been driven out by the revolt known as the " Sicilian

Vespers " in 1282 and by the attack of Pedro III of Aragon, whom the rebels had called to their aid.

Thenceforward the two dynasties reigned side by side, Aragon in Palermo, Anjou in Naples. In 1438 Joan II, Queen of Naples, died childless, leaving her realm to René of Provence, the legal heir. René hastened to Naples, but was beaten by another Aragonese, Alfonso V, who disputed the validity of the Queen's will. His loss did not trouble him unduly, and he returned to France and a life of luxurious ease among his artists and his poets.

The two Sicilies were thus reunited under a prince of the house of Aragon, but on the death of Alfonso V (the Magnanimous) his lands were again divided, his brother John receiving Sicily, while his natural son Ferdinand had the Kingdom of Naples. Meanwhile the exiled René had passed on his rights till they finally fell to Louis XI and after him to Charles VIII, whose attention was drawn to them by the Pope.

The rights of Charles have been disputed by historians, but without good grounds. The wills of Joan and of René of Aragon have been said to clash with the Bull of Clement IV. The Pope, however, in his grant of the investiture of Naples to Charles d'Anjou, had no power to alter feudal custom, and in any case Innocent VIII was fully qualified to modify the decisions of his predecessor. Louis XI, cautious and practical, would never have risked the Italian adventure, however sound his claim and however pressing the Pope. Charles VIII, on the other hand, was young and romantic, a child of the Middle Ages and the romances of chivalry. Louis XI would certainly not have restored Roussillon and Cerdagne, which were pledges for a loan of 100,000 crowns, to the King of Aragon, as Charles VIII did by the treaty of Barcelona. Louis would never have restored them against the money, much less, as Charles did, without it, simply to have a free hand in Italy. Louis would not even have given the Emperor Maximilian Artois and Franche-Comté in return for his benevolent neutrality, though they were part of the dowry of Maximilian's daughter Margaret, who was betrothed to Charles VIII and returned by him to her father so that he could marry Anne of Brittany.

Before, however, condemning as light-headed and fantastic the Italian adventure on which Charles VIII is about to embark, we must consider, firstly, the relations between France and Italy at that time, and, secondly, his own personal position and surroundings. Burckhardt maintains that French intervention in Italy was a matter of necessity, and would have occurred if the Neapolitan and Milanese questions had never arisen. Communication and trade between the two countries, France and Italy, had made great strides in the preceding half-century. Every French town of importance had its group of Italian merchants and bankers. Lyons, in particular, was almost an Italian colony. The bankers, especially the more important ones who acted as money-lenders to the King, enjoyed high favour and were accorded far-reaching commercial privileges and often the grant of French lordships. The Sauli financed Charles VIII's Italian campaign, as later the Albizzi were to provide the sinews of war for Louis XII and Francis I. Those commercial and financial houses naturally formed alliances in France, so that a contemporary author could well speak of the district on both sides of the Alps as " French Tuscany ".

Even more important, politically speaking, were the alliances of the nobility. The Orsini of Rome were traditionally pro-French. The royal house of France intermarried with the Visconti and later with the Medici, the Guise with the Este of Ferrara and so on. The Italian wars were to leave

these relations in inextricable confusion, Italian titles having
been bestowed on French lords, and French lordships awarded
to those pro-French Italians who had suffered for their political
faith. In every sphere the same phenomenon was to be seen.
Italian condottieri served under the French banner : it was
an Italian, Renzo Orsini, who defended Marseilles against
the French traitor Bourbon who commanded the Imperial
Army. At sea, the Florentine Giovanni Verazzano led the
French expedition to Newfoundland, and the Genoese Andrea
Doria commanded the French fleet in the Mediterranean.
Italians swarmed about the courts of all the French kings,
from Charles VIII to Henri II, and were often employed on
diplomatic missions.

In the world of letters Aleandro may serve as a type of
the Italian humanist in France, while on the other hand the
University of Pisa counted many Frenchmen among its
teachers.

Lastly, but probably of most importance in determining
the moment and nature of the Italian war of Charles VIII,
we have the presence in France of the " fuorusciti "—the
Italian refugees from the internecine strife which flourished
in almost every Italian state and city. The vanquished enemies
of the Medici, the momentary losers in the perennial Orsini-
Colonna feud, and a hundred others like them, were compelled to seek a refuge abroad. The Florentines were the
most numerous in France, and chief among them the Strozzi,
one of whom, Piero, became a Marshal of France. It is interesting to note that two Neapolitan exiles, Giulio Brancaccio
and Vespasiano, distinguished themselves at the taking of
Calais from the English in 1558.

The immediate cause of Charles VIII's invasion of Italy
was the invitation of Innocent VIII, which, on the latter's

death, was renewed by Alexander VI and eagerly seconded by Ludovico il Moro of Milan, who had usurped the throne of his nephew Gian Galeazzo Sforza. Gian Galeazzo had succeeded at the age of eight, and had later married Isabella of Aragon, daughter of Ferdinand of Naples, who naturally wished to reinstate him. Ludovico was therefore impelled to ally himself with the Pope in opposition to Naples. In addition, the rebel Neapolitan lords who had fled to France used every effort to stir up the French King against Ferdinand, as did Giuliano della Rovere, a Cardinal who had fled as a result of a feud with the Pope.

To the young and romantic Charles the conquest of Naples was only the first step to a greater objective : it would provide a base for the project dearest to his heart, the reconquest of Constantinople and the deliverance of the Holy Land. He was then twenty-four, with only four years more to live. Physically he was a weakling, very short, with spindly legs, too long for his body. His face was hideously ugly : he had prominent and rather wild eyes, large nose and mouth, and straggling straight reddish hair. He was nervous by nature and loved strong scents, but was nevertheless brave enough in battle. He resembles the Emperor Maximilian in his affectation of story-book chivalry. Such a man had naturally little appeal for the Italians, the Venetian orator saying of him that he was of little worth either physically or mentally. He was innocent enough to be genuinely horrified at the manifold duplicities of his Italian allies and enemies.

Charles's wife, Anne of Brittany, was also very small of stature and lame of one leg, but more intelligent than her husband, of whom she was said to be jealous. She and his sister, Anne de Beaujeu, whom Louis IX called " the least foolish woman in France ", tried to deter Charles from his

Italian adventure, but in vain. War with Naples was decided. At the beginning of 1494, he set off with the Queen for Lyons, where the expedition was being prepared. The army was concentrated and transport assembled for the crossing of the Alps, the serious business being varied with a round of fêtes and tournaments.

On Friday, August 29th, 1494, Charles heard mass, took leave of his wife, and rode away. On September 3rd he crossed the frontier of Savoy at the head of his army. " It was horrible to see," writes Brantôme ; " full of cutthroats, rascals fleeing from justice and criminals branded with their crimes. A gallant company, but with little discipline." There were 3,600 lances, 6,000 Breton archers, 6,000 crossbowmen, 8,000 arquebusiers, 8,000 Swiss pikemen and a powerful train of artillery. As Guicciardini says, " With them there spread through Italy a fire and pestilence which changed not only the conditions of States but the customs of government and war."

There were at that time five principal states in Italy : the Holy See, Naples, Venice, Milan and Florence, all mutually suspicious of any gain by one which might endanger the rest. They watched each other like cat and mouse, and the capture of a village by one shook the others to the depths. If their quarrels ever reached the stage of open war, their resources were so evenly balanced, their troops so long in mobilizing, and their artillery so cumbrous to set in motion, that the siege of a castle took a whole summer and a campaign might be ended with little or no bloodshed. But with the arrival of the French all things were turned upside down as by a tempest ; the balance of power was wrecked and with it all regard for the common interest.

Cities, duchies, and kingdoms were invaded and plunged in disorder, none caring for any but his own interests. Unexpected and cruel wars broke out. Whole states fell in less time than used to be needed for the taking of a country house : there were sudden storms and cities taken in a day instead of in many months, bold and bloody deeds of daring. From that day States were no longer preserved or lost, given or taken, by patient negotiation, but in the field by force of arms.

By September 9th the French force had reached Asti, but two events were about to upset the whole expedition. Ferdinand I, King of Naples, had died in January 1494, and Gian Galeazzo of Milan, the victim of Ludovico il Moro's usurpation, was at the point of death. Ludovico therefore, secure in possession of his dominions, had no interest in the overthrow of Naples, nor had the Holy See, when both Ferdinand and Innocent VIII were dead. Of the two who had invited Charles into Italy, neither had now any cause to wish him success.

Charles marched on Florence by way of Pavia and Pisa. The Pisans, who had groaned since 1406 under the Florentine yoke, thought the moment propitious for obtaining their independence and greeted him with shouts of " Long live the French ! Long live Liberty ! "

In Florence Piero, son of Lorenzo dei Medici, was cordially detested. " He was," in the words of a contemporary, " passionately devoted to pleasure and women, irascible but weak and of mediocre intelligence." Like most incapable rulers he governed by a series of rash follies. He was terrified at the approach of the French and hastened to conclude with them the Treaty of Sarzana, one of the clauses of which ensured the independence of Pisa. The Florentines thereupon drove him out and re-established a popular government, which had, however, willy-nilly, to speak the French fair.

The solemn entry of Charles VIII into Florence was a most splendid affair. The streets were freshly sanded and tapestries and hangings festooned the windows. Unfortunately rain fell and drove the officiating clergy to helter-skelter flight.

The procession was led by the King's four drummers with drums as big as barrels ; then came the fifes, and then, in order, the sergeants-at-arms, crossbowmen, archers and Swiss. These last bore their national weapons, the heavy partisan or the huge two-handed sword slung at their back, with another broad, short sword in front. Their parti-coloured hose were in the King's colours of red and yellow. Then came the halberdiers, also in the King's colours, and then the men-at-arms, the heavy cavalry, on heavy horses, wide-toed shoes in bucket stirrups, legs encased in greaves, surcoats glittering with gold, and ample plumes tossing on their leathern headgear. Above them waved the flag of France and the ensigns of the various companies. Then the royal household ; eight hundred noblemen in gorgeous armour, and pikemen in doublets of velvet and gold, and then the King himself under a splendid canopy. He rode Savoy, his black charger. He was dressed in golden armour set with pearls and precious stones, over which a long blue royal cloak fell from his shoulders and spread over the crupper of his horse. His hat was white, encircled with a crown and topped by a black plume. He bore a lance at his knee. The rear of the procession was brought up by civilians, members of the Florentine council, magistrates and merchants.

In spite of this and the Italian warmth of their welcome, the Florentines were suspicious. They had brought in large numbers of peasants from the country, poor troops in a pitched battle, but ready enough for knife-play in a crowded city.

Charles obtained permission for Piero dei Medici to return to Florence as a private citizen, and then led on his army toward Rome. Suddenly he was stupefied to hear that the situation at the Papal court had completely changed. Innocent VIII had called in the French against Naples ; now Alexander VI was calling on Naples to attack the French. Alfonso or Ferdinand of Aragon might be bad neighbours for the Pope, but the powerful King of France would certainly be worse. Alexander, terrified, fortified himself in his castle of Sant' Angelo and crammed it with men and munitions : he cried for help to every court in Europe and even appealed to the Sultan. Bayazid replied in a letter, written in Greek, which fell into the hands of the French. Its contents amazed and horrified Charles, who continued on his way, but now as a declared foe to the Pope. At Viterbo the French troops captured Giulia Farnese, the Pope's beautiful mistress, and though she was treated as beseemed her rank her ransom cost the Pope 3,000 ducats. Meanwhile, reinforcements had arrived from Naples and Rome was being put in a state of defence. The gates were bricked up, but the people showed no sign of a desire to aid in defending the Pope. " Wherever cannon appeared," writes a poet, " buildings bowed low before them."

The Pope was regretfully compelled to welcome the conqueror. Charles VIII made a triumphal entry into Rome on December 31st, 1494, amid shouts of " France ! " and " Colonna ! " from the crowd, for this time it was the Colonna who had called in the foreigner to aid them against papal oppression.

At Florence, Charles's design had been to impress by his splendour ; at Rome, it was to be by a display of force. First came his dreaded Swiss and German mercenaries, giants in stature, armed with the lance or the huge two-handed sword. They marched to the sound of drum and fife in close formation, which they kept in a way that astounded the Romans. Then came Gascons and Bretons with cross-bows and arquebuses, the Gascons' ragged disorder contrasting strangely with the disciplined Germans, and then the gentlemen of the bodyguard in all their beribboned, bejewelled and beplumed magnificence, mace or lance in hand ; then the King in full armour with red cloak and six cardinals around him.

Alexander VI came to meet him in the ordinary garb of a nobleman : gold-embroidered doublet, with Spanish sword-belt and rapier, his bonnet cocked rakishly over one ear. He was followed by a clamorous guard of Spaniards. Pope and King outvied each other in protestations of friendship, but when Charles demanded the investiture of the Kingdom of Naples as granted by Clement IV to Charles of Anjou, the Pope only redoubled his declarations of goodwill, and to such purpose that when Charles left Rome a month later with an army already suffering from lack of provisions, they still followed him, but without any sign of the investiture. The King also received from the Pontiff a solemn benediction in a ceremony well calculated to display the majestic presence of the latter.

The King, during his sojourn in Rome, had astonished the natives by his piety and his daily attendance at Mass, where he remained kneeling with bowed head and hands folded in prayer throughout the service.

Moved by his distrust of the Pope, Charles had immediately on his arrival taken in charge the policing of Rome, and when he departed, thought it prudent to take with him as a hostage Alexander's too celebrated son Cesare Borgia. Cesare, however, was no easy bird to cage, and as soon as the royal army went into camp at Velletri he escaped under cover of night, disguised as a groom. Meanwhile the Pope was strengthening the defences of the Castel

159

Sant' Angelo, doubling its garrison and laying in war-like stores.

Alfonso II, the successor of Ferdinand I on the throne of Naples, had made himself thoroughly hated. " No man was ever more cruel and vicious," says Commines. On the approach of the French the Neapolitans revolted, and Alfonso abdicated in favour of his son Ferdinand II, and fled to Sicily (January 1495). The new King, Ferrandino as the Italians called him, was only twenty-five. The French appeared at the gates of Naples, the populace welcomed them, and Ferrandino fled in his turn. On February 22nd Charles VIII attained the object of his expedition by taking possession of Naples.

Rapidly and without much difficulty he extended his power over the whole of the kingdom, and then arose the question of its defence and organization. His first measures were liberal enough. The " capitulations " of Naples, which ensured the " liberties " of the people, were confirmed. Among these liberties was the license to patricians and rich merchants to keep slaves, " whether black or white ". The sight of slavery under the Renaissance would be amusing were it not so tragic, but its survival is not astonishing when we find it formally authorized by Papal bull.

Charles was in the seventh heaven of delight with all he found in Naples ; palaces, castles, gardens—and ladies. He wrote to his brother-in-law, Pierre de Beaujeu :

You cannot believe what beautiful gardens I have in this city. Upon my faith, I think that only Adam and Eve are wanting to make them the earthly paradise, so fair are they and so full of good and extraordinary objects. Also I have found here the best possible painters of ceilings, and there are no ceilings in Beauce, Lyons or any other part of France which can approach in beauty and richness those I have here. I will engage some of these painters and bring them with me to work at Amboise.

And without more ado the young King charged his " tapissier ", Nicholas Fagot, to take to France an advance-guard of twenty-two Italians, painters, architects, embroiderers, cabinet-makers and goldsmiths.

A reaction to his first impressions soon set in. His conquering army, composed, as we have seen, largely of rabble, soon got out of hand. Monte San Giovanni was stormed, and the surviving defenders flung over the ramparts into the moat. Custom, it is true, sanctioned the sack of towns which resisted their attackers, but here the victors went too far. Throughout Naples they behaved in a way which paid little regard to the welcome they had received on arrival. First occupation, then exploitation. All lucrative positions were given to Charles's men : he himself, young and avid for pleasure, was blind to the misuse of his authority. In any case he could hardly have hoped to put an end to it, since his few sage advisers tried in vain.

Disaffection in Naples gradually increased, while outside it the whole of Italy was terrified of this powerful guest with his train of brutal soldiery. At the instigation of the very two who had invited him to Italy, a league was formed against him. The formal treaty was concluded at Venice on March 25th, 1495, and united against France the Pope, Ludovico of Milan, the Venetian Republic, Ferdinand and Isabella of Spain and the Emperor Maximilian. On April 1st the Vatican guard made a totally unprovoked attack on 150 French troops who were returning to France and killed fifteen of them.

Charles was furious when he heard the news. He saw that he had been betrayed, and that by those he had a right to consider his most faithful allies. His quick mind determined on immediate return, but first he must have the satisfaction of a solemn entry into Naples as some visible token of his triumph. This time he passed through the streets before the admiring eyes of the Neapolitan ladies robed as the Emperor of the East, with crowned head and sceptre and orb in hand and the Imperial mantle flowing from his shoulders. Thus attired he atttended a solemn service in the cathedral, and next day gave a great banquet to the nobles and patricians of the country, who came the more readily to swear fealty since they knew that it committed them to little or nothing.

On May 20th, 1498, the return journey began. The King left as his lieutenant in Naples the Comte de Montpensier with about 10,000 men. Meanwhile, the armies of the League were already in the field. On June 1st Charles passed through Rome. He found the Pope fled. At the prayer of ambassadors sent to meet him he avoided Florence. Then came the dangerous crossing of the Apennines, made yet more dangerous by the appearance of the Venetian contingent under Gian-Francesco de Gonzaga, Marquis of Mantua. This force, more than double that of the French, mustered 40,000 men. The two armies met on July 6th, 1495, close to Fornovo, at the foot of the Apennines and on the banks of the Taro, a tributary of the Po. Regardless of the enemy's superior numbers, Charles gave the order to charge and the Venetians were broken and utterly routed. Charles himself fought valiantly. Meanwhile certain bodies of the enemy had turned his flank and pillaged his baggage. The whole battle lasted an hour and cost three thousand lives.

Both sides claimed Fornovo as a victory. The French had ridden over their enemies and killed more than twice as many as they themselves lost, but the Marquis of Mantua had concrete spoils to show. At all events, he proceeded to celebrate his own triumph by ordering from Mantegna a commemorative picture for the Chapel of Our Lady of

Victory at Mantua. It shows him kneeling, in the armour he wore at Fornovo, at the feet of the Virgin, who holds out a hand in benediction. She sits under a triumphal canopy decorated with fruit, flowers and birds. To right and left are the patron saints of soldiers, St. Michael and St. George, in full armour. The portrait of the Marquis is a faithful likeness.

By the end of October Charles was back in France and Naples had hailed the return of Ferdinand II as warmly as it had the first coming of the French. Gilbert de Montpensier, whom Charles had left as lieutenant-general of the kingdom, was, according to Commines "a good knight and bold, but of small wit and one who never rose till midday". The young Ferdinand gave proof of strength as well as magnanimity, and, with the help of the Pope and of the "Great Captain" Gonsalvo de Cordoba, he was within a month again master of his realm. Montpensier capitulated with what men he had left on July 20th, 1496.

Cardinal Briçonnet, writing to Anne of Brittany from Florence, describes it as the earthly paradise, a description that often recurs in French letters of the time. A single convoy of the art treasures which Charles carried home weighed 87,000 pounds.

Louis XII, in spite of the efforts of Anne of Brittany, continued his predecessor's policy. His first act on his accession was to add to his French title of "Very Christian King" those of Duke of Milan and King of the Two Sicilies.

The war which ensued was of the same character as the previous one, a series of easy victories over the troops of the condottieri, who were usually as poor generals as they were good braggarts. Guicciardini, who knew them and had sat in their councils, says of them that "they had neither art nor strategy and would only make slow marches along a highway"; and Erasmus said of their men, "Behold, who are the fighters? Murderers, outlaws, gamblers, thieves, the vilest mercenaries caring more for their miserable pay than for their lives."

In 1499 Louis XII reconquered the Milanese as a base for his attack on Naples. As usual in the states of the Italian Renaissance, there were two factions in Naples, the Aragonese party of the Spanish princes and the Angevins who were pro-French. Louis met with precisely the same good and ill-fortune as his predecessor. He saw that his only serious rival was the Spaniard and so proposed to Ferdinand of Aragon, cousin of the reigning King of Naples, Frederick III, an arrangement which should have "satisfied" both, the partition of Naples.

Ferdinand seized the opportunity to introduce his troops into Naples, but when Louis arrived in his turn, Ferdinand thought it better to keep the city for himself. After a struggle lasting several years, Louis was compelled to withdraw.

The Italian wars might well have ceased then, but for Julius II. The Papal States had a long common frontier with Naples. Julius, that most bellicose of all the Popes, desired the overthrow of the powerful Signory of Venice, so that he might himself dominate the whole peninsula. He achieved the famous League of Cambrai, which included the French, the Emperor Maximilian and Florence. The French beat the Venetians at Agnadello in 1509, forcing them to sue for peace, and Julius, his own objects attained, immediately turned on his French allies with the war-cry of "Away with the barbarians!" Against France he called in the Swiss and the King of England, and a new campaign opened, remarkable chiefly for the inspired generalship of Gaston de Foix, nephew of Louis. A great captain at twenty-two, he beat the allies in succession under the walls of Bologna, at Brescia and finally at Ravenna, where he was slain in the pursuit of the fleeing Spaniards.

He had many wounds [writes Bayard's biographer, the " Loyal Serviteur "], fourteen or fifteen between chin and brow, which bore witness that he had not turned his back.

Every man soon learned of the death of this noble and virtuous prince, and so great was the sorrow for him in the French camp that I think that if no more than two thousand infantry and two hundred gendarmes of the enemy had come upon them, the French could not have withstood them, so worn out were they from the fatigues of the long day and the sorrow they bore in their hearts for the death of their leader.

The same author adds that " there was some secret plan to make him King of Naples had he lived ".

The Italians named Gaston de Foix the " thunderbolt of war ". He was slim and straight of body and pale of face, with a boyish growth of beard. It was as a boy that he fell, famous almost before he had the chance to achieve fame.

The French armies were finally crushed by the Swiss at Novara (June 6th, 1513), whilst the English were appearing before Calais and the Swiss landsknechts marching on Dijon. Louis XII was forced to sign a truce with the Pope and return to France, where he died soon after. The second Neapolitan adventure had ended like the first.

X

THE ARTS IN FRANCE AT THE END OF THE FIFTEENTH AND BEGINNING OF THE SIXTEENTH CENTURY

THE principal result of the "pomps and vanities" —the expression is Commines'—of the Italian wars was the lively admiration for trans-alpine civilization brought back by Charles VIII, with his train of artists and artisans who were to "ply their crafts after the manner and customs of Italy". From this beginning dates the footing, soon to become a monopoly, of the art of the Renaissance in France. It was not that Italian art was previously unknown and without influence in France. The architectural and decorative elements in the miniatures of Jean Fouquet were in the Italian taste. Fouquet himself had won the admiration of the Italians by his portrait of Pope Eugenius IV. The oldest known Italian work of art in France dates from 1472. It is the monument to the Duke of Anjou in the cathedral of le Mans. There are sculptures in Avignon and Marseilles by the Italianized Dalmatian Francesco Laurana and Mantegna's magnificent St. Sebastian in the church of Aigueperse, the gift of a Gonzaga lady married to a Bourbon. This lady also brought first Ghirlandaio and then other Umbrian painters to France to do the frescoes of St. Servin in Toulouse and Albi Cathedral. All these, however, were mere disconnected episodes, unlike the events which followed the return of Charles VIII.

Among the artists who accompanied Charles to France, the first name of note is that of a sculptor, the Modenese, Guido Mazzoni. He executed several works for the château of Gaillon, among the medallions in relief of classical warriors. He carved the tomb of Charles VIII at Saint Denis, which perished at the Revolution. He was a member of the colony of Italian artists established in the Hôtel du Petit Nesle, which included Guido Paganino, Montorsoli, the Della Robbias and that bragging genius Benvenuto Cellini.

There was also at Amboise a small town of Italian workmen of all kinds, from painters to cabinet-makers, working on the decoration of Charles's favourite residence. Among them was a landscape gardener, Pacello da Mercoliano, who laid out Italian gardens in the style Charles had so admired in Naples. A small majolica factory was founded in 1502, at Amboise, by Girolamo Solobrini.

There were also two famous architects, Fra Giocondo and the well-known Domenico da Cortona, called " il Boccador ". Fra Giocondo was a native of Verona, where he planned the Palazzo della Ragione. He was in France from 1495 onwards, working both for the King and for the city of Paris, for whom he built the Pont Notre-Dame, which, like old London Bridge, had houses on each side. In 1505 he was recalled by Julius II to Rome to take charge of the work on the Vatican. Domenico da Cortona came to France at the same time, but his influence there was much greater than that of his colleague. While Fra Giocondo returned to Italy after ten years, " il Boccador " spent the rest of his life in France. In the royal accounts for 1497 he figures as a " castle-maker ", probably because he made wooden models of his buildings for his princely clients. With the master-mason Pierre Chambiges, he was responsible for the town-hall of Paris, burnt by the Commune in 1871.

Charles VIII's taste for Italian art was shared by his successor, Louis XII, but still more by Francis I, and this royal patronage was of the utmost importance for its diffusion, since the time was one of unification and centralization of the country. Italy was a collection of small states, each of which had its own peculiar school of art, and the same is true of Germany. But in France, the royal power, in unifying the country, tended to the destruction of all local peculiarities. All the great fiefs had become merged into the kingdom, and only Flanders remained as a separate unit, with a living and brilliant art of its own. Thus Italian art was enabled to spread unchecked through the whole country, once it had been adopted as the " official " and royal art.

Another ingenious suggestion has been made to explain the spread of Italian taste. The marble used in sculpture came chiefly from Italy and entailed the employment of Italians who were accustomed to handle it. The marble, too, needed to be worked in motifs suitable to its grain, in contrast to the native Gothic freestone.

The way of the new art was not equally smooth in all directions. Architects and draughtsmen were easy converts : less easy were the trade guilds, masons, wood-workers, smiths and all the other craftsmen producing works of art. The taste of the King or of the patrons who aped him, the drawings of " il Boccador " or Fra Giocondo had little or no effect on this class, so that the first years of Italian art show not an Italianization of French forms, but rather the two existing side by side. It was only later, towards the end of the reign of Louis XII and in that of Francis I, that a new style, the product of a fusion of the two, begins to appear.

The first outstanding monument of the new style is the

château of Gaillon. Its construction, which took ten years, was due to the Cardinal d'Amboise, the minister of Louis XII. The architect is unknown, though he may have been Fra Giocondo. The conception is Italian, but the details of sculpture betray the hands of Frenchmen not yet used to the new style. It also was destroyed at the Revolution.

It has often been stated that by the time of the Renaissance Gothic art had reached a stage of such excessive complication in the extravagance of the flamboyant style, that it stood in need of the simplification brought by Italian art. The same was later to be said of the effect of the art of David on the ultra-refined mannerisms of the school of Watteau and Fragonard. The accusation, in the case of Gothic art, is wholly untrue. Never had it been richer or more active. It was not in decadence, but in process of renewal in the best truly French taste. All that had happened was that the artists of the fifteenth century, instead of working endlessly on the simple forms handed down to them from the eleventh and twelfth, had sought and found newer and richer subjects, while the architects of the same period were attaining a degree of skill in handling the problems of their art which was unequalled till the coming of metal-framed buildings.

Furthermore, Gothic art, after the short and sudden outburst of the flamboyant period, was itself returning to a purer and more classical model. Proof of this is easily to be seen in Notre-Dame de Cléry near Orleans and in the Tour Saint Jacques in Paris. This latter was constructed in 1508–22, that is to say at a period when the Renaissance itself was on the wane, when Leonardo da Vinci and Rafael were dead, and, in the judgment of some critics at least, it is far superior to the famous Campanile of Florence, the work of Giotto.

Some of the finest towers and spires of France are the work of the sixteenth century, such as the tower of Chartres cathedral for example, built by Jean Texier in 1509, or the open-work spire of Amiens, or that highest of all Gothic spires, that of Beauvais. The cathedral of Metz, the Butter Tower and the doorway of Rouen cathedral all date from the same century. The list is endless.

With civil architecture it is the same. Not all the great lords copied the royal taste in buildings, as is seen from many châteaux in Touraine and from the Hôtel de Cluny in Paris, while in Blois and in Orleans and in the half-timbered houses of Lisieux and Rouen we may see the adaptation of the flamboyant style to the needs of everyday life.

The same holds good for sculpture. Except for the ecclesiastical sculpture of the thirteenth century, which is indeed unrivalled, no period other than the sixteenth century was so rich and attractive. From one end of France to the other we find a marvellous wealth and variety, in which the school of Champagne holds the palm. There are carvings in stone and carvings in wood, the latter coloured to conform to the popular taste, but expressive of simple faith ; Martha grave and thoughtful, cooking-pot in hand : Paul bearing the sword : Eve, the embodiment of feminine slyness : Joseph, a bucolic figure leaning on his heavy staff, stern and solid as befits one who has to watch over the Holy Child : graceful Virgins, not lacking a touch of coquetry, and others, more maternal, who tenderly clasp their Child.

The artists of this period drew their inspiration direct from life and not from an art already dead. Sometimes their subjects were taken from the mystery-plays.

All this variety and colour was soon to be submerged

beneath a flood of Italianism which washed away the popular tints of the true French sculptor. The nymphs of Jean Goujon are indeed exquisite, but there are many statues in the old style in the churches of France which are infinitely more impressive. Take, for example, the reliefs of the choir of Chartres cathedral, portraying the life of the Virgin. Before this marvellous array of life and movement—one might almost say of colour, though they are in plain stone—before these figures, which run through the whole gamut of human life, experience and emotion, one can only regret the abandonment of a national tradition for the soulless imitation of a foreign art.

It would not have been so bad if French sculptors had followed those of the early and middle fifteenth century, the vigorous and realistic school of Donatello and Verrocchio, whose works live in figures taken from actual life, with natural gestures and " speaking " countenances, such as Verrocchio's David or Donatello's St. George and the Prophets, or many admirably conceived Florentine Virgins. The French imitators, however, took for models the works of a later period, which, except for the mighty and inimitable Michael Angelo, were definitely inferior. The decline in sculptural taste has been clearly shown by Vasari :

It was left to the successors of Donatello and Verrocchio to discover perfection when the Laocoön, the Hercules, the Belvedere Torso, the Cleopatra, the Apollo and a hundred others were disinterred. Their softness or severity, the bold yet supple treatment of the flesh in these most lovely figures, their unstrained attitudes combined to banish the harsh and crude directness which hitherto had been so much admired.

These very works to which Vasari alludes were nothing but the products of an outworn paganism, which had already lost the glow of faith illuminating its greatest works. The

Venus de Milo, the Apollo of Praxiteles, the frieze of the Parthenon and the Victory of Samothrace were as yet unknown. The Italians, in imitating second-rate works, lost what little vigour they possessed. Faced with such an academic work, at once frigid and pompous, as Jehan Boulogne's Rape of the Sabines, one can only conclude with Marquet de Vasselot that it was not a Renaissance of Greek art that was in progress, but of a decadent Florentine art.

Even if the Renaissance had drawn its inspiration from the purest forms of Greek art at its highest, from Phidias or Praxiteles, it would still have lacked the thought, the emotions, the very spirit which moved these great artists. The utmost that could have been achieved would have been a formal and soulless imitation. Instead of looking to the nearest ploughboy or peasant lass for his models, we find the aspiring young sculptor measuring up fragments of antique statuary with the meticulous care of a jeweller designing a trinket. The living art of the French Gothic churches merged into the cold theatrical pompousness of the Italian school : the architectural decorative motifs—drawn from the gardens, woods and fields of France, and adapted to French light and climate—gave place to Doric, Ionic or Corinthian capitals, friezes, architraves, oves and triglyphs and all the paraphernalia which the Italians had taken from the Romans, as the Romans from the Greeks, and which had been deformed and degraded at each step in its descent.

Viollet le Duc gives an admirable definition of French architecture in the Middle Ages :

Every necessary element becomes a decorative feature ; gables, rain-pipes, windows, entrances and stairways, even such minor details as iron and lead work and means of heating and ventilation, are not concealed, as they often were after the sixteenth century, but rather revealed and made to contribute by their skilful arrangement and tasteful execution to the general architectural effect. A fine building of the thirteenth century would have not a single decoration to spare, since each would correspond to some necessity.

An architecture which had its origin in the Greece of Alcibiades and Pericles could not possibly supply the needs of a modern Frenchman. Their manners and customs were different ; they passed their lives in another climate and beneath another sun.

In the fourteenth and fifteenth centuries architecture was practical and style gave way to convenience, but later a rigid ideal, a formula, a convention, was imposed on the architect. Conservatism and ancient usage prevailed for a short time and to a limited extent against the flood of novelty, but soon gave way. Decoration then became an object in itself and constructional necessities things to be hidden, however clumsily.

The appropriateness of the two styles can easily be judged from two buildings in Paris, the Madeleine and Notre-Dame, the latter beautiful in any weather, while the former, though passable with bright sunshine to display its pillars against a background of shadow, on a grey day is nothing but a huge box.

Till the time of Francis I, when the Italian avalanche buried all beneath its weight, the essential structure of French buildings was maintained in its traditional form, only the decoration being borrowed, but this was the last stand of domestic necessity and religious tradition against the taste of the court.

In the Middle Ages the ruling spirit in the arts had been unity, congruity and concord ; with the Renaissance appeared individuality. The creators of a thirteenth-century cathedral and the ceremonial it enshrined were not individual workers but parts of a vast whole, a common labour in which the details were completely harmonious. Architect, sculptor, glazier, the composer of sacred music and the author of the mystery play whose theatre was the church porch, all lived, thought and created as a body. Within the craft guilds architects and master sculptors lived a life in common with their humbler fellows. Master-craftsmen were paid, like labourers, by the day, and a day's holiday meant to all alike the loss of a day's wage. This was as true of Germany as of France. A great artist, sculptor and bronze founder such as Peter Fischer of Nuremberg calls himself a " cauldron maker " ; a famous wood-carver like Surlin of Ulm appears as a " carpenter ". The arrival of the Italians brought about a change in this simple, patriarchal system. The artist became a person of importance. He became a courtier and held a court post, he was sent on embassies, or held benefices like poets, captains and royal favourites. First came the separation of the arts from one another, and then the division between masters and workmen. Finally came the separation of art from the people. Mediæval art had sprung from the soul of the people, as a plant springs from the soil, but on the arrival of the formula of Greece, Rome and Italy this fruitful contact was utterly lost.

The imagery of the churches, whether in glass, in sculpture or in painting, had been the living expression of the feelings and beliefs of the people. The people inspired and gave direction to the artist ; the artist was one with the people. Now all is changed. With a flourish of trumpets enter Mars and Jupiter, Venus and Adonis, Apollo and the nine Muses, the story of Procris, the Trojan War, the triumphs of Cæsar and all the rag-tag and bobtail of antiquity, in decorated chariots straight from Rome and Florence.

Even in its presentation of the figures of the Bible the new art made no appeal to the people. The herculean Deity and naked Virgin of Michael Angelo's Last Judgment would only have disgusted and appalled them. As Louis Gillet very accurately says :

With its own hands the Church destroyed the shining imagery of its stained glass and the mystery of its velvety shadows. Soon the bright colours, the long and edifying stories, the gentle Gothic saints like Geneviève of Brabant, the touching Paradise of the Golden Legend, all the marvels of old, beloved by the simple people, which had produced a Joan of Arc, were utterly cast forth, to survive only in the gaudy lithographs printed at Epinal to be sold from cottage door to door by wandering pedlars. Such is the loss the Renaissance inflicted on France : the breach between art and the people.

Then, after " art for the few ", we have " art for art's sake ". Until the Renaissance, art had been a production of the people for the people. Poets sang, painters and sculptors worked to express for the people their own thoughts and feelings. The conception of beauty for its own sake, of art for art's sake, of the artist as useful in himself was non-existent. We do not know the name of a single one of the great sculptors of the thirteenth-century cathedrals. Writing was valued for its matter and not for its manner—until the Renaissance brought in the " promising young artist " and the " literary lion ".

Literature followed a course precisely similar to that of the plastic arts. Poetry underwent the same changes at the same time and for the same reasons. Thus we find among artists of all kinds the same freely expressed contempt for their predecessors. As Rabelais and Ronsard speak of the old poetic forms, so do Philibert de l'Orme or Jean Bullant of Gothic barbarism.

Montaigne, who was hopelessly unjust to his literary predecessors, could nevertheless appreciate mediæval churches.

They seemed to touch him through some ancestral feeling. His art criticism, too, is sound and strangely modern. "If I were an artist, I should treat art as naturally as possible. I would naturalize it as much as they Italianize nature."

In breaking with tradition and popular inspiration, the artists of the Renaissance had entered on a perilous path. In future, unless they had genius, they could not avoid the pitfalls of insignificance and platitude, and even if they achieved true greatness they could not hope to excel the old masters whose work was the sincere expression of a truly popular emotion.

It is permissible [writes Emile Mâle] to prefer the simple Christ of a French cathedral, the unassuming work of a modest artist following a tradition consecrated by time, to the " Christ cursing the damned " created by the genius of Michael Angelo without reference to any tradition whatsoever.

The necessities of domestic life and of climate, and also, to some extent, the limited resources of the builders, contributed to preserve French architecture against the Renaissance, but in painting and sculpture the harm was more serious. One department only remained almost untouched —that of portraiture. The absolute necessity of a faithful reproduction of features, expression and dress proved an insurmountable obstacle to Italianization, and so it is that we possess the incomparable series of portraits collectively known under the name of Clouet, and the equally unrivalled collection of portrait busts which constitute the lasting glory of French sculpture from the Renaissance to the present day.

In short, the chief emotion left by a survey of the plastic arts of the French Renaissance is the same as that aroused by the contemplation of French literature of the same period

—regret that artists who might by working out received traditions have achieved true greatness should have been led astray into by-ways of mere imitation of an imported and inappropriate art.

XI

SAVONAROLA

CHARLES VIII had entered Florence on November 17th, 1494, a week after the expulsion of Piero dei Medici. The red circles on the golden field which adorned the palace built by Michelozzo for Cosimo the Elder had given place to the cross of the city coat-of-arms, and the city had fallen under the sway of one of the strangest and most striking figures in all History—Fra Girolamo Savonarola.

Savonarola had already, in one of his fiery sermons, predicted the coming of the King of France with his army, as a new " Scourge of God " to chastise the corrupt Italians. The Frenchman was to come " like a new Cyrus, armed by the Lord with the sword of vengeance ".

Savonarola was born at Ferrara on September 21st, 1452. His family was of the middle class and came from Padua. He was destined for the medical profession, in which several of his family were well known, and received a good literary and scientific education. He soon showed a pensive, wild and enthusiastic nature, seeking solitude to pore over the philosophy of Aristotle and Thomas Aquinas. His vocation for the Church showed itself unmistakably after a sermon he heard in Faenza. On April 23rd, 1475, he fled from his home to Bologna, where he donned the white robe of the Dominicans.

At whatever cost [he said later] I was compelled to don the

monastic garb. The thought of entering a monastery kept me awake at nights and took away my appetite, but as soon as I obeyed the commands of my mind I became utterly contented. Now that I am a monk I would not change places with any man on earth.

Two days after he had entered the Convent, Savonarola wrote to his father that he had done so to escape the impiety and filth of a world which emulated Sodom and Gomorrah. His ultra-sensitive and nervous nature found congenial surroundings in the monotonous peace of the cloister.

Two things I love above all [he writes], freedom and rest. These two have brought me safely home. I would have no wife, since I wished for liberty, and to attain peace I have fled the world and found asylum in religion.

At his own request the humblest offices of the convent were allotted to him, those of gardener and tailor, but after a year of these his superiors insisted that he take up teaching. His first subject was metaphysics, but hair-splitting subtleties so disgusted him that he soon devoted his whole attention to the Scriptures. Henceforth the Gospels were to him the only source of truth, a doctrine which makes him appear a forerunner of Luther and Calvin.

The book from which divine law in its entirety is to be learned is the book of Our Lord Jesus the Crucified. Read this book : it contains everything. You wish to love : then read the book of the Crucified. You wish to have charity : then read the book of the Crucified, where you will find all the virtues.

In 1482, he was transferred from the convent of Sta. Maria degli Angeli at Bologna to the famous house of San Marco at Florence, which had just been rebuilt by Cosimo the Elder on the plans of Michelozzo and decorated by Fra Angelico and Fra Bartolomeo, and which was also famous as the home of St. Antony. There Savonarola was promoted " lector ", or instructor of the novices, a post he held for four years. At the same time he used to preach the Lenten sermons at the Church of St. Laurence. It is astonishing to learn that his first efforts as a preacher were most unsuccessful. When he spoke, his large black eyes shot forth flames and his whole body trembled with the ardour of his passionate conviction, but his voice was hoarse and inaudible, his intonation false, his carriage awkward and his style dull. In 1483 hardly a score of people followed his Lenten sermons till the end.

From 1484 dates his tendency to interfere in politics. He was seized by an irresistible urge to reform the state in a democratic sense on a basis of virtue and religion. A council had been established in Florence to work out a new constitution for the republic. Savonarola demanded to be heard by it and put forward the most radical proposals. He passionately loved Florence and Italy, the poor and the humble, the " popolo minutissimo ". He loved liberty, which seemed to him prerequisite for virtue, and therefore hated the tyranny of the Medici.

He was an exemplary monk by the purity of his life, by his modesty, his devotion to his work and his deep piety. He passed whole nights in prayer and meditation, till his thoughts were transfigured and he believed himself in contact with God, who imparted directly to him the teachings of Christ which the poor monk himself had vainly endeavoured to comprehend. He ended by believing in an identity of thought between himself and God and hence was convinced that his own moral and political conceptions had been implanted in his mind by the hand of God, and that God was to speak through his mouth. He was a prophet, as Isaiah, Jeremiah and Daniel were prophets. This was no sudden flash of conviction, but a gradual process, which took complete possession of his mind when it was confirmed by the realization of his early predictions of the deaths of Innocent VIII and Lorenzo the Magnificent, the fall of the Medici and the French invasion. From this conviction sprang the motives which ruled his life in word and deed and the mistakes which brought about his downfall.

By nature he was modest, but the conception of God thinking with his mind and speaking through his lips raised the demon of pride within him : he was naturally good and kind, but the conviction that those who opposed him went against the will of God made him intolerant and ruthless : his own character was at once feeble and fickle, but the feeling of his prophetic gift gave him a strength and energy which drove him into the pitfalls dug by his own timorous and hesitant nature. Herein lies the secret of the contradictions of his life.

Perrens, in his *Life of Savonarola*, shows how he may have been influenced by a fellow-monk, one Silvestro Maruffi, who was a sleep-walker and subject, during his attacks, to visions which he described aloud. At that time it was generally held that sleep-walkers were closer to God than other men.

Savonarola was full of doubts and scruples :

As God is my witness I never closed an eye in the night from Saturday till the dawn of Sunday, and could see no help. My knowledge had left me, I knew not what to do. When day came, and I was weary with long watching, I heard a voice which said, " Madman, seest thou not that it is the will of God that thou shouldst foretell the future as heretofore ? " That is the reason of my furious discourse the next day.

Here we have the true enthusiast, carried away by his passions, though it is true that his passions sprang from the noblest sources. But side by side with this was another Savonarola, a human being with human desires and ambitions, a calculating, reflective, prudent and circumspect human, of singularly acute observation and penetrating thought. The prophet is an observer of men and events and shapes his course by them. He takes due note of the tasks, tendencies and ambitions around him. Thus he goes cautiously forward among the obstacles in his path, only now and then bursting forth into wild harangues of furious indignation.

He was a small, thin man, narrow-chested and sickly. He stooped and hung his head as if weighed down by thought. His large deep-set eyes were black, his eyebrows red and bushy, his nose large and aquiline. His mouth too was large, with thick fleshy lips, and his prominent cheek-bones seemed on the point of bursting through the flesh. In the Uffizi in Florence is a fine portrait of him in profile by Fra Bartolomeo : his face is thin, wasted by fasting and the unending ardour which consumed him. His brow is deeply lined, his hair thick under his hood.

Meanwhile, his reputation had grown. His lessons to the novices soon drew the whole community to hear them, and an ever-increasing number from without. The lector was soon compelled to take the largest room in the convent for his lectures, and this in its turn was found too small, so that eventually he had to speak in the convent garden, standing against a tree of white roses by the chapel door. At last he was called to preach in the Cathedral of the Madonna del Fiore, where during the eight years from 1490 to 1498 he gave a considerable number of sermons. The ten volumes which survive are far from exhausting the total.

As a speaker he had made great progress in a short time. Villari says that his voice was superhuman. It was deep and cavernous, but his conviction pierced through his words in a flame which set heart and mind afire. People flocked to hear him till they were packed like herrings even in the largest churches. They clung in clusters to the rails of the choir, and those who failed to get into the church remained motionless outside, gazing at the walls within which flowed the torrent of eloquence. Peasants walked long hours through the night from distant villages to be in time for the opening of the church.

Ah ! the wondrous word which compels the heart [writes Fra Domenico Buonvincini, one of his disciples], the word which makes the breath come gustily, which holds all heads erect with eyes bent upon the speaker ! I have often seen the crowd hanging on his lips, as if drawn by their mighty breath, trembling and fevered with dread, weeping and sometimes crying aloud in anguish at the terrible words which set forth the anger of the Lord.

When the preacher spoke against the extravagances of female dress, the women who had heard him hastened to cast aside their costly dress and jewels, to sell and give to the poor. When he preached against ill-gotten riches the money-changers, speculators and merchants went straight from the church to restore a part of their wealth : one of them, one day, thus returned three thousand gold ducats. The very scribe whose duty it was to take down the speaker's words interpolates in his text, " Here tears and emotion prevented me from writing ".

The preacher thundered against the vices of his century, against the corruption which pervaded the world ; but the scourge of God, the coming of the barbarians, would not be long delayed. They would cross the mountains to slay and burn and ravage.

They will lead our tyrants into captivity with rings of iron through their noses, like beasts in the ring. In vain shalt thou flee to right or to left, the scourge of God will be on all sides, on all sides will be the darkness. Thou shalt have no place to hide thine head. Darkness here and darkness there, all things in tumult, earth and sky, sun and moon.

And the curse goes on till it is broken by an outburst of piercing anguish :

" Pity, pity, O God ! In the name of the blood of Christ ! " And the people, sobbing, fell to their knees, repeating : " Pity, pity, O God ! In the name of the blood of Christ ! "

" An inward fire consumes my bones," said Savonarola, " and compels me to speak." At these moments he seemed to be carried away by some superhuman ecstasy, with heaven and the future revealed to his eyes.

So far did the fame of his sermons spread that Sultan Bayazid, in distant Constantinople, requested the Florentine envoy to obtain them, that they might be translated into Turkish.

Amid these resounding successes, Savonarola himself remained humble and modest, kind and gracious to all. He was greatly beloved by his companions of the Convent of San Marco, and in 1491 they elected him their Prior, in which post he introduced reforms which display his faith and his desire for a simplicity like that of the early Christians, in conformity with the Gospel. He writes to the prior of a Pisan monastery :

We know no other way of life than our rule, and have suppressed certain unessential matters contrary to the customs of our fathers. We are determined to build the most simple convents, to wear only coarse cloth and to eat and drink simply after the manner of the saints, to dwell in cells devoid of all luxury, to keep silence and live a life of contemplation.

But the new prior also founded a school of oriental languages in his convent, where the necessary knowledge to read the Scriptures in the original texts could be acquired. This school was largely attended, not only by the monks but by many other Florentines.

In his sermons he continued to criticize the Medicean tyranny and now began to attack the depravity of the Court of Rome under Alexander VI. Lorenzo dei Medici endeavoured to appease his opposition, which had an ever-increasing influence on the people. Savonarola ignored his most attractive offers. "Go and tell the Medici to do penance, for God maketh ready to punish both him and his."

In 1492 the tyrant felt that his sickness was mortal. "I know no truly religious man but this," he said, and sent for Savonarola to be with him at his death.

The next year, the prior of St. Mark was called to preach at Bologna, and from there he maintained an active correspondence with his monks. In this he appears as a man full of tenderness for those whose leader he was. He enters into the minutest detail, with deep thought for the good and happiness of each one of them. On his return he was appointed Vicar-General of Tuscany, which placed under his rule all the monks of his order in the province. He had now become the most important personage in the State. Lorenzo being dead and his son Piero an exile, Savonarola was charged with the negotiations between Florence and Charles VIII.

From the pulpit he spoke frankly on questions of government. The downfall of the Medici and the troubles brought about by the French invasion had plunged Florence into anarchy.

The disturbances that were in prospect [writes Guicciardini] would have brought disunion into the government, revolution, proscriptions, and perhaps, as a last resort, the return of the Medici amidst general slaughter, and finally the ruin of the city.

Savonarola now ruled in Florence, like Cosimo dei Medici before him, without any official title.

His talents [writes Varillas in his *Anecdotes of Florence*] made him act with greater authority than if he were a sovereign prince ; his advice was followed in the public assemblies ; he was arbiter in domestic troubles and settled the strife between husbands and wives without appeal against his decision or delay in carrying it out.

[He proclaimed Christ Lord of Florence and called upon every citizen to model himself on the Christian virtues.] Love one another and strive to understand and help one another.

As the organ of government he set up a council of all citizens more than twenty-nine years of age whose families had held one of the " major offices " of state within three generations. This council made the laws and appointed all officials.

Savonarola was devoted to the people. He was so carried away by his love for the humble that he went too far in his attack on the rich and powerful. Debtors were freed of their debts, a bank was founded to make loans without interest to the needy, the Jewish money-changers and money-lenders were driven from Florence. All this produced a fruitful crop of hatreds which later became dangerous. He meant his flock to follow in the footsteps of their Saviour, who was now the official " tyrant " of Florence.

" He could move the Florentines at will by the tones of his voice," says Gabriel Naudé, one of his earliest historians. And Florence, that magnificent city, the jewel of the Renaissance, the city of luxury, of art and of pleasure, swiftly became like a cloister or a convent. Taverns were closed, fast-days multiplied till the butchers were ruined : on all sides, on the square before the Signoria, on the Ponte Vecchio, in every street, nothing was to be heard but lauds and canticles, hymns and psalms. People ran into one another in the streets through walking with their noses buried in their Gospel or their prayer-book. They were like a people chained to their breviaries. As for their amusements—and this in Florence, the city of gaiety and pleasure—

They meet [says Burlamachi] in groups of thirty or so, men and women together, and seek out some pleasant spot, in town or country. There they hear mass and communicate, and spend the day in singing lauds and psalms. They gather round some image of the Infant Jesus, and pray amid tears. They listen to moral sermons and carry a Madonna in procession.

All this was achieved by persuasion and not by force. Savonarola had touched them with his own emotion. Meanwhile his attacks on the morals, then on the doctrines, and finally on the authority itself of the Papacy continued with ever-increasing violence. Savonarola finally attacked Papal authority. He desired the convocation of a General Council for the reform of the clergy. He desired the return of the Church to its primitive state of simplicity, stating plainly that the papal office was more often than not obtained by most reprehensible means. He never thought either of a separation from Rome or of doubting any one of the fundamental dogmas of Catholicism, to which, to the end of his life, he remained devoutly attached.

Alexander VI, alarmed as Lorenzo dei Medici had been by the first onslaught made on him, endeavoured to appease the terrible preacher by the offer of the highest offices it was in his power to bestow, the archbishopric of Florence and the Cardinal's hat. The monk's most ambitious dreams could not have gone further, but he repulsed the Pope's offers as he had repulsed those of Lorenzo. As his criticisms continued, he was summoned to Rome to justify himself by an order of the Pope dated July 25th, 1495. He refused to obey, and was forbidden to preach by two further Papal briefs of the 8th September and 15th October, 1495.

Savonarola took the pulpit again with renewed vigour, and now his eloquence burst forth with unmeasured force. Under some irresistible impulsion, he perpetrated the first of the series of mistakes which brought about his fall, the famous auto-da-fé, the " burning of the vanities " which he fixed for the last day of Carnival, the seventh of February, 1497. He had proscribed from the pulpit all manner of worldly pleasures : dances, cards, backgammon, dress, masks and masquerades, frivolous instruments of music, mythological pageantry and all imaginative literature. He had collected bands of street urchins to carry out his orders. They stopped ladies in the street and despoiled them of their jewels, they entered houses to seize pictures they held to be indecent, playing cards, musical instruments, beads, lace and books of verse. The proceeds of these pious robberies were collected in a heap which Savonarola declared anathema.

On February 7th, 1497, a huge bonfire was built on the Piazza della Signoria, in which were collected all the objects which the prophet had devoted to the flames. The first layer, counting from the bottom, consisted of carnival masks, false beards, clowns' dresses, silken vests, gilded helmets, bells and tinsel : above them the gorgeous pile of feminine adornment, brocade gowns, lace, jewellery, powder, rouge and perfume, and above them again secular instruments of music, pipes, tambourines, mandolins and viols, with cards, chess and backgammon ; and, to crown all, those works of art which were adjudged immoral, that is to say all those displaying the human body in the nude, however great the artist.

Such was the fever-heat of emotion excited by the preacher

that works by Baccio della Porta and Lorenzo di Credi were freely brought by their painters to add to the pile. The signal was given, and fire applied at the same time to the four corners of the pile, while trumpets sounded and all the bells of the city gave forth a joyous peal. The crowd around the bonfire sang canticles, but when the excitement of the moment was passed the clearer-headed of the citizens declared that the " saint " had gone a little too far. Burning the poems of Pulci, Petrarch and Boccaccio, and the exquisite portraits of fair women simply because their dresses were rather low, seemed sacrilege to the Florentines, who had never lost their love of beauty.

From that day forward Florence was divided into two camps ; the " Piagnoni " or weepers (so called from the tears they shed as they listened to the preacher) and the " Arrabiati " or madmen (from their rage at Savonarola's reforms). Foremost among the Piagnoni, who were also called the " Whites ", were the adherents of the popular party, while the others, the " Greys ", were mainly of the aristocratic party which desired the return of the Medici. Passions rose, threats and blows were exchanged, and Savonarola's party would no longer let him go out except with an armed escort.

An incident now occurred which greatly increased the tension. Certain of the notables had been condemned to death for a political offence, namely, that they had plotted for the return of Piero dei Medici.

Their relations [says Guicciardini] appealed against the sentence to the Great Council in virtue of a law proposed by Savonarola himself. But the judges who had passed the sentence, fearing that compassion for old age and nobility and the multitude of these relations might move the people to mitigate the severity of the judgment, arranged that it should be left to certain citizens to decide whether the appeal should be proceeded with or forbidden. By a majority it was decided that it should not be proceeded with—as dangerous and likely to arouse sedition, the law itself allowing laws to remain in abeyance if riot could thereby be avoided. Thereupon the members of the government were compelled, almost by force and threats, to consent to the execution of the sentence that very night, in despite of the appeal. The prime movers in this deed were precisely those who most favoured Savonarola, and he himself bore the shame of making no effort to oppose the violation of a law which he himself had proposed only a few years before.

Though this last detail is disputed, the prophet's opponents did not fail to make capital of his alleged cruelty and bad faith.

Finally sentence of excommunication was pronounced by Alexander VI on May 31st, 1497, and received with contempt by Savonarola. " In these days," he said, " excommunications are four a penny. Anyone can buy them for use against an enemy." This is already the voice of Luther.

A brief has arrived from Rome [he says] calling me son of perdition. I who am thus addressed have neither favourite nor concubine, but preach the faith of Christ. Those who listen to my doctrine do not pass their days in deeds of darkness, they confess, communicate and lead an upright life. I strive to exalt, you to destroy the Church. Patience ! The time will come when the casket must be opened (and the corruption of Rome revealed). One turn of the key, and such a stench will come forth as will poison all Christendom.

Speaking of Alexander, Savonarola wrote to the princes of Europe : "I swear that this man is no Pope and no Christian. He does not believe in God."

But there was to be an interval of calm. The plague descended on Florence. The prior of St. Mark dismissed seventy of his monks and shut himself up in his convent with the forty who remained. " We are rather more than forty, and the citizens attend to our wants and see we lack for nothing. As we do not go out, they bring us all we need." Savonarola adds that he had remained in Florence to comfort the afflicted. It was certainly an odd way of bearing consolation to the sick and the families of the dead, to shut himself up out of danger of infection ! It was the weakest moment of his whole life. Within him two ill-assorted beings were striving for supremacy, his timid, fearful, rather selfish nature and his exalted mind, full of devotion and virtue.

When the plague was past, his adversaries the Greys did not spare their criticisms of his conduct. His person and his deeds became a subject of strife, not only between Whites and Greys, democrats and patricians, but between husbands and wives, parents and children. Some took his part, others opposed him : some from conviction embraced the Christian life he wished to impose on all, others called him a bigoted hypocrite. " Every day threats and curses were to be heard : a mother-in-law would drive her daughter-in-law from her house, a husband leave his wife . . . a wife would secretly warn the ' prophet ' of her husband's opposition."

Meanwhile, the Augustinians and Franciscans, jealous of the prestige which Savonarola had brought to the Dominicans, went about fanning the flame of discord. Savonarola, nervous and irritable, was deeply troubled by the growing opposition round him. He had moments of dejection, which he sought to conquer.

I have worshipped the Lord in all sincerity, only seeking to follow His divine footsteps : I have spent whole nights in prayer ; I have given up my peace and used up health and life in the service of my neighbour. Nay ! It is not possible that the Lord should have deceived me !

In his agitation at the course of events he lost not only

his calm but his moderation. One day he was so far carried away as to proclaim in a sermon that he was so certain that he was in the right path, that he was ready to appeal with his opponents to the judgment of God.

The ordeal by fire was in his mind. A Franciscan accepted the challenge, and on Savonarola's side Fra Buonvincini, his most ardent supporter, offered to pass through the flames in place of his prior. Public opinion was aroused. All Florence spoke of nothing but the ordeal. Arguments between citizens of different factions took on a new violence. After the first excitement had worn off, both sides were inclined to regret their own rashness. The Franciscan champion alone still kept his spirit. "I am certain to perish in the flames, but Savonarola or his representative will perish too, and the false prophet thereby be unmasked."

The Signoria appointed a commission of ten, drawn in equal number from both factions to fix time and place for the ordeal. The seventh of April, 1498, the eve of Palm Sunday, was the day chosen, and a pile sixty cubits long was built on the square before the Palazzo Vecchio. A narrow passage was left between the stacks of faggots through which the two champions must pass amidst the flames. The nascent hostility of the Florentines to Savonarola burst forth with greater violence so soon as it was known that he himself would not submit to the test.

On the day appointed an impatient mob filled the square. Heavy clouds in the sky threatened to deluge the ceremony. Fra Buonvincini appeared with Savonarola, bearing the consecrated wafer in his hand. Savonarola claimed that his representative should brave the flames armed with the Sacrament. His opponents protested. It was sacrilege to expose the Host to the flames, and if it should happen to be consumed the faith of the people would suffer. Savonarola stood firm. An interminable discussion began and continued till the storm broke in torrents of rain. The faggots were drenched beyond all possibility of lighting them, and the assembly broke up when Savonarola pronounced the rain to be a sign of God's disapproval of the proposed ordeal. The faith of the Florentines in their prophet had received a mortal blow. It was said that he had raised so many objections at the last moment because he expected, not from God but from the lowering clouds, a way out of his difficulties.

The next morning, April 8th, the convent of St. Mark was attacked by a howling mob, raised and led by the Arrabiati. The monks had shut themselves in and defended themselves vigorously, opening fire with bombards and arquebuses. Five of the attackers and three monks were slain, among them Savonarola's brother.

Alexander VI immediately convoked a court to try Savonarola. Its members were the General of the Dominican order and the Archbishop of Sorrento. His condemnation was assured. He was executed on May 23rd, 1498, on the square of the Signoria, with two faithful friends who insisted on sharing his fate. They were Fra Domenico Buonvincini and Fra Silvestro Maruffi the sleep-walker. Their punishment was accompanied by disgusting barbarities on the part of a frenzied mob. This same mob which used to kneel when he passed, now hooted him, cursed him and pelted him with filth and stones. The three Dominicans were hanged, their bodies cut down and burnt and the ashes thrown into the river. They met their deaths bravely, without a word.

Savonarola was then in his forty-sixth year.

Next day a letter arrived for the Signoria from Louis XII, who had just succeeded Charles VIII, forbidding them to put to death the great Dominican.

Afterwards came the reaction. All that could be saved from

the pyre was piously collected. The nephew of Pico della Mirandola boasted that he possessed a fragment of Savonarola's heart and that it worked miracles.

Marcantonio Flaminio wrote this Latin epitaph upon him :

> Whilst the savage flame devours thee, O Girolamo !
> Alarmed religion wets her dishevelled hair with tears.
> " O cruel flames," she cries, " spare that breast
> Which is our breast."

Botticelli glorified the three martyrs in his painting of the Nativity, in which angels bear them to Paradise. Rafael, in the Vatican itself, placed Savonarola beside Dante in his " Triumph of the Sacrament " ; Michael Angelo remained his faithful admirer. Two years after his death, during the pontifical jubilee in Rome, there were on public sale medals struck in his honour. For years afterwards, on the anniversary of his execution, pious hands strewed flowers on the place where he had drawn his last breath. Luther declared that he had died a martyr.

Guicciardini, historian, statesman, and fellow-citizen of Savonarola, judges him thus :

Never was seen a monk of such parts, or who gained such authority and credit. Even his foes admitted his learning in many sciences, especially in philosophy. For centuries there had been none to compare with him in knowledge of the Scriptures. In eloquence he surpassed all his contemporaries. His speech was never artificial or constrained, but flowed simply and naturally, with unequalled authority.

How shall I judge his life ?

There was in it no trace of avarice, nor of luxury, neither weakness nor passion : it was the model of a religious life, charitable, pious, obedient to monastic rule, not only the externals but the very heart of piety. On none of these points could his enemies find the slightest fault in him, however much they tried during his trial.

He achieved a holy and admirable work in his reform of morals. There was never so much religion and virtue in Florence as in his day, and after his death the fall of piety and virtue gives us a measure of the good that he had done. There was no more public gaming, and gambling in private was kept within limits. The taverns were closed, women dressed modestly, and children led a life of holiness. Conducted by Fra Buonvincini they went in bands to church, wore their hair short and pelted with stones and insults gamblers, drunkards and women of immodest dress.

Fra Girolamo's work in the sphere of government was no less beneficent. After the fall of the Medici the city was divided against itself, and the supporters of the late government were in peril. He put a stop to violence. He founded the Grand Council to put a curb on ambition, and by leaving the appeal to the Signoria brought the excesses of the people within bounds. And lastly, by proclaiming a " universal peace ", he prevented any too close scrutiny of the past and saved the supporters of the Medici from the vengeance that threatened them.

These measures were beyond all doubt for the good of the Republic, of victors as well as vanquished.

In short, the works of this great man were excellent. Since some of his prophecies had been fulfilled, many people continued to believe in his Divine inspiration, in spite of his excommunication, trial and death on the scaffold.

Guicciardini ends with a remark that is worthy of his fellow-citizen Macchiavelli : " If Fra Girolamo was sincere, our age has seen in him a great prophet : if he was a rogue, a very great man."

XII

ALEXANDER VI

POPE ALEXANDER VI, who was responsible for the condemnation of Savonarola, is a strange figure. He was large and lusty, quarrelsome, splendid in figure, overflowing with life and spirit. There has perhaps never been so majestic a figure on the throne of St. Peter. As the Milanese envoy Giasone Maino said, "He is of royal aspect : he seems a god." He doubtless committed crimes enough, and, as Pope, appears a monster, but in spite of all he evokes a certain degree of sympathy by the very scale of his deeds and misdeeds.

Michele Ferno, a pupil of the famous humanist Pomponio Leto, gives us this portrait of him :

His Holiness rides a snow-white horse. His brow is full of brightness, his dignity strikes like lightning ; the crowd acclaims him as he blesses it. His presence makes men glad and is taken as a good omen. What dignity is there in his gestures, what nobility in his features, what magnanimity in his gaze ! How greatly does his imperial stature, his proud though benevolent air add to the veneration he inspires !

Alexander VI was tall and broad-shouldered. His eyes were large and black, his complexion ruddy. His lips were sensual but good-humoured. His health was thoroughly sound, and his great strength and endurance enabled him to triumph at sixty over excesses which would have killed a young man. His face wore an expression of utter serenity.

He was always content with life, except for certain grievous wounds dealt him by fate and certain moments of despondency and despair from which he soon recovered. His chief characteristic was exuberant gaiety. He was a good fellow with a glass in his hand or when he watched pretty women dancing, his favourite pastime when he was Pope. He was impulsive and loved travel and the chase. His temper was sometimes uncontrollable, even in grave diplomatic negotiations, but he used it skilfully in combination with his natural cunning. The ruling passion of his life was love for his children, of whom he had six at the time when he became Pope, while others were yet unborn. After the murder of the Duke of Gandia, Cesare and Lucrezia were his favourites. He would do anything, sacrifice anything for them. " The Pope grows younger every day," writes the Venetian envoy in 1502 ; " he is joyous by nature and thinks of nothing but the aggrandizement of his children."

The ambassadors accredited to the Vatican soon found out this weakness. When Giustiniani wanted something from the Pope, some hint on an interesting subject, he began by talking of Cesare. The aged Pope's emotion could hardly be restrained. He laughed and cried together, forgot himself and was touched by his own tender words. And the wily Venetian waited on the moment when the flood of emotion would bear with it a word, perhaps a promise, which he could seize as a cat seizes a mouse.

The life of Pope Alexander VI is certainly stained by crimes, the more horrible when we consider that the father of Christendom was the criminal. Nevertheless he may be accorded some degree of indulgence, if only because he has been accused of too much. In his lifetime his anti-feudal policy and the unscrupulous and bloodstained brutality with which his son Cesare sought to hack out for himself a principality, raised against him a host of libellous enemies, and afterwards it so happened that his weightiest historians were Protestants, great and honest historians such as Bayle, Ranke, Burckhardt and Gregorovius, who were, however, bent on finding in his misrule the cause and justification of the Reformation and so were too much inclined to believe the worst insinuations of his contemporaries.

The stories, for example, of cardinals poisoned for their wealth are incredible. It might even be maintained that the famous Borgia poison only existed in the wild imagination of the enemies of Alexander and of Cesare. Passing over Lucrezia, who has already been sufficiently justified, we will go so far as to state that we do not believe that Alexander ever poisoned anyone, and we cannot understand how serious historians could possibly pay any attention to fantastic stories such as that of the death of Alexander as presented by them.

Rodrigo Borgia was born at Jativa in the province of Valencia in Spain on January 1st, 1451. His family was noble, and had been established by Jaime I in Valencia after the conquest. He first studied law, and even his enemies grant his merits as a jurist. In 1455 his mother's brother became Pope under the title of Calixtus III, and he abandoned the legal profession for the Church. His uncle made him cardinal the next year, and from 1457 onwards entrusted him with the important post of vice-chancellor of the Church. He was then twenty-six, young and handsome, amiable and elegant. His teacher, Gaspare da Verona, speaks of him thus :

" He is handsome—always smiling and gay ; his conversation is amusing and witty. He has an amazing gift for attracting the affections of women, who are drawn to him as by a magnet."

Pius II writes to Cardinal Borgia in 1460 complaining

of his conduct in entertaining ladies of doubtful virtue in the gardens of one Giovanni Bichi in Siena.

Your conduct is the talk of Siena. Everyone is laughing at it. It is the talk of the stews. You are Chancellor of the Church and head of the diocese of Valencia ; you sit among the cardinals and a cardinal's life should be above reproach.

The young priest failed to mend his ways. Years later Cardinal Jean Balue told him openly at a meeting of the Consistory that he led the life of a swine, and called him a " wine-skin ".

In spite of his questionable amusements, the Cardinal, who was active, painstaking and intelligent, gained much knowledge and much practice in administration from his position in the Papal chancery. At the same time, through his rich benefices and his lucky speculations, he gradually became one of the wealthiest of the cardinals.

When Innocent VIII died he was sixty-two, almost an old man, but in character still young and vigorous. There were four candidates for the succession ; the two nephews of Sixtus IV, Rafael Riario and Giuliano della Rovere, Cardinal Sforza, brother of the Milanese tyrant Ludovico il Moro, and Cardinal Borgia.

The Borgia calmly set about buying votes by promises of future preferment and lavish gifts from his private fortune. Once Pope, he would find it easy to recoup himself. The election was held on the night of the 10th-11th August, 1492. Although bargaining was an old-established custom in the conclave, bribery was on so great a scale and so openly practised that it became a public scandal.

The Florentine envoy, Manfredo Manfredi, writes : " It is known that His Holiness has paid out vast sums ; some say as much as 150,000 ducats." The Venetian declares for his part that the election had been held under conditions such that neither France nor Spain would recognize it. But the Borgia was a Spaniard and a skilful diplomat to boot. On the very day of his enthronement he appointed his son Cesare, who was then sixteen, Archbishop of Valencia and Primate of Spain : soon after he gave one of his nephews the red hat and the next year made Cesare a cardinal.

The day of Alexander's enthronement was a day of pride for Vannozza Catanei, a woman of humble birth but great beauty and the mother of several of his children, among them probably the first Duke of Gandia, who died in Spain in 1488, and certainly Cesare, Giovanni, the second Duke of Gandia, Lucrezia and Geoffredo Prince of Squillace. She was a plebeian and uncultured, but energetic and prudent, and probably took her part in the advancement of Rodrigo Borgia's career.

Now she had to yield to a younger and more beautiful rival, the golden-haired Julia Farnese, whose hair was so long that it fell to her ankles. Her brother, Alexander Farnese, had handed her over to the Pope, who in return made him a cardinal at the same time as Cesare Borgia. This same Alexander Farnese afterwards became Pope Paul III and gave proofs in his tenure of the papal office of intelligence and liberal views.

Innocent VIII had left the Papacy in a deplorable state both financially and politically. Alexander VI was exactly the man to deal with the situation. He knew by heart the complex mechanism of papal administration through long experience as Vice-Chancellor, and as a diplomat he was second to none.

Alexander VI [says Macchiavelli] never had a thought but of double-dealing, and he was right. None was ever more skilful in making a covenant or supporting it with the most solemn oaths

—which he always broke—and nevertheless no one ever succeeded better by trickery. He knew the weakness of man.

His dealings with Charles VIII are a good example of his style, but later he drew closer to France to help his son Cesare. He remarked, apropos of the war between French and Spaniards in Italy,

We are for France, and will continue on that side if France sends enough troops to beat Spain, but if she hesitates and wants us to fight for her, we will take good care not to lose what we have, and if it be the will of God that the Spaniards are the stronger, it is not our place to will it otherwise.

His financial capacity was of the same degree of skill and crookedness. The cardinals themselves may well have thought, when they elected him, that one who managed his own fortune so well could also manage that of the Church. To this end he used the most varied means ; he placed a tax of ten per cent on the incomes of his cardinals and his clerics. He may not have killed the princes of the Church to inherit their goods, but at least he saw that all whom he raised to the cardinalate paid heavily for their promotion. A single creation, that of May 1503, is said to have brought him 150,000 ducats, about half a million pounds. He found the jubilee year 1500, which brought a huge crowd of pilgrims to Rome, an excellent occasion for lining his coffers, and used all kinds of means to attract the generosity of the pilgrims. To save expense on the papal kitchens he laid his tributary towns under contribution, making them supply fixed quantities of game, poultry and other comestibles.

His most fruitful source of revenue was the sale of Indulgences, which he confided chiefly to the begging friars. He had the brilliant idea of declaring pontifically that the Pope had the power to release souls from Purgatory, and then proceeded to use the power as a source of steady revenue.

It will be remembered that the Holy See received a sum of 45,000 ducats yearly from Sultan Bayazid for the "expenses" of Djem, his brother and pretender to his throne. Forty thousand ducats of this sum were pure profit. Not only did the Pope draw through Djem this handsome revenue, but he also improved his relations with the Sublime Porte. Thus we have the spectacle of candidates for the cardinalate, such as Niccolo Cibo, Archbishop of Arles in 1494, appearing with the Sultan's recommendation to the Pope.

When in 1499 a French ambassador informed Alexander that his master was preparing a Crusade against the Turk in response to an appeal from Rome, the Pope was staggered. "I hope he was not serious," he told his familiars afterwards.

Alexander was in perpetual need of money, for the purposes of the Church, to keep up the blatant luxury of the Roman Court, and to pay the armies which his son Cesare used in his policy of conquest. "His Holiness takes money for anything he can sell," wrote Ferdinand of Aragon in 1493. He went so far as to sell bishoprics.

The plans of father and son were complementary to each other. The great families of the Orsini, Colonna, Savelli, Santa-Croce still existed in the Papal States. Alexander's predecessors had endeavoured to secure their own independence by a balance of power among their great vassals, or by an alliance with some of them against others more hostile. Alexander himself determined to rid the Papacy once and for all of these petty princes by destroying them. "I will not be the slave of my barons," he said. And he found help ready to his hand in the person of that energetic, ruthless, capable soldier and statesman, his son Cesare.

The objectives of the Pope's whole policy were threefold : firstly, to destroy the remnants of feudalism in Rome ; secondly, to extend the papal authority over the neighbouring states, such as the Marches and Romagna; and thirdly, to maintain the suzerainty of the Papacy over the Kingdom of Naples. If these three ends were won they would achieve Italian unity by forming, under the rule of the Pope, a power unrivalled in the rest of Italy.

These plans were pursued by Cesare Borgia, backed by his father's wealth and authority, with a skill and perspicacity which filled Macchiavelli with admiration. It is well known that Cesare is the hero of *The Prince*. Cesare, however, still young, had an aim which he kept to himself. He wished to carve out for himself, on the death of his father, a secular state on the basis of the papal dominion. So he went on his bold and unscrupulous way. His methods involved murder, treachery, perjury and most other crimes, but when once they had made him master of a town or principality he brought in an ordered and equitable government which soon won him the love of its inhabitants.

The two Borgias were relentless against the Orsini. Alexander confided to the French ambassador that he aimed at their total destruction. He told the Florentine envoy: "Our hands are red with the blood of the Orsini. We have gone so far that we must make sure that none is left to harm us." Men, women and children were slain, estates, castles, money, all was seized. Cardinal Battista Orsini and all the ecclesiastical dignitaries in the family were arrested in the Vatican itself. The ambassador Giustiniano writes: "The Pope's people have taken everything, down to the straw from the stables." The cardinal's aged mother was driven from her home with a few faithful servants and could find no lodging. "The poor wretches wander about Rome," writes the Venetian envoy, "and no one dares to take them in."

Alexander VI raised the Papal Court to a degree of brilliance such as it had never yet attained. It was like any other

European court ; there was the same luxury, there were the same amusements, meals washed down with fine wines, dances, plays, fools and clowns and elegant women.

Some Christians, however, were scandalized at the excesses they saw. Ferdinand of Aragon, for example : " The Pope leads such a life that it is an abomination to all men : he takes no thought for the seat he sits in, nor does he care for anything but to make his sons great and powerful."

The foreign ambassadors, even the Spanish and Portuguese, between whom Alexander had thought to divide the New World by his Bull of May 1493, made their remonstrances to the Pope. They threatened him with a General Council to try him, but he grew angry and returned their threats. To the French Ambassador he justified himself by explaining that " even the French do not understand that the Pope is a man like other men ".

At carnival-time, he closed the Vatican to the ambassadors so that he could amuse himself in his own way with his cardinals, some in their purple, some in fancy dress, and a few not too prudish women. He took out masked women in his coach. Arnold de Werf, who was present at the carnival of 1497, declared that he dared not write down all he had seen.

A servant of Cardinal Briçonnet said on his return from Rome : " Now I have seen how the prelates live. If I had stayed longer among them I should not only have lost my faith, but come to doubt the immortality of the soul." And Luther, while yet faithful to the Roman Church :

Every kind of iniquity is here allowed : people absolved from their vows, bastards legitimized, ignominy ennobled and vice held for knightly virtue. There is naught but avarice and cupidity. The laws of the Church are chains that money can break. Here the devil would seem a saint.

In spite of all this, it would be well to suspect exaggeration and not too readily to believe the stories of monstrous happenings left by certain contemporaries. The jubilee year of 1500 was a date of great splendour in the annals of this riotous Pope. Pilgrims appeared from all the ends of Europe. On April 15th of that year it is estimated that 200,000 of the faithful were present in Rome to receive the papal benediction.

Cesare returned triumphant from his campaign of conquest, Imola, Cesena, Forli, Forlimpopoli among his spoils. He had laid the foundations of the kingdom of his dreams. He entered the Eternal City on his black charger, clad in black velvet, with a black hat bearing a falcon's plume held in place by a huge diamond. The Roman ladies were wild with enthusiasm for this young and handsome conqueror as he rode through their streets, his hair like gold against the black velvet of his coat. They thronged around him. They threw him flowers and kisses ; but the pilgrims, the thousands upon thousands of pilgrims who had come to Rome for the jubilee, went home with stories of papal corruption.

Alexander VI himself was neither wicked nor cruel, but he was entirely dominated by his terrible son. Cesare initiated a reign of terror in Rome. " Every man lived, not only in the belief that his life and property were threatened, but that he might, and indeed would be, attacked in some devious and insidious way. This made fear itself more fearful." The Pope despised the pamphlets, libels, satires, epigrams and pasquinades which were posted up in Rome against him and his family. His natural impetuosity led him to laugh and pass them by. With his son it was otherwise.

Antonio Mancinelli was a celebrated humanist. One day of solemn procession, when the crowd was assembling, he appeared on a white horse and harangued the Romans on the scandalous life of the Vatican. His speech finished, he distributed printed copies of it. He was seized and both his hands were cut off. He returned to the attack, and again he was arrested and his tongue cut out. From the effects of this he died.

A Venetian, Lorenzo di Veni, had composed lampoons in Greek on the Borgias. His house was searched and the incriminating documents were found. He was arrested. The Venetians, who held him in high esteem as an author, instructed their envoy in Rome to speak for him. "For my own part," answered the Pope, "I think the best thing is to laugh at such nonsense, but my son Cesare holds that it is high time authors learnt politeness. The man of whom you speak is already condemned, strangled and thrown into the Tiber."

According to Giustiniani, the city of Rome, packed with Cesare's ruffianly mercenaries, was nothing but a "den of brigands". People were attacked in the street. The nights were filled with the noise of conflict between soldiery and citizens eager to avenge their dead or protect their own lives.

The district of Siena had just been ravaged. At San Quirico, as we learn from the diary of the Papal master of ceremonies, the troops of the Borgia had found only two old men and nine old women ; the rest had fled. The soldiers seized the eleven, and hung them up by their arms with their feet in a fire to make them reveal where their money was concealed. As none of them possessed anything, they all died under the torture.

At seventy-two, Alexander was still in the best of health. His cheeks were ruddy and his black eyes full of fire. His deep, rich voice was as sonorous as ever. He had just returned from a trip in the Romagna and was about to visit his daughter Lucrezia in Ferrara, whose Duke, Alfonso d'Este, she had married. He had just formally handed over to the Church all the castles and fortresses taken by his son from the Colonna, the Orsini and the other feudal lords, and had asked in return that the Sacred College should recognize Cesare lord of the Romagna, the Marches and Tuscany, the conquest of which last he had already begun. Suddenly, on the night of August 18th, 1503, the Pope died. Some historians, including even Ranke and Burckhardt, give the following account of his death : Alexander had planned to murder one of the cardinals present at the Consistory in order to seize his property. The cardinal learned of the plot and bribed the papal master-cook to put the poison into the Pope's dish instead of his own.

This fantastic account, however, is based on the flimsiest of evidence. Another author declares that Alexander fell a victim to one of those poisons of fifteenth-century Italy the result of which has been lost. The secret has been so well and truly lost that the famous " Borgia poison " probably never existed.

While the Pope was dying, abandoned by all, as was usual with a Renaissance Pope, his son lay seriously ill. As soon as the Pope was dead, Cesare Borgia's villainous condottiere and right-hand man Michelletto appeared with a troop of mercenaries. Sword in hand, they demanded the keys of the papal treasury, and when Cardinal Casanova, who had charge of them, hesitated to hand them over, they threatened to throw him from a window. Then they rushed into the treasury and sacked it. The estimate of 300,000 ducats in coin and 200,000 ducats' worth of jewellery is probably an exaggerated figure of their loot. What is certain is that they stripped the treasury to its bare walls.

The swollen corpse of the Pontiff soon became too offensive to be touched, so that it had to be dragged to the bier by a servant by means of a rope round the ankles. The bier was too small, and the body had to be stripped to get it in, while Swiss guards and papal servants fought with pikes and candlesticks over the spoils. No one would watch the corpse through the night, no candles were lighted around it. " The funeral was a horrible sight," wrote Gebhardt. The covering of the coffin was an old rug.

During his last illness the Pope spoke no single word of his children, and suffered from the delusion that he saw the devil dancing round his bed.

With his death the result of Cesare's arduous labours fell at once to the ground. As he told Macchiavelli : " I thought I had provided for every possible result of my father's death and the action I should have to take thereafter, but I myself was seriously ill when he died. That event was the only one which I had not foreseen." Cesare was arrested and handed over to the Neapolitans, but escaped once again. He managed to reach Spain, took service with the King of Navarre, and died obscurely but valiantly in a night sortie under the walls of Mendavia, near Pampeluna, on March 12th, 1507.

The Cardinal of Viterbo, a contemporary of Alexander VI, left this portrait of the Pope :

He was gifted with the most penetrating intelligence ; he was clever, industrious, and eloquent. He was unequalled in the dexterity of his actions, in persuasiveness, in his obstinate power of resistance. He was so great a man that he would have been a great prince, in thought, word and deed, had his natural gifts been allowed to develop and not been overlaid with so many vices. There seemed, to a witness of his speech and action, that there was nothing lacking to make him ruler of a world ; he was ever ready to give up his sleep, yet was greedy for pleasure. His pursuit of it, however, never prevented him from assuming the burdens of his office, such as giving audience and appearing and speaking whenever his position made it necessary. And yet, in spite of all his qualities, his reign cannot be called auspicious. All was dark as night. We need not speak of his domestic tragedies and their background of incest and crime : but never, in the lands of the Church, were seditions more threatening, robberies more frequent, murders more cruel, the peace of the public highways more brutally disturbed, or the way of travellers more dangerous. Never was Rome in a more unhappy state. Never were seen more informers, never was the insolence of the police more unbridled, never were robbers more numerous or more daring. None dared to pass beyond the city gates, yet how could one remain in the city ? It was lése-majesté or treason to possess gold or precious goods. A man had no security in his own house, in his own room, even in his own stronghold.

Orestes Ferrara writes of Alexander in his book on Macchiavelli :

Politically, he discharged his functions better than many other Popes. The successes which fell to Julius II were the fruits of Alexander's skill. Any sincere investigator of the facts must admit that the decadence of the Roman Curia only set in after his death. Julius II enjoyed only Pyrrhic victories, preparing the way for a later and greater fall, since Julius, imprudent to the last degree, had neither plan nor system nor any reasoned conception of the future. In place of Alexander's balance of power, Julius inaugurated a system of leagues and alliances. Leo X, who did not reckon with the advancing tempests in religion and in the world at large followed the same course.

Alexander VI is one of the Popes whose deeds have had most effect on the destiny of the Church. Julius II is credited with the restoration of the power and independence of the Papacy, without regard for the fact that the plan was that of Alexander and the execution already partly carried out by him and by Cesare Borgia.

Alexander took a prominent part in the development of the cult of the Virgin Mary, who, as he believed, was his especial patron. He never wearied in his letters to his children, of reminding them to pay her special devotion. He restored the ringing of the Angelus, which had been allowed to lapse. His faith was deep and his piety sincere, to the astonishment of certain witnesses of it.

The two most famous Popes of the Renaissance, Julius II and Leo X, inherited from the financial policy of their predecessor the vast resources which enabled them to make Rome the artistic capital of the world in a blaze of splendour which even Florence had never attained. But by this very policy, which depended on the sale of Indulgences, Alexander had exaggerated to unheard-of proportions the vices and abuses to be found in every papal government since that of the great and noble Nicholas V, and through this he contributed to bring about the Reformation.

XIII

JULIUS II

ON the death of Alexander VI, Cardinal Giuliano della Rovere used all his influence to secure the election of Cardinal Antonio Todeschini, who ascended the papal throne under the name of Pius III. Della Rovere himself had designs on the tiara, but, being uncertain of success, he determined to support a candidate whose age and ill-health promised a short reign. The new Pope, in fact, died on October 15th, 1503, after a reign of only a few months.

Cardinal della Rovere had been a candidate at the election of 1492, when Alexander VI was chosen, and had then been supported by the King of France, whose professed adherent he was. The future Julius II was born at Albissola Superiore in Liguria. The day, September 18th, of his birth is known, but the year is variously given as 1441, 1442, or 1443. He was a nephew of Sixtus IV, who, after the custom of the age, had showered upon him every possible favour, benefice and title. He became Bishop of Carpentras (1473), Bishop of Mende (1474), Archbishop of Avignon (the bishopric being raised in degree for him) (1475), Papal Legate to France (1480), Cardinal of San Pietro ad Vincula (1495), and Bishop of Ostia.

He was of obscure birth. Some authors go so far as to say that he was a boatman in his youth : Louis XII says he came of peasant stock, but as soon as the hand of Sixtus IV had bestowed high dignities upon him, the discovery was not delayed that he was akin to the noble family which, by a happy chance, bore the same name of della Rovere. He assumed their badge, the oak-tree, which was very appropriate to his rugged nature. The noble della Rovere, as soon as he became Pope, were only too ready to accept him as an authentic member of the family.

Innocent VIII succeeded Sixtus IV without lessening the favour in which Cardinal Giuliano stood. On the contrary his influence became preponderant in the circle of the Vatican. Some of his contemporaries go so far as to call him the real Pope. His fortune changed with the coming of the Borgia Pope. Both of them were dominating and aggressive by nature, so that Rome was too small to hold two such great men. In fear of the Pope, the cardinal fled to his see of Ostia, and, not finding there the safety he sought, to France (1494), where Charles VIII welcomed him with open arms.

Thus the career of the future Julius II evolved under the protection of France. Of all the confidants of the young King, it was della Rovere who did most to urge him on to the conquest of Naples. This he did out of pure hatred of Alexander VI and in the hope that the King, if victorious, might call a General Council to depose the Pope or declare his election invalid by reason of simony. Of this Cardinal della Rovere himself could bear truthful witness, since he himself had been one of those whose votes had been bought.

" The very man who later raised Italy against France," writes Emile Picot, " was the most eager to call in the French." Rodocanachi is very harsh on the conduct of the cardinal at the French court.

This man, who appears in history as inflexible and indomitable in his energy, more the warrior than the churchman, was at that time a wavering and undecided diplomat, intriguing against the country where he lived, and advising its enemies, never losing an opportunity to express his devotion to the Pope who had treated him so badly, and to his son, and acting as go-between for them. He went so far in defence of Cesare Borgia as to talk of his " virtue ".

When Pius III died after his few months' reign, Giuliano della Rovere was elected on November 1st, 1503, and took the name of Julius II in honour of Julius Cæsar, whom he esteemed the greatest man in history and whose conquests he endeavoured to emulate. In spite of his indignant protests at the simony to which Alexander VI owed his position, he hastened to follow his example. " The bargaining," writes the Venetian Giustiniani, " goes on in the open street." He doubtless spent less in hard cash than had Alexander, but was in revenge much more lavish of promises to the cardinals who elected him. A veritable rain of honours and benefices was to fall upon them and their families after his election, but his aim achieved, he showed not the slightest sign of keeping his word.

One of his first official acts was to take possession of the papal fortress of Sant' Angelo, which he entered on November 15th, 1503, to the thunderous welcome of its culverins and sakers. On July 27th, 1505, he reviewed on the Campo di Fiori the papal army, which he had completely reorganized.

Julius II stands out in almost terrifying relief from the canvas of the Italian Renaissance, where there are so many salient figures. He was sixty-two when he was called to the papal throne, and then suddenly this priest, on the threshold of old age, amazed the world by a violent, turbulent, impetuous activity which would have been surprising even in a young man or a condottiere well versed in the arts of war. All Italy was filled with the tumult and the shouting of his activities. By all the standards of his age, an age when Macchiavelli held up Cesare Borgia as a mirror to princes, he was a great politician and a great statesman. " The Pope keeps his word," writes a correspondent of the Marquis of Mantua, " if it suits his interest."

Julius II was bold, resolute and indefatigable. In him the soul ruled the body : the soul was overflowing with life and energy while the body was exhausted and drew its strength solely from the compelling force of the will. In age he kept the foppish airs of a young man. When he seized the splendid wardrobe of Cesare Borgia he did not hesitate to keep the best of it for himself. He displayed with pride to the Cardinal of Portugal a green silk cloak from that source. He paid the sum, a great one for the time, of two hundred ducats for red silk bed-hangings and kept a French and an Italian tailor to dress him in their respective styles. In 1512 he is known to have paid the former one bill of 480 ducats, and that at a time when the papal treasury was so depleted that his plate was sent to be melted down.

Like Alexander VI, he had a passion for jewels and costly rings. Immediately after his accession he published an edict forbidding the Roman ladies to wear more than two rings, but his own fingers were laden with them. He once paid the Fuggers of Augsburg 1,800 ducats for a single diamond. The Holy See possessed a splendid tiara dating from the pontificate of Paul II, but it did not suffice for Julius II. He had two new ones made, of gold and sparkling with diamonds, one of them the work of the famous Francesco Foppa. According to an eye-witness, this tiara could only be compared with the sky when the stars shine most brightly. It is still to be seen, but only in Rafael's frescoes in the Vatican and on Julius's tomb in San Pietro ad Vincula. Alexander VI had loved to acquire pearls and jewels for his daughter Lucrezia : Julius had a daughter, Donna Felice, who had married the Prefect of Rome, but his delight was to summon her to the Vatican to admire the jewels he himself wore. He was also like Alexander in his taste for amusements. He organized bull-fights in the Vatican courtyard. Again like Alexander, he was a great eater. " It is terrible to see how His Holiness eats," writes a contemporary to the Marquis of Mantua. But if he ate heartily, he drank still more, in spite of his gout. He could always be appeased by the gift of a butt of malmsey. " We have no Pope after midday," said the Romans, meaning that after that hour their sovereign was at least tipsy.

Julius II was devoted to the chase. Grossino, servant to Federigo de Gonzaga, wrote : " The Pope has been several days hunting with Signor Federigo. His Holiness was delighted every time he brought down a plump pheasant and showed it to all and sundry amid roars of laughter."

Even in his exalted station he remained at heart the Ligurian boatman, rough, brutal, crude and coarse. His character was so rigid that even thought had no power to move it. He habitually carried a stick, but not merely to support his tottering steps ; it was often seen to descend on the shoulders or even on the head of any so rash as to disagree with him. If the Venetian ambassador at an audience in the Vatican should utter a displeasing word, the Pope would turn his back. When one of his secretaries submitted to him certain papers with whose content he disagreed, he flung not only the papers, but his own spectacles at the secretary's head. He was the first Pope to let his beard grow, a fact which moved Rabelais to mirth. Rafael painted him, beard and all, in a picture which Vasari thus describes : " Rafael painted a portrait of the Pope so true to life that in beholding it one is seized by the same fear as when in the presence of the original."

Francesco Vettori, Florentine ambassador in Rome, said of him that he was " more lucky than prudent in his enterprises, rather bold than courageous, ambitious and greedy for power beyond all measure ". He wished to raise the Papacy to a height from which it should appear to the nations no longer merely a spiritual power over Christendom, but its temporal overlord. " The Pope," said the Venetian envoy Domenico Trevirano, " desires to be lord and master of the play of the world." It was the old dream of Boniface VIII, but with a new will, a new energy engaged in its pursuit.

Julius II determined to drive out the foreign powers who had established themselves in Italy, the French in the Milanese, the Spaniards in the Kingdom of Naples, and the Germans who had settled all over Italy in the shadow of that historic fiction the Holy Roman Empire. His war-cry was " Out with the barbarians ".

His first care on his accession was to strip Cesare Borgia —whose praises he had sung and who had been largely responsible for his election—of his lands and in general of all the property he had received from his father. He first compelled Cesare to give up his fortresses and then stole his wardrobe.

As early as January 3rd, 1504, the new Pope had declared that it was his duty to recover the lands that in times past had been usurped from the patrimony of St. Peter. His imagination set the limits of these lands very wide. From his first day he had declared himself the enemy of all the works of Alexander VI and Cesare, and immediately proceeded to follow in their footsteps.

Meanwhile, in France, Charles VIII had been succeeded by Louis XII. The new Pope hastened to express his devotion to the new King. Had he not himself accompanied Charles VIII on his invasion of Italy ? Louis XII, in the goodness of his heart, lent a ready ear to the Pope's protestations and put at his disposal eight thousand troops for the attainment of objectives which the Pope had explained, but with many disingenuous reservations.

So Julius donned his armour and set off boldly for the wars. On August 26th, 1506, surrounded by a crimson staff of cardinals, he took command of an army of 600 lancers and 1,200 crossbowmen. His first objectives were Perugia and Umbria, which were under the lordship of the Baglioni. With his son-in-law and his cardinals he made his triumphant entry into Perugia on September 12th, 1506. The Baglioni were constrained to accept the Pope as suzerain. Then he suddenly burst forth. From Forli, on October 18th, he hurled incredibly violent anathema at the head of Giovanni Benti- voglio, hereditary lord of Bologna. Bentivoglio and all his kin were declared rebels against the Church and traitors. If in ten days they did not submit, leave their palaces, quit the city and dismiss their troops, they would forthwith be excommunicated, their possessions forfeit, their property the prey of any who cared to take it, themselves the slaves of any who could seize them, their subjects free from all and every obligation to them. The students of Bologna University who did not desert them would fall under the same ban. As for the princes, captains and soldiers who should come to the aid of the Church, in the person of Julius II, they were to receive a plenary indulgence. Four messengers were entrusted with the dangerous task of posting up this effusion in the city of Bologna, but the Pope took hostages for their safety in the persons of eight delegates sent to him by Benti- voglio. When Louis XII had seen the text of this tirade of the papal chancellery, his only comment was, " The Pope has been drinking ".

The Pope and his staff were at Imola when he heard that

Bologna was ready to admit him. The news was greeted with exultation, salvoes of cannon were fired, and comedies prepared in advance to lampoon his enemies were played before a well-satisfied audience, with the Pope in the front row leading the applause.

His entry into Bologna on November 11th, 1506, was like a Roman triumph. Dressed in white satin, he passed under no less than twenty-two triumphal arches. His helmet had given place to one of his new bejewelled tiaras, and he cast small change in handfuls to the kneeling crowds. A deputation of the Jews of the city came to meet him bearing olive branches. Erasmus, that peaceable philosopher, who was then at Bologna, found the spectacle infinitely sad. "I could not but groan when I compared this triumph, which many a secular prince would have thought too pompous, with the majestic tranquillity of the Apostles, who conquered the world by the word of Christ."

The aged Bentivoglio, his wife Ginevra and his children had fled. The privileges granted by Nicholas V to the Bolognese were abolished and they were made to pay 30,000 ducats to the Pope. Meanwhile, their late ruler's wife Ginevra had died of sorrow and was refused the last offices of the Church as sharing in her husband's excommunication.

It should be remarked that Julius constantly followed the course of policy exemplified in his dealings with Bologna. It was lawful for a Pope, as temporal ruler, to resort to force of arms. It was equally lawful for him, in his capacity of Head of the Church, to excommunicate those whom he held to have sinned against orthodoxy and morality. But it was definitely an abuse of his powers, and one which had never been tolerated, for him to attack his enemies at one and the same time with temporal and spiritual weapons. The frivolity and scandal of the Court of Alexander VI

certainly played their part in bringing about the development of Protestantism, which was to deal Rome so grievous
a blow, but no less important a factor was the brutal, vindictive and often wholly iniquitous policy of Julius II.

The return of the conquering Pope to Rome was greeted
with demonstrations which surpassed in splendour those
accorded to Alexander VI and Cesare Borgia, and vied with
those of the golden days of the Roman Empire. The warrior-
Pope made his triumphal entry on Palm Sunday 1509. The
patricians of Rome had erected triumphal arches adorned
with pictures and statues and inscriptions in honour of the
" expeller of tyrants ", prominent among which was the
famous " Veni, vidi, vici " of the greater Julius. The streets
were strewn with flowers. A chariot drawn by white horses
bore a load of children dressed as angels, who presented the
palm of victory to the Pope and sang songs in praise of his
glory and valour. A host of prelates, nobles and officers
escorted the hero. The procession is well described by the
author of a famous pamphlet *Julius excluded from Paradise*.

Never was seen so great a concourse of cardinals in their crimson
robes, never so many servants, never so many horses caparisoned
like a King's, never so many mules covered with fine linen and
gold and precious stones, and shod with gold and silver. The
Pope sat in a chair borne by soldiers, and the people knelt when
his hand moved in blessing. Bombards thundered, trumpets pealed,
the crowd shouted madly. The eye was dazzled by the blaze of
torches and bonfires.

But Luther in his *Antithesis between Christ and Antichrist*
does not fail to draw the comparison between this pompous
entry of a military conqueror and the humble and pious
entry of Christ into Jerusalem on the same Palm Sunday.

Having thus, with French assistance, conquered Umbria
and the Bolognese, Julius II turned his eyes to Romagna,

which Cesare Borgia had seized, and which after his fall had been the object of Venetian covetousness. The Venetians had taken Rimini, Ravenna, Imola, Cervi, Faenza and Forli to mark out a defensive line tenable against Lombardy and Rome. These towns, however, were also coveted by the Pope. Another element in the situation was the traditional hostility between Venice and Genoa, arising from their commercial and maritime rivalry ; and the Pope was a Genoese by birth.

The Venetian Republic could at this time bring into the field forces vastly superior to any that Rome could produce.

The campaign opened with wordy warfare.

Said the Pope : " I will reduce Venice to the fishing village from which she has sprung."

To which the Venetian envoy retorted : " We will reduce Your Holiness to the rank of a village priest."

Julius II, in his usual shameless manner, began to set on foot secret negotiations for a combination against the Republic. The result was the famous League of Cambrai (1503). Under the high patronage of the Holy See, France, Spain and Austria and later Ferrara, Mantua and Urbino were allied against Venice.

Hostilities began in the usual way with the imposition of a papal interdict on the Venetians, who were accused of " combining the cunning of the wolf with the ferocity of the lion, and flaying the skin by tearing out the hairs ", the which was held good and sufficient reason for the sentence of excommunication. It was left to France to give substance to the papal thunders by the victory of Agnadello (May 14th, 1509), where, as Saint-Gelais put it, " was vanquished a nation wise, powerful and wealthy, which had never been conquered since the days of Attila ".

Venice was conquered. Julius II had attained his ends. He

immediately perceived that he must not humiliate too deeply the Republic, since it had a part allotted to it in his policy, and that the French, who had so far been useful allies, might in their turn become a menace. Louis XII already held the Milanese ; if he could add the Venetian domain to it he would possess a power in North Italy proof against every onslaught of Papal ambition. Accordingly, in the underhand manner characteristic of all his dealings, he changed his tactics. Thanks to France his conquests were safe ; now he had to get rid of the French.

Julius sent to Louis XII the young Cardinal Alidosi, the object of his particular confidence and affection. His mission was to persuade the King that after the victory they had shared, Pope and King should draw even closer the bonds which united them. The King's province in Italy was now no longer necessary, since the Pope would watch over French interests as his own. The ingenuous Louis allowed himself to be convinced and recrossed the Alps with his army. The Pope raised the interdict on Venice, and turned his back on the French cardinals who protested against this violation of the Treaty of Cambrai. " These Frenchmen," he growled, " would have me the chaplain of their King," and immediately made a separate peace with Venice (February 15th, 1510).

Ten days later there was a touching ceremony on the steps of St. Peter's in Rome. In front of the old church, already half demolished by Bramante, five delegates of the Venetian Senate in their long crimson robes knelt at the feet of His Holiness, who touched each of them on the shoulder with a long golden wand while a Miserere was sung. As regent of God on earth he pardoned the Republic and Venice and lifted the sentence of excommunication he had pronounced on its subjects. The same Pope who a little before had boasted that he would reduce Venice to a fishing village now told its envoy that if his state had not existed it would have had to be invented.

Julius II next abruptly called upon Alfonso d'Este, Duke of Ferrara, to cease hostilities with Venice. The Duke sent Ariosto, author of the *Orlando Furioso*, then at the height of his fame, as his delegate to the Pope. Ariosto endeavoured to bring the Pope to recognize the binding nature of his master's engagements to France, who had always been his faithful ally. The Pope's only reply was to threaten to have the unfortunate poet-ambassador flung into the Tiber, and as the Duke still persisted in his inappropriately honest courses, he was forthwith excommunicated in the most violent terms, his title was declared void and his lands forfeit to the Church, his family, friends, allies and adherents being placed under an interdict which extended even to the King of France (August 9th, 1510).

Louis XII, as can well be imagined, was thunderstruck at the news, but he had other surprises in store. Julius II remarked, " The Gallic cock wants my hens, and he shall not have them " ; and swore, after his fashion, like a trooper ; " God's blood ! I will drive the French across the frontier and beyond if I have to finish the war single-handed."

He won over Ferdinand of Aragon to his side by investing him with the Kingdom of Naples, in spite of Louis XII's claim. On March 4th, 1510, he made a treaty with the Swiss cantons which gave him for five years the exclusive services of their infantry, which, since the battles of Granson and Moret, was held to be the finest in Europe. " They could conquer the universe," said Macchiavelli. From this time dates the existing Swiss guard of the Vatican, with its black-red-yellow uniform and black velvet bonnets.

Finally, to back his military preparations, he launched a

direct and formal excommunication at the head of his faithful ally, and all who should presume to help him.

The French had been the constant supporters of Julius II ; they had protected him against Alexander VI and he owed to them his career, his papal dignity, his conquests of Perugia and Bologna and his triumph over Venice. Julius II had twice called the French into Italy, the first time marching with them, but now, having taken all they could give him, he turned on them with frenzied rage and shrieks of " Down with the French ".

He proclaimed it lawful to kill any Frenchman, wherever found. He declared the fair of Lyons transferred to Geneva. To ensure that in future no Frenchman could mount the Papal throne he created eight new cardinals : six Italians, an Englishman, to please Henry VIII, and one Swiss, as a compliment to his new allies.

The French Cardinal of Castelnau-Clermont-Lodève, Archbishop of Auch, was frightened into flight by the vehemence of the Pope's language, but was arrested at the Porta del Popolo and cast into prison in Sant' Angelo (June 29th, 1510). The Frenchmen who had helped in his attempted escape were beaten, and when the Italian cardinals themselves protested to the Pope that the charter he had signed on his accession prohibited the imprisonment of a cardinal, he retorted : " He deserved quartering and his imprisonment will be of long duration."

The interdict law in France caused much perturbation in that country. Queen Anne of Brittany was beside herself with fear, thinking herself irretrievably damned. The greater part of the French clergy, however, as it had done in similar cases from the time of Boniface VIII and Philippe le Bel onwards, preferred its duty to the King to that to the Pope. A synod was convoked at Orleans and another at Tours.

Guillaume Briçonnet, Cardinal of St. Malo, raised an eloquent voice against the policy of the Pope. The Pope, the representative of God on earth, had no right to make himself the apostle of discord, stirring up the kingdoms and rulers of Christendom one against another. His condemnation of the French had no validity.

Jean de Ganay, President of the Parlement of Paris and Chancellor of France, spoke for the King.

Who alone was the aggressor ? The Pope. A league had been made at Cambrai to further the Pope's designs against Venice and Bologna. The Pope had treacherously broken it. He had invaded the lands in Italy which the King possessed as Duke of Milan, and had sent briefs to Henry VIII of England to inform him that he recognized his claim to the throne of France.

Thereupon the French clergy voted the King 260,000 livres to assist in the struggle with Rome (September, 1510).

Another synod met at Lyons in March 1512, where the clergy determined to appeal to a General Council against the proceedings of Julius II. This decision provoked the excommunication of Cardinal Briçonnet, who, however, was consoled by Louis with the gift of the great Abbey of St. Germain-des-Prés and the governorship of Languedoc.

Meanwhile, the Parlement had decided on the measures to be taken against Roman aggression. The Pragmatic Sanction of Charles VII was reversed, as were the decisions of the Council of Basle. A decree of August 16th, 1510, forbade any French subject to visit the Roman Court, on any pretext whatsoever.

The people followed the examples of Church and Law in rallying to the King. During the carnival of 1512 was played the famous " sotie " of Pierre Gringoire, *The Play of the Prince of Fools*, followed by the " morality " of *The Obstinate Man* (Julius II). Gringoire himself took the part of

"Mother Fool", who represented the Church as personified by Julius. The Church knew nothing but hypocrisy and perjury:

> Good faith is out of date.

The Pope strove to raise all Europe against the King of France:

> I will find inventions
> To set prince and prelate against him . . .

and he sets off for the wars:

> Up! ye prelates! The tocsin sounds!
> Leave church and altar . . .

Meanwhile, the people, in the person of Dame Commons, go in fear of the result of war in the shape of death and taxation. The King, however, is compelled to draw the sword, if only to assure a lasting peace.

The war began. The generals of the Papal army were two cardinals, with the Pope as Commander-in-Chief.

He left the throne of St. Peter to take the title of Mars, to plant the standard of the three crowns in the field of battle, to sleep in a sentry-box. His mitres, his crosses and his pastoral staves made a brave show straying in the fields (Du Plessis-Mornay).

"Our Pope," wrote Guicciardini, "has nothing of the Pontiff but the dress and the name." And Rabelais: "I have seen him helmed instead of mitred, making cruel and treacherous war when all Christendom was at peace."

Julius II, full of fire, led on his troops, dangling before them the bait of plunder. Guillaume Budé calls him the "bloody chief of gladiators". Le Maire des Belges depicts him bent on a war which befitted him "as dancing befits a monk".

He had set his heart on taking Ferrara, but his captains advised him to begin with the siege of Mirandola, the key of the duchy.

He took the field in person.

The vicar of Christ against a Christian town, a thing till now unknown. He was old and infirm, and was engaged on a war he himself had stirred up against Christian princes, yet he was so fiery and impetuous that nothing went quickly enough for his taste. He stormed at his captains in a perpetual rage ; he slept so close to the firing-line that two of his cooks were killed, and this in spite of the protests of his cardinals at his scandalous conduct (Guicciardini).

He slept in his clothes and, when his followers begged him not to expose himself, he only replied : " I will not go till a cannon-ball takes off my head ! " which very nearly happened to him near San Giustinio on January 18th, 1511. The siege of this small town was no common spectacle. It was resolutely defended by a woman, Francesca Trivulzio, the widow of Count Ludovico, and equally resolutely attacked by the septuagenarian Pope. Julius II went from trench to trench, correcting the fire of his bombards and encouraging the men who were suffering from the weather. The winter was unusually hard, but the aged and infirm Pope would not give way to it. He was seen erect among his men, cloaked in a mantle of snow. There exists in a small town in Italy a picture of the scene, apparently drawn from life. The Pope's dress is no longer clerical ; his armour is covered by a long grey cloak which falls from chin to ankle. He wears a helmet, but it is covered by a great grey hood. His beard has been allowed to grow, but has not yet reached the dimensions which led the Mantuan envoy to dub him the bear. His whole appearance is wild.

The Pope on two occasions narrowly escaped capture.

226

The first time he was almost taken by Chaumont d'Amboise, commander of the French army ; the second he had an even narrower escape from falling into the hands of Bayard, who had laid an ambush close by the castle of San Felice, where the Pope had spent a night. The enterprise failed, since the bad weather led to a postponement of the Pope's departure. It was touch and go, and the Pope had to beat a hasty retreat. " Swiftly and without assistance," writes the Loyal Serviteur, " he leapt from his litter and helped to raise the drawbridge, and therein showed his presence of mind, for if he had stayed but the time it takes to say a Paternoster, he would have been taken." The bold knight, " sans peur et sans reproche ", was deeply dejected at the failure of his plan. He had no artillery to besiege the castle, but the Pope was " in a fever the whole day long from the fright he had received ".

Mirandola capitulated on January 21st, 1511. The Pope was so impatient to enter that he would not wait for the barricades at the gates to be thrown down, but was hoisted over the walls in a basket.

The following day the ultra-refined diplomat Baldassare Castiglione, the author of *The Courtier*, appeared bearing the congratulations of the Duke of Urbino. It must have been a quaint sight to see the courtly and elegant diplomat delivering his harangue to the booted, spurred and helmeted Pope, who habitually used the language of the guard-room.

In April Julius II returned from Mirandola to celebrate another triumph in Bologna. The people were amazed to see the aged Pope control a spirited horse as if he were a young man. The Holy Sacrament was borne before him and twelve cardinals followed in his train. After this he spent the winter in negotiations and journeys in the Romagna to put its towns into a state of defence. Through snow and rain and tempest he toured the country in a heavy waggon drawn by white oxen.

Meanwhile the war was putting a heavy strain on the Papal finances, which were so depleted that the Pope was compelled to pledge the tiara of Paul II with the Sienese banker Agostino Chigi against a loan of 40,000 ducats. The next year he sent one of his myrmidons to the banker to withdraw the pledge, with orders to arrest him if he made any difficulty. The tiara was handed over, and Chigi heard no more of the money he had lent.

With the coming of spring hostilities recommenced vigorously. Chaumont d'Amboise, the French commander, had died in February 1511. His successor was Marshal Trivulzio, father of the lady who had defended Mirandola with such valour. He succeeded in raising the Bolognese against the Papal rule. On May 21st, 1511, the Papal Legate was driven out and Bentivoglio returned triumphant. Michael Angelo's giant statue of Julius II was overthrown by the mob, and, by a stroke of irony, Alfonso d'Este, who had been excommunicated for holding to the French party, had it melted down and cast into one of the finest guns in his arsenal. In honour of the Pope he named it " Julia ". Alfonso d'Este regained Modena and Reggio : Francesca Trivulzio returned to Mirandola. The whole situation seemed to have changed, the more so when Louis XII placed the great captain Gaston de Foix at the head of his troops.

Louis, to protect himself against the Pope's spiritual attacks, had called a Council at Pisa. This was in conformity with the decisions of the French clergy, but hardly any but French churchmen attended. On January 19th, 1512, the Fathers of the Council summoned the Pope before them and on the 21st suspended him for non-appearance. Julius II retorted by excommunicating the whole Council and laying an interdict on Pisa, the inhabitants of which immediately showed their hostility to their guests.

The Pope had already summoned a Council to meet in the Lateran. The French Council, driven from Pisa, was moved to Milan, and from Milan to Asti, losing prestige all the way and finally falling to pieces after a final move to Lyons. Meanwhile, Julius II had placed not only the King and his supporters, but the whole of France under an interdict. At the beginning of August 1511 a report was spread through Rome that the Pope lay dying in the Vatican. He had caught a fever while hunting at Ostia. The great nobles, the Orsini, the Colonna and the rest mounted the Capitol and harangued the people. Pompeo Colonna, the youthful Bishop of Ostia, described in impassioned language the decadence of Rome under the Papal tyranny. Rome was humiliated, the slave of idle and depraved wretches. The ancient republic should be restored. He called the people to arms to storm Sant' Angelo. Then came the news of the Pope's recovery. The conspirators, finding themselves unsupported, took to flight, two of them going to France.

The Lateran Council met on May 3rd, 1512. It consisted of fifteen cardinals, the Latin patriarchs of Alexandria and Antioch, ten archbishops and fifty-six bishops. The King of Naples, the Venetian Senate and the Florentine Republic were represented by their ambassadors. The Council's advocate proclaimed the abolition of the Pragmatic of Bourges, the French clergy were called upon to justify their actions, and the anathema against Louis XII was renewed.

Thanks to the energy and skill of the Pope, the King's situation was becoming critical. On October 5th, 1511, Julius II had made public the conclusion of the Holy League, which united Rome, Spain and Venice against France, while his skilled diplomacy soon added the King of England and the Emperor Maximilian to their number.

The outlook in France was gloomy. The people were suffering under the interdict, there were no more processions or " pardons " and no more holidays, for all holidays were at that time religious festivals. Taxes showed a disquieting increase, being tripled in the course of a few years. Urged on by Rome, the English appeared before Boulogne, the Spaniards in Guyenne and the Swiss before Dijon, while Maximilian prepared for an invasion of Picardy.

Thus, after the death of Gaston de Foix, the French, attacked on their own territory on almost all their frontiers, were compelled to abandon Italy. At the division of the spoils the Pope detached Parma and Piacenza from the Milanese to add them to his own dominions, but still he would not disarm. He desired the dismemberment of France. The King of England was to have Normandy, Picardy and Brittany, the Swiss Lyonnais and Dauphiné, the Empire Champagne, and the Papacy Paris itself.

Julius II could rest on his laurels for the years that remained to him, surrounded by the acclamations of the Italians, who were amazed at the superhuman energy with which their aged Pope had restored to Rome its ancient glory. " Formerly," wrote Macchiavelli, " the smallest among the barons despised the Papal power, but now even the King of France must respect it." Poets hymned his rule : Rafael, Bramante and Michael Angelo adorned it.

Even on his death-bed Julius's mind was busy with great designs. The Spaniards had still to be driven from Italy. He enjoined upon the cardinals who gathered round his couch that they should press on relentlessly with the war against the King of France and his " accomplices ". He added, however, that those whom he condemned as Pope he absolved as priest. He refused to see his daughter Felice, who came to ask for the cardinal's hat for her half-brother. He said that he had been a sinner all his life, and desired but the simplest funeral. His last official act was the bull which founded the famous Schola Cantorum. On February 31st, 1513, at three in the morning, the "obstinate man" drew his last breath. He was then seventy-two, and had reigned nine years and three months.

He had turned the Vatican gardens into an enchanted pleasaunce. Statues, steles, and architectural fragments were skilfully placed among groves of orange-trees and laurels beneath the towering cypresses. There were aviaries alive with the song and movement of exotic birds, or in which the weary eagle slowly spread his wings. There was a menagerie of strange beasts, and pools shot with the gold and brilliant colours of rare fish. And among them strutted the gorgeous figures of the Renaissance : red-robed cardinals, Roman ladies in their finery, glittering men-at-arms, particoloured Swiss in their liveries of red and black and yellow, all against a background of greenery and flowers.

In Rome a transformation began which was to continue under Leo X. From the sight of Rome to-day, with broad streets and fine buildings, it is hard to conceive what it was like at the beginning of the sixteenth century or to imagine the contrast between the pomp and splendour of the Church and the savagery of the remainder of the place and the people. A small population of 40,000 was lost in the vastness of Rome. The campagna, still haunted by the wild ox, was a place of dread to the traveller. Mercenary soldiers, turned brigand in times of peace, and professional banditti made it a place of murder. The narrow, dark and twisting lanes of Rome itself were hardly safer. Macchiavelli wrote that it was unsafe to venture forth after dark. Most of the houses

231

were still of wood, with projecting eaves and balconies and outside stairs which overhung the street. Poles stretched from house to house across the street and bore washing which dripped upon the passers-by. Grass grew freely in the streets, and many of them were rutted like a country lane. Within the walls were here and there waste places filled with ancient ruins, where Benvenuto Cellini went pigeon-shooting. There were vineyards, patches of corn and market gardens like those which flourished in Paris at the same date. Cattle, goats and sheep were pastured within the city. Rabelais described the Colosseum rising from a mound of broken columns and statuary, with kids gambolling among the marble blocks and the great oxen couched upon the grass. While the new St. Peter's was building it was once invaded by maddened bulls which were only dislodged with difficulty. The ancient Forum had become pasture-land and was called the Campo Vaccino, the field of cows ; and the Tarpeian Mount the Campo Caprino from the herds of goats. At night these herds had to be driven in, since wolves roamed close outside the Vatican. The Quirinal was covered with wild olives, from which rose the dilapidated but splendid marble horses which gave it its name of Monte Cavallo. A filthy, stinking stream, the Mevrana, flowed at the foot of the Palatine Hill, and its marshy banks were the home of pestilent fevers.

Roman ruins, their marble mellowed by time, alternated with the new palaces and the decaying churches which great men's vanity had raised and failed to maintain. Palace cellars and church crypts alike sheltered a host of criminals. Those palaces which still stood were uninviting structures with gloomy, windowless walls and evil-smelling moats, turrets and battlements, where the Roman barons lived as in a fortress with their retainers and their " bravi ", hired ruffians always ready for murder on their masters' account or on their own. In the courts and outbuildings of their palaces the nobles could always find a mob ready for any outrage. While he was still a cardinal, Julius II had fortified his house with cannon.

Julius, seconded by Bramante, made a remarkable effort to transform Rome, the more amazing when we consider the shortness of his reign. His methods showed his customary vigour. He imprisoned a property owner who would not demolish a building out of alignment with one of his streets. For the same reason he demolished the palace of the Cardinal of Auch, in spite of his protests. Under the hand of Bramante new buildings arose in wider and more airy streets, contrasting pleasantly with the picturesque and rugged constructions of the past. The vast projects of Julius drew to Rome a throng of painters, sculptors and architects.

All this change and improvement was not achieved without a certain amount of vandalism. New buildings only too often destroyed ancient monuments. The Pope allowed his contractors to take the material they needed from the Roman ruins, and often from the finest of them. Lime-kilns were set up beside the larger ruins for the burning of the marble, and many statues, bas-reliefs, columns and inscriptions were thus destroyed.

Rafael reported to Leo X in 1518 that in the reign of his predecessor the triumphal arch of the Thermes of Diocletian had perished in this way, as had the temple of Ceres, a part of the Forum of Nerva, and the basilica of Constantine.

I go so far as to say, [he wrote] that the new Rome we behold to-day in all its grandeur and beauty is built with lime made from antique marbles; [and added] It is barbarous and a shame to this age which even Hannibal would not have surpassed had he taken the city.

The so-called Meta of Romulus, which was as high as the Castel Sant' Angelo, was destroyed to make way for the streets converging on St. Peter's. Bramante, the director of the new construction, was nicknamed " Ruinante ". The Pope cared as little for Early Christian buildings as for the relics of Rome : his objective was a Rome in the " style of Julius II ". Fortunately, most of the masterpieces of ancient art, sometimes whole temples, were buried deep in the accumulated débris of the ages, far below the present level of the soil.

Julius contemplated the building of a mighty tomb to enshrine his glory ; it was to be a splendid sarcophagus amid a forest of columns and statues. He entrusted its construction to the young Michael Angelo. A whole mountain of Carrara marble was cut into blocks to serve as the raw material of the sculptor. So that the tomb should have an appropriate resting-place, Bramante and Michael Angelo planned the new St. Peter's on the lines of the ancient Pantheon. Ranke disinterred a pamphlet of Panvinius *On Memorable Antiquities*, in which he said :

The Pope had against him men of all ranks, but especially the cardinals. They bewailed the destruction of the ancient basilica, revered throughout the world, famed for the tombs of so many saints and renowned for the memory of the many religious festivals that had been held there.

The following is a description by André Michel of the tomb as planned by Julius II and Michael Angelo beneath the mighty dome of St. Peter's :

An enormous oblong base bearing a platform on which rests the sarcophagus beneath a kind of triumphal canopy. Forty colossal figures and bas-reliefs without number fill the corners, the sides and the pilasters. There were to be the Papal victories, Fame, the Arts, every conceivable subject. Only one detail was forgotten for a tomb placed in a church—God.

Perhaps Julius II alone was enough.

It proved impossible to carry out the original design for the tomb. It stands to-day, not in St. Peter's but in St. Peter ad Vincula. The plan is vastly changed, and for the worse. It is a miserable failure. Even the Pope's ashes do not rest there, for they were scattered in the sack of Rome by the army of Charles V. Only the "Moses" of Michael Angelo remains as a constant lure to every pilgrim of the arts.

The German historians Burckhardt and Pastor summed up their studies on the reign of Julius II by calling him the saviour of the Papacy. Ranke saw in him the creator of the modern Papacy. But perhaps a better judgment was that of Orestes Ferrara : Julius, he wrote, lacked prudence. This violent and unstable man, devoid of any political plan, "fails to call forth our admiration in spite of all his resounding phrases. It was his histrionic talent which gained him the plaudits of a world content thus to be deceived". Other historians have pointed out that though he drove the French from Italy, he failed to move the Spaniards and brought in the Germans.

Finally, we must consider the results of this fatuous conflict. Jean d'Albret, King of Navarre, was excommunicated by Julius II as the ally of Louis XII. Ferdinand of Aragon seized his Spanish domains, and he became a French prince, whose granddaughter was to embrace the reformed religion and give birth to Henri IV. Henri IV certainly was converted to Catholicism, but his uncle remained the recognized head of the Protestant party in France, a lasting memorial to the activities of Julius II.

Michael Angelo wrote in one of his sonnets : "Here they beat chalices to swords and helmets : they sell the blood of Christ in spoonfuls."

Erasmus, the wisest, the best balanced and the calmest mind of his century, was moved to write of the warrior-Pope :

He is an old man, and displays the energy of a young one. He stays neither for cost nor for weariness nor for toil, nor does he scruple to overthrow law and religion and peace and all other human things. He does not lack learned flatterers to gloss his fury of piety and boldness : they easily find arguments to justify the hand which holds the murderous sword and plunges it into a brother's heart without, as they say, breaking the charity which is the greatest of Christ's commandments.

Ritter Ulrich von Hutten, who was to be Luther's right-hand man in spreading anti-Roman propaganda, arrived in Rome towards the end of the reign of Julius II. He was stupefied at the sight of the successor of the Apostles " taking fortresses and hunting down a woman who sought to defend her children's heritage ". When he returned to Germany he published his *Description of Julius II* with an engraving of the Pope in armour, bearing this legend :

The Sovereign Pontiff Julius, stirring up the Christian world to strife.

The Reformation tore Christendom in twain and destroyed for ever the dream of humanity bowing to the authority of the Vicar of Christ. There is no doubt that the reigns of Alexander VI and Julius II contributed largely to bring this about.

Who, then, was the saviour of the Papacy ? In a negative sense, it was none other than Louis XII, King of France. If he, with much greater cause, had followed the example of Henry VIII and cut himself off from the Pope, clergy and people would have followed his lead, and the Papacy, having lost England, France, most of Germany, Switzerland, the Low Countries and Scandinavia, would have been doomed.

XIV

THE ITALIAN POLICY OF FRANCIS I

WE have already dealt with the ties which bound Italy to France at the end of the fifteenth and beginning of the sixteenth century. Francis I and Henri II carried on the Italian policy of their predecessors.

The "vanities" of Italy had apparently ended in the withdrawal of the French under the shadow of defeat, but we must scrutinize all the circumstances before we can judge the earlier rulers who had fallen to their lure and the two kings who continued in the same policy. The wars of Italy might well be dismissed, in the language of the school-books, as "wars of ambition and conquest", but for one fact taken from contemporary documents. Francis I desired that an Italian of standing should sit in each of the courts of his kingdom and that Frenchmen should sit in the Senate of Milan and the Parlement of Turin. Thus we have a Gentile in the Parlement of Paris, Emilio Ferreti, a Counsellor in the Parlement of Grenoble, and so on. One of them, Niccolo Panigarola, who sat in the Norman Parlement at Rouen, found it difficult to vote, as he knew no French.

The King had good reason for his actions. It was one thing to summon artists from Italy to gratify his taste for the Italian art of the Renaissance, but quite another to introduce Italians into his courts to deal with matters of French law, and to place Frenchmen in equivalent positions in Italy.

This fact is supported by another equally curious. To-day, when one Power declares war on another, the subjects of each hasten to make their way home, if possible before hostilities begin. But when Charles VIII and his mercenaries crossed the Alps in 1494 precisely the contrary was the case. Not only did the Italians established in France remain there, but others flocked to join them in numbers greater than ever before. " The French were at home in Italy and the Italians in France," said Emile Picot in his study of Franco-Italian relations at the time of the Renaissance. " France," wrote Orestes Ferrara, " was considered the protector and ally of the princes and republics of the peninsula."

Piedmont was for twenty-three years, from 1536 to 1559, in French hands. " Piedmont," according to Lucien Romier, " was during the reign of Francis I a typical French province : it had been legally naturalized and its conquest had received legal recognition." This historian shows up the work of the royal lieutenants-general for the prosperity of the country. " The Piedmontese had become so attached to France that they considered the rest of Italy as a foreign country." A Piedmontese delegate to Henri II declared :

Though Piedmont used to love the King of France, you are now recognized as its rightful and sovereign lord, and with good cause. Piedmont has taken a sincere oath of fidelity to Your Majesty and will never fail in its duty.

An agent of the Duke of Florence, writing to his master from Siena, reported : " The whole city is so devoted to France that no trace of feeling to the contrary is observable. If it exists, it is well hidden."

After the treaty of Cambrai (August 3rd, 1529), which followed the captivity of Francis I in Madrid, the Florentine envoy in France, Baldassare Carducci, lamented bitterly that Francis, by his treaty with Charles V, had abandoned

Tuscany. Guicciardini ascribed to his countrymen " a natural inclination toward France " and, dealing with Ferdinand of Aragon's government in Naples, " The past recalled to him his subjects' affection for French rule."

As is well known, the city of Genoa was spontaneously surrendered to Charles VI in 1396, and Marshal Boucicaut became its governor. He was recalled by the disasters of the Hundred Years War, and Genoa was lost to France, but the Genoese again surrendered to Charles VII in 1458, and, after a further separation, wished to hand over their city to Louis XI, who declined the proffered gift.

When, after the Treaty of Cateau-Cambrésis (1559), the King of France had to evacuate Casale and Montferrat, it took a week's struggle before the people could be persuaded to give up French rule and pass under that of the Duke of Mantua.

Most moving, however, is the story of the republic of Montalcino, the capital of a small independent state in Tuscany, to the south-east of Siena. It is a mountainous country of terraced vineyards producing a fine wine and a few fields of corn. Besides the capital it contains about sixty rocky fortresses and a few villages. When Siena fell before the Spaniards in 1555 a number of its citizens, led by Montluc, left their homes and took refuge in Montalcino. They insisted on remaining under French rule. " There were more than a hundred young girls following their fathers and mothers," wrote Montluc, " and women with their infants in cradles borne on their heads." The journey was of some thirty miles. The story is confirmed by the Florentine Strozzi, who wrote to Henri II : " Sire, many of these people have left Siena with their wives and children, carrying with them what little they can, abandoning home and everything else to follow Your Majesty's men." These

people, who gave proof of a loyalty of which few Frenchmen of the time were capable, arrived in the evening at
Montalcino " haggard and looking like death ".

Montalcino was famous for its firm loyalty to France.
The army of Charles V, led by Don Garcia de Toledo,
besieged it in vain from March 27th till June 15th, 1553.
The little garrison, commanded by Giordano Orsini, and
seconded by the entire population, beat off every assault,
and finally the Imperialists were forced to retreat, leaving
three thousand dead beneath the walls.

Montalcino possessed a curious constitution, of which the
first article ran : " A republic and sovereign state, dedicated
to the Virgin under the protection of the King of France."
The King for his part undertook never in any circumstances
to withdraw his protection from the republic, which swore
eternal fealty to him. The news of the taking of Calais by
the Duc de Guise reached Montalcino on January 24th, 1558,
and was celebrated more joyfully than in any town of France.
There were bonfires on the Rocca, a thanksgiving mass in
San Agostino : the courts did not sit and the shops were
closed, and all the bells of the city pealed day and night
without ceasing for three days.

But Calais followed St. Quentin (1557), where the French
army, led by the Constable de Montmorency, was annihil-
ated by the Spanish forces under Emmanuel Philibert of
Savoy. Peace negotiations were begun. The citizens of Montalcino, terrified, sent a petition to Henri II, imploring him
to allow them to " live and die his subjects ". Babou de le
Bourdaisière, French ambassador in Rome, strove to console them. " These are difficult days ; the King of France
has so much on his hands that circumstances are stronger
than his will."

The treaty of Cateau-Cambrésis followed, by which France

gave up all her territories in Italy and surrendered a hundred and eighty-nine fortresses. The work of four reigns was undone.

Some years later Montaigne visited Montalcino.

On Sunday morning [he said in the account of his Italian journey] we left Buonconvento because M. de Montaigne wished to see Montalcino for the sake of its associations with France. Montalcino, a town of about the size of St. Emilion, lies upon one of the highest mountains of the district, almost inaccessible. The people's affection for the memory of the French is so great that they can hardly be reminded of it without bursting into tears.

Lucien Romier wrote : " The good work of the King's men in the Alpine regions was proof against the worst shocks of war, but the diplomats destroyed it with a little paper and ink. Its growth was cut off in its prime." We have contemporary testimony as to the sorrow thereby caused in Italy.

The Battle of St. Quentin had been a disaster. The treaty of Cateau-Cambrésis, which followed it, was arranged by the Constable de Montmorency and the Marshal de Saint André, both prisoners of Emmanuel Philibert. While still in the hands of their enemies they negotiated with unseemly haste a peace which was to set them at liberty. In any case Montmorency had always disliked the Italian adventure. The Duc de Guise was beyond the Alps when Montmorency lost his army. If only this famous soldier, who ranks with Gaston de Foix among the finest soldiers in France before Napoleon, had been at St. Quentin, the event of the battle would have been otherwise. The treaty of Cateau-Cambrésis, too, would have been of quite a different character, and the King of France would have retained his Italian possessions.

The Milanese remained two centuries under Spanish rule,

which might well have been French, since, as has been shown, Francis I did not aspire to dominate Italy, but to bring about a fusion of the two nations in every possible way, even to the amalgamation of their judicial systems by an exchange of magistrates. The modern idea of nationality, of united nations hostile one to another, had not yet appeared. On both sides of the Alps there existed in Latin a common language in law, in medicine, theology, science, even in history and in the greater part of poetry.

We have shown the extent to which the two nations had interests in common, and to what degree they shared a common activity. It thus appears that the policy of the French kings of the Renaissance was both useful and productive, and that the efforts of Francis I to extend it were wholly admirable. It is not always just to judge the ideas and actions of men by the event. As Danton said before the Revolutionary tribunal : " It is easy to judge when events have spoken, but not so easy when the veil of the future conceals them."

These two battles, Pavia, which left the King a prisoner, and St. Quentin, which destroyed a French army close to the capital, were both disasters which might well have turned out otherwise. Charles VIII and Louis XII had no means of foretelling that their rival in Italy, the King of Spain, was in the next generation to mount the Imperial throne and weigh down the balance against France. Charles VIII, Louis XII and Francis I could hardly have suspected the treachery which they met at the hands of Alexander VI, Julius II and Leo X.

The facts we have adduced throw a further light on the somewhat neglected question of Francis I's Italianate tastes and the prodigality of his favours to Italian artists. It would be better, instead of speaking of Francis's enthusiasm for Italian art, to speak of his artistic policy, which appears as a part of his general policy. He attracted to France not only artists and architects, painters and sculptors, but magistrates, jurists, churchmen, soldiers and sailors, bankers and merchants, artisans of all kinds, humanists and teachers. His sons received an Italian education and he married his heir to an Italian. He endeavoured to imbue not only French art, but French jurisprudence with the Italian spirit and vice versa. He was fully aware of the great prestige enjoyed by artists in Italy, and saw in it a useful means to aid in the rapprochement of the two nations. He therefore endeavoured to obtain as much publicity as possible for the favours he granted to Italian artists, his princely reception of Leonardo da Vinci at Cloux, near Amboise, his establishment of that braggart genius Cellini in the Petit Nesle in Paris, and his autograph letters to Michael Angelo.

Fontainebleau, which is throughout of his creation, he made into a " French Italy ", as Michelet described it. Brantôme has left a marvellous description of it. It was an Italian palace decorated by Italians, Primaticcio, Rosso, Benvenuto and a score of others, rising amidst a small town of princely mansions built for the most part on Italian plans and many of them the homes of Italian nobles and churchmen. The royal palace was open to all comers, and was thronged with Italians of every station. They were allowed to look on while the King dined. Brantôme gave an amusing description of the conversations which took place between the King, seated at table, and his audience, conversations often held in the tongue of Petrarch, which Francis spoke fluently.

We thus discover a vast political project, capable of unlimited extension, in complete contradiction to the accepted idea of " wars of ambition and conquest ". The success of

the Italian policy of Francis I was well within the bounds of
possibility, we might even say those of probability, at the
time when it was decided upon and the King attempted to
realize it. It was not a question of a conquest of Italy for
profit and increase of power, as the Spanish conquest proved
to be. The King of France desired the union of the two
peoples for the prosperity and happiness of both. If he had
succeeded, the destinies, not only of France and Italy, but
of the whole world, would have been changed.

It was not to be. In the words of Goethe : " Es wär zu
schön gewesen, es hat nicht können sein."

XV

THE CONCORDAT

TOWARD the end of 1515 Leo X went to Bologna to meet the young King of France, Francis I. His object was the settlement of the weighty question of the relations between the Church of France and the Holy See. The Pope was then forty and Francis a youth of twenty-two.

Leo X was a member of the powerful Medici family, from whom he inherited his artistic tastes. Throughout his whole life he retained his pride in the honour and greatness of the family, which he celebrated by the hand of Michael Angelo in their sculptured tombs in Florence. He was a short, thick-set personage with weak and spindly legs, fat-cheeked and thick-necked ; his eyes were large, short-sighted and vague without spectacles, but his finely modelled hands betrayed his breeding. Rafael has left a portrait of him which clearly shows his character.

Leo X was known to his entourage as an elegant humanist. His appearance was imposing, and his natural dignity concealed his misshapen body and the effects of his gluttony. His morals were beyond reproach, a rare quality in a Pope of that day, if we except the pious Adrian IV. He had an astonishing memory, which made him appear more intelligent than he actually was. He could express himself well, both in Italian and in the purest of Latin. His voice was his most charming feature, being both soft and clear. He had great powers of persuasion and conciliation. His character was such as might be inferred from his physique, cautious and undecided. His predecessor Julius II nicknamed him " His Circumspection ". He was reluctant to take any definite decision, hoping that time would settle the question and spare him the trouble of making up his mind. His contemporaries, comparing him with his predecessors, said, " When Leo X speaks of a matter he is considering it ; Julius II spoke and acted together ; when Alexander VI spoke the deed was already done." " His Holiness," said the Venetian envoy, " dislikes effort and does all he can to avoid it ; he wishes neither trouble, nor enemies, nor war."

He was generous and tolerant and protected Jews, of whom he had a number about him whom he treated with consideration. There was certainly no place in Europe at that time, outside the Vatican, where there was such freedom of thought. In 1515 Ulrich von Hutten, Luther's lieutenant, published his virulent pamphlet against the Roman Church, *The Letters of Obscure men*—and published it with papal privilege. In 1520, Luther addressed to Leo X a letter comparing him with Ezekiel surrounded by scorpions. " The Roman Church," said the German reformer, " surpasses the Turks in impiety." Leo X read it, and simply remarked, " Brother Martin is a genius ".

Leo X carried out the duties of his office with dignity, even with majesty, but in private life his easy-going ways and his unmeasured love of the chase and fishing were the despair of his master of ceremonies. Luther, in impassioned speeches and writings, daily anathematized this good-natured dilettante as Antichrist and the incarnation of the devil.

Leo X loved the arts, and patronized them with unerring good taste : he was also interested in science, particularly in astronomy. Having heard of a mathematician who had written on his subject in good Latin, Leo fetched him all the way from Portugal. He collected fine copies of classical texts, but his greatest delight was in music. His rooms were full of instruments of all kinds, which he imported from Nuremberg at great expense. He had a good voice and was fond of vocal music, humming one or other of his favourite tunes the whole day long. Even on his death-bed he asked for music. He took in hand the reformation of the calendar.

He was deeply convinced of the truths of the faith of which he was the supreme head, and most conscientious in carrying out his religious duties, never missing Mass a single day, which should be accounted to him for merit, considering his bad health. He suffered greatly from malaria, which brought on fits of melancholia.

He was generous and even prodigal. Vettori said that it was as difficult for him to keep a thousand ducats in his drawer as for a stone to fly up to heaven. "In pomp and generosity," said Guicciardini, "Leo X squandered the treasure which Julius II had laid up for warlike purposes." He spent 50,000 ducats on his coronation alone. His largesse was divided among all classes : it went to painters, architects and scholars as well as to the poor and to hospitals and churches. His insatiable need for money was the cause of the excesses to which the Church was driven, in the sale of Indulgences and the traffic in ecclesiastical dignities. Money was obtained from the faithful on every possible pretext, such as a tax for a crusade, a tithe for the building of St. Peter's, the many foreign branches of the Medici bank working hand in hand with the clergy at the task of raising funds. The result was the commencement and then the spread of Protestantism in Germany.

The Papal Court had never been so animated or pleasant a place as under Leo X. As Cardinal Bibiena remarked, only women were lacking, and they not always. The Vatican was guarded by the Swiss, whose uniform Leo X changed to green, white and red. The Papal banquets were on a lavish scale, sometimes lasting a whole day, with intermissions. These intermissions were not, as now, sweet courses, but amusements, such as dances, music, short plays or clowns, which filled the intervals between courses. There were comedies in Latin or Italian, ballet dancers and comedians who sang and jested, not always in the best of taste. A wretched monk who composed a play which his audience found boring was pitilessly " ragged ", his clothes half torn from his back, and he himself consigned to bed for some days to recover from the effects of his ill-treatment. The Pope regarded the whole affair as a capital joke.

Among the Papal clowns should be numbered the Vatican " archpoet " Quernus. He took his meals standing in a window and eating the morsels which the guests threw to him, for which he had to give thanks in at least two Latin verses. If these verses were not approved, his punishment consisted in drinking watered wine. Leo X was himself a skilled maker of verses, and sometimes amused himself with a dialogue with his archpoet in Latin verse.

> Archipoetus facit versus pro mille poetis
> (The archpoet makes verses enough for a thousand poets),

improvised Quernus ; and Leo X retorted :

> Et pro mille aliis archipoeta bibit
> (And drinks for another thousand).

To which, nowise abashed, Quernus replied :

> Porige quod faciat mihi carmina docta Falernum
> (Bring forth the Falernian which inspires my learned song),

and the Pope, parodying Virgil,

Hoc etiam enervat debilitatque pedes
(But which also weakens the feet) ;

a play upon real feet and the feet of the verses.

A good idea of these banquets can be obtained from the description, left by the chronicler Sanuto, of one given by a Roman cardinal to the ambassadors of Venice. It began with veal soup and continued with gilt stags' heads, each of which bore a streamer with the arms of the server. These courses were served to the sound of trumpets. Then followed seventy-four dishes of poultry, handed round to the mellifluous strains of harps, cymbals and viols ; then the roast in eight dishes and eighteen other dishes, each of two pheasants and a peacock, served in the French manner with neck and tail plumage intact. This course was enlivened by the antics of a troupe of buffoons. Then came stuffed capons and a Spanish clown, dressed in cloth of gold, and playing on a silver tambourine. Finally, the sweet consisted of bowls of whipped and sweetened cream with wafers, accompanied by poems recited by children dressed as shepherds and a Moorish girl who performed her native dances. Before rising each guest was presented with a bowl of perfumed water to wash his hands and clean his teeth.

Leo X was fond of the theatre. Even the lightest of pieces, such as the *Calandra* of his favourite Cardinal Bibiena, were played before him. Indeed it is believed that the Pope himself had a hand in this trifling comedy. The *Suppositi* of Ariosto was performed in the Vatican, and the Pope supervised the production down to the smallest detail. The staging, by Rafael, filled the audience with admiration. On September 27th, 1520, the day of SS. Cosmo and Damian, a comedy was performed which, according to the Papal master of ceremonies, Paris de Grassis, was much more fitted to arouse mirth and aid digestion than to encourage its audience to a pious life. Leo X even had performed Macchiavelli's obscene *Mandragola*.

The cardinals modelled their manner of living on that of the Pope. They often had from 150 to 250 servants, Cardinal Farnese having as many as 300. They dressed luxuriously in brocade and ermine, velvet and fine lace, which was constantly changed.

Rome itself attained at this time a height of prosperity, luxury and splendour which it had not known since the age of the great emperors. Everything became a pretext for shows and festivities, from the entry of an ambassador to the masking of the carnival, from the crowning of a poet to the most solemn religious feast. In the years when Leo X was Pope the population increased from 40,000 to 90,000, and 10,000 houses were built. The whole nature of the city was altered. Within thirty years Rome changed from a mediæval city to a city of the Renaissance, full of grandeur and beauty. Palaces adorned it : the most intractable barons had become courtiers, and even the pamphleteers had found flattery more profitable than their everlasting lampoons.

The secret of the vast influence of Alexander VI, Julius II and Leo X over their contemporaries lies in the fact that they conformed to the tastes and inclinations of the crowd, with perpetual festivities, processions, banquets, plays, song, dance and music in the streets, racing and bullfights. All this could not but increase the financial stringency. The work on the dome of St. Peter's and the decoration of the Vatican had to be slowed down, greatly to the annoyance of Rafael. Indulgences had ceased to bring in money, their sale in France being restricted by the Pragmatic of Bourges and in Germany by the spread of Lutheranism. There were protests even in Italy. In March 1515 the Republic of Venice prohibited the sale of Indulgences throughout its territories.

Leo X even tried without success to make money by gambling, and finally had recourse to loans, first from private lenders, and then from the Communes of Florence, Siena and Ancona. He increased the number of Cardinals so as to profit from their thank-offerings on their promotion. In 1520 he obtained 400,000 ducats in this manner. Posts in the Papal Court were put up for sale. Defendants brought before the Papal tribunals were condemned to fines of astronomical proportions. Leo X pledged his plate and considered putting Lake Trasimene up for sale. "The Pope," wrote the Venetian envoy Marco Minio, "never has cash in hand ; he is hopelessly generous, and the Florentines who claim kinship with him never leave him a farthing."

Leo X disliked the French for several reasons. They had helped to bring about the downfall of his family, the Medici, when first his brother Piero II and then his nephew Lorenzo II were driven from Florence. We have already pointed out that his first preoccupation was the fortune and prosperity of his house. To restore the Medici to their former greatness he began negotiations with Venice, which was then at war with France, and allied himself with Charles V. He even offered the English soldiers engaged in the war with France the spiritual privileges reserved for crusaders, an ironical touch, seeing that Henry VIII was to bring about the rupture between the Church of England and Rome.

When Francis I won the battle of Marignano (1515) Leo X was terrified lest he should retake Parma and Piacenza, which Julius II had succeeded in detaching from the Milanese. Leo had also in view the renewal of Julius's designs on the duchy of Ferrara, which he desired to bestow on his nephew Lorenzo dei Medici, Lorenzo being already master of Urbino, whose legitimate ruler Leo had dispossessed by force of arms. France, the traditional protector of Ferrara, stood in his

way. The combined pressure of political and financial necessity finally compelled the Pope to consent to meet Francis I
at Bologna. He counted on his diplomatic skill and powers
of persuasion to prevail upon the young King to abolish the
Pragmatic of Bourges, the charter of liberties of the Gallican
Church, and the barrier which prevented the flow of French
capital into the coffers of the Holy See. He succeeded so
far that Francis guaranteed the Medici rule in Florence,
though he would not restore Parma and Piacenza.

One of the chief reasons for the Pope's dislike of the
French was the effect of the Pragmatic of Bourges, which
defined the liberties of the Gallican Church and prevented
the exploitation by the Roman Court of French piety.
Luther himself said : " In France they do not suffer the
religious abuses we tolerate "—the continuous and open sale
of indulgences, the raising, in every possible form, of dues
and rents from religious bodies, and arbitrary nominations
to the higher posts in the Church. This Pragmatic, which
even Luther admired, was in Rome denominated a " diabolical
pestilence ", a " thorn in the eye of the Church ". If the
constitution of the Gallican Church gave the Pope no reason
to love his neighbours beyond the Alps, it at least made
him strongly desirous of a meeting with the young King
for the purpose of extracting this painful thorn.

The royal edict known as the Pragmatic Sanction had
been issued at Bourges by Charles VII in 1438. Its general
tenor followed the decisions of the recent Council of Basle,
which, among other things, had definitely laid down that
the canonical elections of bishops should be held by the
chapters, and of abbots by the monks of their convent.

At this time practically a third of the land of France was
in the hands of the clergy, and neither the King nor the
dignitaries of the Church were disposed to see their vast

possessions serve as a milch-cow for the Papal treasury. The Pragmatic began by declaring the Pope subject to the decisions of the Councils, which, it claimed, should be called at regular intervals. It limited the Pope's reversion to the right of nomination of bishops and abbots. During the regency of Anne de Beaujeu the Pope's nominees were expelled from the bishoprics of Tournai and Gap. When Alexander VI desired to appoint André d'Epinay, who was already Archbishop of Bordeaux, to the archbishopric of Lyons, in opposition to the chapter's nominee, Talaru, the latter prevented the Pope's favourite from taking possession.

Also in conformity with the Council's findings, the Pragmatic abolished the so-called "expectatives", the Papal right to make nominations to ecclesiastical offices, to take effect as soon as the said offices fell vacant. It likewise suppressed the custom of allotting to a person other than the incumbent the pecuniary profits of a given benefice, which had served as a pretext for providing, out of Church funds, for people unfit to hold ecclesiastical office. The Pragmatic also abolished the "reservations", the right, which the Popes had usurped, to nominate candidates to certain vacant benefices. A hundred years before, Gerson had attacked the abuses resulting from this practice. "The reservations," he declared, "are a usurpation, manifest robbery and a diabolical custom which lead to all kinds of evils." Henceforth the Pope's right was restricted to a maximum of one post in ten.

"Annates" were suppressed : that is, the payment to Rome of a part (usually amounting to a year's income) of the revenues of all benefices on the accession to them of a new incumbent. The Pragmatic further forbade direct appeals to the Pope from the decisions of the lower ecclesiastical courts, and left to the Pope only the right of "confirmation" of duly elected candidates for ecclesiastical posts. The elections, according to the Gallicans, were divinely inspired.

These provisions easily explain the hatred of the Roman Curia for the whole Pragmatic. A second assembly at Bourges in 1452 confirmed and renewed the provisions of the first, and proclaimed it the " immutable constitution of the Church of France ".

In his Bull " Execrabilis " (1460) Pius II attacked in violent language all those who " tear the seamless coat of Christ ", and accused them of trying to turn the Church into a many-headed beast. The Parlement of Paris replied : " The Pope should take thought before he commences open strife with a multitude of good Christians : in any case he has no business to meddle in French concerns."

Charles VII, however, died the next year, and his son and successor Louis XI, having lived in constant strife with his father, was prompt to annul any decision Charles had taken. He accordingly decreed the abolition of the Pragmatic Sanction. Pius II and his court were unbounded in their expressions of joy. " The Pragmatic is abrogated. This deed is one of the best and most solemn ever performed. We have celebrated it in Rome with festivals and processions." Pius II sent Louis XI a consecrated sword and a copy of verses of his own composition. In France, on the other hand, there was discontent. Jean de St. Romain, procurator-general of the Parlement of Paris, adamant to both threats and promises, obstinately refused to give legal effect to the royal edict, eventually losing his office rather than give way. The Parlement itself followed his example and, after vigorous protests had been disregarded, refused to register the edict, thus depriving it of all validity. The University of Paris, which for centuries had been hailed as the " torch of Catholicism ", appealed against it to the next Council ; the highest and best qualified ecclesiastical persons of the Kingdom declared it null and void. France asserted almost unanimously its desire "to maintain the ancient liberties of the Church in Gaul against all attempts of the Pope". A Concordat arranged between Louis XI and Sixtus IV (1491) was equally unsuccessful.

These facts suffice to show the importance of the meeting arranged at Bologna between Leo X and Francis I.

The Pragmatic of Bourges had been a clear and definite expression of opinions held by almost the entire clergy of France, who displayed a lively independence. After the death of Philip the Fair, Pope Boniface VIII, in memory of the feud which had raged between them, solemnly conferred on him the title of Philip the Catholic. At the close of the fourteenth century the "evangelic doctor" Gerson had brilliantly maintained the Gallican doctrine. In 1482 the faculty of theology in Paris, which was regarded as the pre-eminent authority, condemned the Franciscan Angeli for recognizing in a sermon the Pope's authority over souls in Purgatory. It thus struck at the roots of the theory of Indulgences. The great majority of the clerical delegates to the States-General were adherents of the Gallican school. "The whole clergy of France," wrote the Venetian envoy Marino Cavalli, "place the King before the Pope," that is, in his ecclesiastical capacity.

About the same time the King's Advocate in the Parlement of Paris, Le Maistre, defined the Gallican Church as "a particular Church under the Church of Rome whose liberties Rome cannot be suffered to take away." The King of France was independent in the exercise of his God-given powers, of which no earthly power could deprive him. He was the sole judge of the limits of his own laws. His edicts were legally valid within his realm. Canon law had no legal authority in France. The Pope was Head of the Church, but not above the Church, being subject to the decisions of a General Council. Christ had not attributed infallibility to Peter, whose successors the Popes are, but to the Church. A Pope may therefore err and be condemned for heresy. Was not Pope Libert an Arian ? The clergy of every country may make its own regulations, which even an œcumenical Council has no power to change.

The French clergy remained fundamentally Gallican, but at the same time invincibly Catholic. While Luther found important adherents even among the higher ranks of the German clergy, French clerics were practically unanimous in their opposition to Calvinism.

The French clergy was supported in its Gallican views by the lawyers, led successively by the Chancellor l'Hôpital, the Advocate-General Etienne Pasquier, the Presidents de Harlay, and the jurist Dumoulin. The Parlement, in the name of royal prerogative and ecclesiastical liberty, refused to legalize the powers of a Papal Legate, stirred up chapters to rebel against bishops imposed on them by Rome, and ordered the confiscation of benefices held by " Romans ".

When the Cardinal of Le Mans posted up in his diocese an ancient statute excommunicating bailiffs who imprisoned clerks, and persons who refused payment of tithes, the Parlement had his placards destroyed and threatened the Cardinal-Bishop with fine and imprisonment if he failed to annul his decisions. Citation before the Roman Court was forbidden, and Louis de Beaumant, Bishop of Paris, was summoned before the Parlement for having made use of a Papal Bull citing his metropolitan, the Archbishop of Sens, to Rome.

The Parlement could thus, in case of necessity, lift an ecclesiastical ban, fine the person imposing it, make a statutory order to priests to hear confession, grant communion and give orders for religious burial if, in its opinion, the offices of the Church were being unjustly withheld. It deliberated on vestments and legislated on the question of whether a bishop should wear a train. It could authorize a private person to take his vows, or a monk to change his monastery, and possessed the right of visitation of convents by a commission charged to oversee the strict maintenance of monastic rules. The authority of the Parlement in these matters was all the greater since at that time there was no cleavage between ecclesiastical and civil law. The two were so closely united that decrees of Councils, Papal Bulls, and statutes of synods were subject to registration by the Parlements exactly like royal edicts, and were only valid after being thus registered.

The Gallican Church comprised practically the whole of the French middle classes, under the triple leadership of the bishops, the universities and the Parlements. " Every day," wrote Innocent VIII to his Nuncio in France, " the authority of the Pope in this Kingdom is more and more abased."

One cause of this, and incidentally of the strength of Gallicanism, was the quasi-sacerdotal nature of kingship in France. The King was God's minister, Head of the Church in France. When he was anointed with the oils brought direct from Heaven, he became a sacred personage, under the direct inspiration of the Holy Ghost. The early Capetian kings appeared to their subjects in full priestly attire, crowned with the episcopal mitre, and their successors kept the ecclesiastical dalmatic. The King was the Head of the Church, and the obedience of the Church to him was canonically ordained. Bishop Catwulf wrote to Charlemagne : " Thou art Bishop in the seat and place of Christ " ; while even in the eleventh century the same view of the functions of the French King persisted in Italy, as is shown by a painting by

a Sienese artist, now in Naples, which depicts Louis IX in
the act of crowning his nephew Robert of Anjou as King
of Naples. The King wears a bishop's mitre and dalmatic,
and bears the episcopal staff in a hand adorned by the episcopal ring. The oldest of the French " chansons de gestes ",
which give an exact picture of life in the eleventh century,
bear out this thesis. The early Capetians blessed and absolved
their subjects like priests : Hugues Capet took his place as
Head of the Church at his coronation in 987 by the oath he
took at Noyon : Robert the Pious was a true priest, and
presided over the councils of his clergy, while Philip Augustus
formally blessed his knights before the battle of Bouvines.

Miracles were of commoner occurrence in the lives of
unsainted French kings than, for example, in that of St.
Francis of Assisi. In the fifteenth century the King was always
considered the head of the French clergy. " The King is a
prelate," said Juvénal des Ursins to Charles VII. The States-
General of 1407 and 1483 declared that the royal authority
took precedence of that of the Pope. Even in the seventeenth
century the pious Fénélon could say : " The King is much
more head of the Church than is the Pope." Renan was not
only dealing in paradox when he declared that the rivalry
between Pope and King from Hugues Capet to Louis XII
sprang chiefly from professional jealousy. From this conception of the kingly office comes the attribution, peculiar
to the King of France, of miraculous powers. An Italian,
Claude de Seyssel, Archbishop of Turin, is witness to this
attribution at the period in question. " God has given this
gift of working miracles to the King of France, not as a
person, but in virtue of his office, and this power is granted
to him alone of all earthly princes, not excepting the Roman
Pontiff."

Francis I had just won the brilliant victory of Marignano

(September 13th, 1515) over the Swiss : he was master of the Milanese, to which he had annexed Parma and Piacenza, greatly to the anger of Leo X. There were, however, matters of moment to be settled with the French Government, and these, with the financial difficulties of the Roman Court, gave the Pope good cause to desire a meeting with the King. The meeting place was Bologna, where Francis made his entry on December 11th, 1515.

A gorgeous company of scarlet cardinals met the King of France at the Porta San Felice. Francis dismounted and uncovered before them, a gesture of respect which Charles VIII had refused to the Pope himself, and made an appropriate reply to a harangue from the dean of the Sacred College. The magnificent procession entered Bologna at one in the afternoon, led by two hundred crossbowmen in the Papal livery, to the sound of a fanfare of silver trumpets and the pealing of bells from all the hundred and nineteen churches of the city. Then came the French heralds in tabards of royal blue strewn with golden lilies, then the splendidly attired officers of the royal household and a crowd of churchmen, in red, violet or black, set off with lace and gold braid and precious stones of every hue. The ambassadors were there, the Venetians prominent among them in the robes familiar from Tintoretto's pictures, wine-coloured togas, gold-embroidered and edged with ermine.

Francis I, tall, elegant, and youthful, rode his black charger between two cardinals mounted on peaceful hackneys. One of them, Ippolito d'Este, son of Lucrezia Borgia, was one of the most devoted friends of France. The young King's tabard was black, embroidered with silver ; his cap and plume were also black. " His face is handsome," wrote Paolo Girvio, " his hands are slender, his height above the average, and his whole person alive with energy." The King smiled

to right and left with an air of condescending majesty, and
as he passed the people burst into shouts of " Francia !
Francia ! " He was followed by a group of French princes,
among them the Duc de Vendôme, the Constable de Bourbon
and others, and by the famous captains of his wars, Bayard,
Lautrec, d'Antigny and La Trémoille. Then came his ministers,
one of whom drew but little attention, being short and
squat and bilious of complexion : this was Antoine Duprat,
Chancellor of France, to-day in the background, but to-
morrow to take first place in importance.

In the rear marched 6,000 archers, their doublets bearing
the salamander badge of Francis I in gold, and mounted
crossbowmen clad in all the colours of the rainbow.

The procession passed beneath a series of splendidly decorated triumphal arches built for the occasion and bearing
inscriptions in honour of the young King. The Pope was
lodged on the second floor of the Bishop's palace. In defiance
of the protocol, he rushed out on to the balcony as the procession approached, dragging with him the Emperor's envoy,
with whom he happened to be talking. Leo X was too good
an artist to miss the gorgeous pageant that passed before his
eyes.

When the King came before the Pope, he fulfilled exactly
the rites required by custom, kissing the Pope's foot, knee
and shoulder, and loudly declaring that his devotion to the
Holy See fully equalled that of his predecessors. This committed him to little, since Louis XII would hardly be called
an enthusiast for the Papacy.

For some days Bologna was given up to rejoicing in honour
of the French, whose hearts were as open as their hands and
their purses. The rough soldiers of France showed such
devotion in their kissing of the foot and knee of the Pope
that he bore for several days bruises as the visible mark of

it. Meanwhile, the dignitaries on both sides were hard at work, and on December 15th, 1515, there resulted from their deliberations an event of first-class importance—the Concordat.

The primary objective of Leo X was to obtain from the King the annulment of the Pragmatic of Bourges, which prevented Rome from receiving what it conceived to be its just due from France. Francis I's advisers on this occasion were his Chancellor, Antoine Duprat and the Bishop of Coutances, Adrien Gouffier. Leo X was seconded by a number of skilled clerical diplomats, chief among them his literary collaborator, Cardinal Bibiena. Francis I was won over with the bait of the Kingdom of Naples, but, said the Pope, it would be better to avoid diplomatic complications by awaiting the death of Ferdinand the Catholic, who had declared Naples to be an integral part of the Spanish dominions. Francis also demanded the Laocoön group of statuary, but this the Pope refused point-blank. Adrien Gouffier was promised the cardinal's hat and Antoine Duprat was overwhelmed with important and profitable benefices. As he left Bologna on December 15th, says Rodocanachi, Francis I saw Gouffier standing amid the cardinals, and could not help exclaiming : " Now you stand among the wolves ! " He spoke more truly than he knew, for Gouffier had succumbed to bribery.

The Concordat of December 15th, 1515, consisted in essence of regulations governing ecclesiastical elections and the payments to Rome of moneys derived from annates, the sale of Indulgences, and so on. According to the Pragmatic of Bourges, archbishops and bishops were to be elected by their chapters, abbots by their monks. By the Concordat Leo X placed these nominations in the hands of the King, reserving to himself only a theoretical right of institution of the royal candidate. Only in cases where a bishop or an abbot died while actually in Rome had the Pope the right to appoint a successor. In return, the King granted the Pope his much-desired annates. These annates were to consist of one year's revenue of all major benefices, or of one-half the yearly revenue of the smaller ones, and were payable to the Papal treasury for the year after the accession of a new incumbent. It can be imagined what a huge sum was involved when it is realized that France possessed 110 bishoprics and nearly 4,000 monasteries. The system of annates, save for short intervals under Henri II and Charles IX, persisted till the Revolution.

The third question at issue was that of jurisdiction. Here a compromise was reached. Judgment in causes clearly defined by canon law as " major causes " was reserved to the Pope, but the infinitely greater number of minor causes, which affected ordinary life, were left in the hands of the local jurisdictions to which law, custom or privilege had already assigned them. The registers of Leo X show how little weight was attached to these legal prerogatives.

As has been very well said, by this Concordat Pope and King each gave the other something which belonged to neither, the election to ecclesiastical posts, which belonged of right to the French clergy, and the money thereto appertaining, which belonged to the French people. But King as well as Pope stood to gain vast sums thereby, for by the ingenious system of " commends " the King could grant rich benefices to laymen who would draw the income and leave their internal administration to a churchman. There was thus opened a lucrative source of rewards for royal servants or favourites.

The whole of the negotiations leading to this result only occupied four days. Before his departure from Milan the young King yielded to the pressing requests of those about him and gave an exhibition of the miraculous powers of " touching " for sickness vested in him as anointed King of France. Hopeful Italians had flocked to him from all parts : a bishop had come all the way from Poland. The ceremony, which was held under the eyes of the Pope, was accompanied by the traditional military pomp of drums and trumpets and waving ensigns. It was hardly calculated, however, to lessen the Pope's detestation of the French.

The Papal side of the Concordat was ratified by a Bull of August 15th, 1516, but the French letters patent were not sealed till May 13th, 1517. As soon as the agreements reached at Bologna became known they called forth a storm of protest. The Lateran Council ratified them on December 19th, 1516, against the opinion of the Bishop of Tortona, who maintained that the Council had no right to annul the decisions of former Councils such as those of Basle and Bourges. The Sacred College was hostile, and its approval was only gained at the end of 1516. The opposition of the Parlement of Paris was unanimous and violent. In vain did the King in person call upon it to give way ; in vain did the Chancellor Duprat endeavour to justify the agreements in a long and persuasive speech. On February 5th, 1517, the magistracy refused to register the Concordat, declaring that they could only recognize the Pragmatic. " Only a General Council, attended by representatives of the Gallican Church, can legislate for the internal organization of the realm." The Parlement was compelled to yield by a royal decree, but added to their formal registration the following commentary :

This Court hereby declares that it has registered this edict by order, and not by vote of the said Court, which hereby protests that it nowise authorizes nor approves the reading and publication of the Concordat aforesaid, and that cases dealing with benefices will be judged by the said Court in accordance with the Pragmatic.

The King did not finally have his way till March 22nd, 1518, and even then the royal advocate and procurator-general formally refused their assent. An ordinance was passed by the Parlement forbidding printers to publish the text of the Bologna agreement. Protests from the clergy were read at sermon-time in most churches. The doyen of the parish priests of Paris protested in the name of all his colleagues. The University of Paris appealed through its Faculty of Theology to a General Council. " The Concordat could not be observed without grave offence to God." Teachers and students were equally excited. The chapter of the cathedral joined the University in its appeal, and for many years afterwards public prayers were said in many churches for the abolition of the Concordat. The King was amazed at the depth and wide extent of the resistance to his will.

In spite of the registration into which they had been forced, the Parlement's ordinances continued to be framed as if the Concordat did not exist and the Pragmatic had never been annulled. When the chapter of Albi Cathedral elected as their bishop a candidate in opposition to the one nominated under the Concordats by the King, the Parlements of Toulouse and Paris declared the chapter's candidate legally elected. The government was finally compelled to withdraw all cases of this nature from the Parlement and to submit them to a more tractable body, the Grand Council.

It was not till the disaster of Pavia and the captivity of the King that this almost unanimous opposition began to lose its intensity. France rallied to its King in an access of patriotic loyalty, but even then the Parlement of Paris renewed its protests against the violence that had been done to the Church of France, and demanded the reinforcement of the Pragmatic.

There had certainly been new abuses in the Church since

the reforms of Charles VII. The elections of bishops and abbots had sometimes ended in violence and disorder. Philippe de Gamaches, Abbot of St. Faron at Meaux, brought in men-at-arms to protect his seat against a rival (1441), while Pierre Bureau, son of the celebrated Grand Master of the Artillery, entered on his episcopal office to the accompaniment of shots and burnings (1447). Sometimes a whole district was set in uproar by some such dispute. Comminges was divided by a quarrel over the bishopric between Guichard de l'Hôpital and Amanieu d'Albret, while in Bigorre there was a civil war between the rival supporters of Gontaut and Theodore de Foix. In 1507 the election to the bishopric of Poitiers of a successor to Cardinal de la Trémoille was the occasion of a pitched battle lasting three days, between men-at-arms and Breton and Gascon mercenaries armed with spears, daggers and firearms. The affair ended by six different people being elected, each of whom celebrated his success with a Te Deum.

The same disturbances signalized many elections to abbacies, where the Parlement was compelled to intervene and sometimes to commit one or both rivals to prison to cool down. Richer monasteries were plundered on similar occasions, the treasury, the granary, and usually the cellars being stripped of all they contained. The Bishop of Angers, commendatory Abbot of Fontaine Daniel, brought up a train of artillery and destroyed the cloister chapel before he could enter by the breach and take possession of his abbey. At other times elections were said to be influenced by plots and intrigues, and there was talk of bribery and the deadly sin of simony. It cannot be denied that such abuses existed, though they were often invention and usually exaggerated by contemporaries. In particular, Pierre de Bourdeille, who was commendatory Abbot of Brantôme, is to be distrusted,

since he drew too much from his own benefice to do anything but detest electoral practice as laid down by the Pragmatic and suppressed by the Concordat, which permitted his
holding his fat living. He himself bears witness to what
happened before the Concordat :

The monks usually elected the jolliest fellow among them, the
fondest of women, dogs and birds, the one who was the stoutest
toper, so that, having him for abbot or prior, they could continue
a disorderly life. Others elected a stupid worthy who dared neither
grumble nor give any order that displeased them, and threatened
him if he assumed the airs of a superior. Others, out of pity,
elected some impoverished wretch who secretly robbed and
starved them.

It remains to notice that in the States-General of 1614, a
century after the Bologna agreement, the Third Estate joined
with the Clergy in demanding a reform of the Church of
France under the following heads : the suppression of commends, pensions and reservations ; the convocation at regular
intervals of provincial councils ; the repression of Roman
fiscal exactions ; in short, a reform of precisely those abuses
in the Church caused by the interference of the Pope.

Both parties to the Bologna agreement hastened to make
use of their advantages. Gouffier was forthwith made a
cardinal, and the Papal master of ceremonies was amazed
to hear him, in his joy, burst forth into a drinking song as
he left the consistory at which he was cardinalized. The
family of Chancellor Duprat was well provided for, his
brother Thomas becoming Bishop of Clermont in his native
Auvergne ; while he himself, a widower, took orders, and
was almost submerged in the flood of benefices and titles
which poured upon him. He was made cardinal, Archbishop
of Sens with primary over the Bishop of Paris, Bishop of
Albi, of Valence and of Die, Abbot of Fleury. The King

did not wait for the formal registration of the Concordat to distribute with lavish hand among his favourites the ecclesiastical honours which were now, by a mere stroke of the pen, his to bestow. Thus began that half-clerical, half-ministerial oligarchy which governed France till 1791. As Imbart de la Tour put it, the Church of France became "an instrument of government, a bait, a reward to secure devotion and overcome opposition". Madelin added that "neither Pope nor King in the sixteenth century seems to have seen the curious immorality of their acts, which had for consequence the consecration of what was really simony, the purchase of religious benefices with political services", and "since favouritism became the source of bishoprics, abbeys and all other benefices, simony was taken for granted". The Church of France was handed over to the rule of a camarilla "chosen at Amboise, St. Germain or Versailles".

Many laymen obtained ecclesiastical preferment. Nay, more, husband and wife were settled in monasteries among the monks. Henri III presented the bishoprics of Grenoble and Amiens to a favourite who promptly sold one of them for 30,000 livres to a lady of the court, and the other for 40,000 to a young nobleman. Some benefices, even bishoprics, were given to minors of fourteen or fifteen. Pierre de Bourdeille became Abbot of Brantôme at sixteen, whence the name he has made so famous. Louise de la Béraudière, whom the Court nicknamed "la belle Rouet", was mistress to Antoine de Bourbon, King of Navarre. She bore him a son, whose illustrious parentage procured for him the Archbishopric of Rouen. When her husband, Louis de Madaillan, died, she married Robert de Combaud, Henri III's *maître d'hôtel*, and the King gave them as a wedding-present the bishopric of Cornouailles, which gave rise to many equivocal puns.

Odet de Coligny de Châtillon was made a cardinal in 1533, at eighteen : at nineteen he became Archbishop of Toulouse and Count Bishop of Beauvais, later acquiring in succession the titles of Vidame of Gerberoy, Abbot of Sainte-Euverte d'Orleans, of St. Lucien in Beauvais, of St. Benoît-sur-Loire, of Ste. Croix in Quimperlé, of St. Germer de Ferrières, St. Bénigne in Dijon, Conches, Vauluisant, and Belleperche, Prior of St. Etienne de Beaune and Fresnoy ; after which he turned Huguenot, but continued to wear his cardinal's robes ; hence his name of " Cardinal de Châtillon ".

Francis I made use of the ecclesiastical patronage at his disposal to pay his beloved artists, among them some Italians. Rosso became a canon of the Sainte Chapelle, Primaticcio Abbot of St. Martin de Troyes, Philibert de l'Orme Abbot of Ivry. Their names often appear in the accounts under their ecclesiastical titles. Under Henri II Marshal Strozzi received the bishopric of Bazas and under Henri IV the redoubtable Crillon found himself possessor of two archbishoprics and an abbey. He was no doubt a good fellow and a stout soldier, but he must have made an odd archbishop and abbot. At the same time Sully, whose study was adorned by the portrait of Calvin, possessed five abbeys.

When the States-General of Orleans, in 1560, put forward a measure to effect a compromise between the old elective system of the Pragmatic and the new one inaugurated in 1515, one Joachim du Chalard, a member of the Parlement, made the following remarks on the abuses which sprang from the Concordat :

If either human or divine law had been heeded by those whose profession it is to carry it out, this proposal might be thought superfluous, but the wickedness of the age, human boldness, avarice and the favouritism of the great have corrupted all things. By

favour, by friendship and by the power of money, idiots and
ignorant men hold the fat benefices, the high offices and great
prelacies, most of them bishops before they were born. The people
are unable to restrain their bitter complaints that they are led by
such men, who dare to impose on the nations of God burdens
too heavy to be borne.

In 1617 the Bishop of Aire, Philippe Cospéan, rose in his
wrath to denounce before Louis XII the "bishoprics and
abbeys granted to sucklings at the breast or to children yet
in their mothers' wombs, and benefices granted to laymen".
Richelieu himself followed in the same course : he re-
warded Godeau for a few verses dedicated to him with
the bishopric of Grasse ; Maugars received a monastery for
his skill on the *viola d'amore*. "An abbey," wrote Voltaire,
"was part of a girl's dowry and a colonel mounted his
regiment on the revenues of another."
There were atheistical bishops like Lavardin and evil-
living bishops like de Broc. In the latter days of the old
régime the conditions under which ecclesiastics were nominated had improved, though even under Louis XVI Loménie
de Brienne, Cardinal Archbishop of Toulouse, was held to
be an atheist, while de Rohan, the light-headed hero of the
"diamond necklace" story, though charming and upright,
was a little out of place as Cardinal, Bishop of Strasbourg,
Abbot of St. Vaast and Arras and Abbot of Chaise-Dieu.
The commendatory abbot did not usually live in the
monastery whose revenues he pocketed, but only visited it
when he chose. His only return for his income was the
maintenance of the buildings : if he were conscientious,
they were well kept, if not, ill. Some commendatories did
nothing at all. Anthyme Saint-Paul drew attention, in his
Histoire Monumentale de la France, to the dilapidated state of
certain French cathedrals in the sixteenth century, of which

the primary cause was " the lack of interest of many dissipated and unworthy bishops in their sees, in which they
will not reside, and for the upkeep of which they have to
be forced by process of law, as at Chartres, Agen and St.
Pons, to disgorge a portion of their income ".

Mézeray, a great historian in the true French tradition of
the age of Louis XIV, pronounced the following judgment
on the Concordat :

> The French clergy, the universities, the Parlements, every person
> of standing presented complaints, remonstrances, protests and
> appeals to the next Council against it. After two years the opposi-
> tion had to give way, and the Concordat was registered by the
> Parlement. Thus, on the pretext of removing the inconveniences
> of the electoral system, which might well have been remedied,
> greater and irremediable abuses were authorized.

It seems impossible not to agree with Mézeray, who was
both a great man and well placed to judge the facts of which
he wrote. Even so, his criticisms err on the side of moderation. The conclusion of the Concordat was one of the greatest
and most harmful mistakes made by any French king. It
was fatal both to religion and to the kings whose purposes
it was made to serve, fatal even to France herself. As all
power and all patronage in the Church of France were concentrated in the hands of the Court, there was naturally
formed around the King a clique of ecclesiastical courtiers,
which demanded the absenteeism of the rulers of bishoprics
and monasteries. Brantôme described this priestly Court :
" Francis I was the first to attract to his Court not only
ladies to form a ladies' court, but churchmen. Before his
time the great prelates lived in their dioceses or their abbeys."
These churchmen would no doubt have done better to stay
at home, but the combination of a " Ladies' " and a " Churchmen's " court seemed to strike Brantôme as admirable.

In a general procession I have seen about this great king twenty
or twenty-two cardinals in full canonicals, some French, some
Italian—Trivulzio, Ferrara, Farnese—yet others English, Scotch
and Portuguese . . . The Pope has not so many about him . . .
And in addition, these cardinals were followed by a crowd of
bishops, abbots and protonotaries, and many noblemen who
adorn the royal Court and keep a great number of pages. So that
such honourable prelates distinguish a Court and bring to it much
wealth and profit.

All this is doubtless true, but what was happening to
bishoprics and monasteries in the meantime ? The first serious
abuse arising from the Concordat was the separation of the
higher clergy from the people and from their inferiors, who
were most active and influential in the religious direction
of the country. The consequence of this was afterwards often
to be seen, notably in 1789 at the time of the " Tennis-court
oath ", when many of the delegates of the clergy joined
enthusiastically with the Third Estate and turned the scale
in favour of the Revolution.

The centuries-old traditions of a great people are not to
be broken off with impunity. We have just described the
conscientious revolt of almost the whole of thinking France,
clergy, Parlements and universities. Gallican tradition had
been, ever since the accession of the Capetian dynasty in the
tenth century, deeply anchored in the hearts and minds of
the people. By the Concordat it was shaken to the depths
and the gates were thrown open to irreligion. This forcible
rupture with Gallican tradition produced the bitterness and
cruelty of the wars of religion. In the seventeenth century
Pellisson, in his treatise on religious toleration, observed
that it would be disgraceful to quarrel over questions which
would be buried in oblivion when the heat of the moment
was passed. " The disputes which made so much stir at the

beginning of the schism are now never mentioned, whether it be justification by faith or by works, efficacy of the sacraments or anything else." The enduring question was that of the independence of the Church of France as opposed to Roman supremacy, and this was the real basis of Huguenot obstinacy, of Jansenism, and finally of the civil constitution of the clergy.

Neither Protestantism, nor Jansenism, nor the Civil Constitution would have roused such bitter strife if there had been in France a national instead of a Roman Church. It is even probable that schism would have gained no foothold in France. The activity of the Jesuits—many of them worthy, intelligent and learned men, but devoted solely to Rome—increased the conflagration. Their Order almost monopolized the teaching profession and its members became the confessors and spiritual directors of princes. Hence we have deplorable events such as the Revocation of the Edict of Nantes, which drove so many good men and good Frenchmen into exile ; the hateful persecution of Port-Royal ; the miracles of the deacon Paris, which were finally exposed by the police ; and, finally, the expulsion of the Jesuits and the revolutionary explosion, which was not so much anti-religious as anti-Roman.

Chancellor Duprat and his successors—for the young Francis I was not of an age or of a mind inclined to such speculations—did not realize that Gallicanism had saved the Roman Catholic Church. " It is largely due to Gallicanism," wrote Imbart de la Tour, " that Catholic France passed through the storms of the Reformation without leaving Rome." Ranke, the historian of the Papacy, was of the same opinion. If France had suffered from the abuses of which Germany had to complain, she would doubtless have followed Calvin's standard of rebellion. Luther said : " Why do the Germans allow themselves to be plundered by cardinals who invade every rich foundation and spend its income in Rome ?—the French do not permit it." As early as the end of the thirteenth century Dante had cast his slings and arrows at the trade in Indulgences " with which St. Anthony fattens his pig and many others worse than swine ". The liberties of the Gallican Church had shut out Indulgences as they had shut out the Inquisition. The Emperor Maximilian was so far convinced of the advantages of Gallicanism that he proposed to put its principles into practice in Germany.

England, most of Germany, Switzerland, Holland and Scandinavia broke away from Rome. Rome counted violent enemies even in Italy. What would have happened to Catholicism if France, the greatest and most powerful nation in Europe, had followed ?

XVI

THE REFORMATION

THE Reformation is one of the principal events of
the Renaissance, perhaps the most characteristic of
all, surpassing in importance both humanism and
the transformation of art under the influence of the classical
ideal of beauty. The real point at issue was neither dogma
nor the interpretation of dogma. Dogma represents an abstract
idea, and endless arguments can be carried on " about it
and about ", without either party to them attaining any
further degree of certainty, simply because dogma is purely
theoretical. We have, for example, Montesquieu's Persian
visiting a library. " And what," he asks his companion,
" are the mighty tomes which fill this whole wall ? "—
" Interpretations of the Scriptures."—" The Scriptures must
then have been most obscure, and must now be perfectly
clear. Does any doubt still remain ? "—" Doubt ! Now there
are as many doubts as lines in these books ! "

There exist, to our own knowledge, eight different interpretations of the words of Christ ! " This is my body. . . .
This is my blood." We need only take two of them : the
Catholic, according to which the bread and wine actually
represent the body and blood of Christ, and that of the left
wing of Lutheranism, which maintains that Christ's words
were merely a figure of speech. A library of commentaries
would fail to give scientific proof of either theory.

Politics played as small a part as did dogma in the

Reformation. At the most, religious differences might give rise to plots and intrigues within a Court, but could not thus give rise to events which affect the lives of nations and carry away a whole civilization.

The immediate causes of the Reformation are to be found in the economic sphere, its more distant ones are lost in the dim beginnings of modern history. They vary from country to country, from class to class, family to family, individual to individual.

In our view the primary cause was the great material prosperity of the age and its unequal distribution. The wealth which flowed from Spain to Italy, the Netherlands, France and Germany in exchange for natural products or manufactured goods, brought about in these countries an excess of activity resulting in a vast industrial and commercial expansion. The gold brought from the New World by the galleons of Spain was distributed through every land. The first result was an excess of currency and an increasing ease in the conduct of business, with a proportionate demand for comfort and luxury. A further result of the same cause was its effect, not only on the relations between the productive and leading classes, but on the ruling class itself. The purchasing power of money decreased by some four-fifths, even nine-tenths, thus reducing in that proportion all fixed incomes depending on such things as rents or feudal dues, that is to say, the incomes of the ruling class. The resultant crisis affected every European country and even the Church, while on the other hand the price of corn and wages rose.

From the beginning of the economic change brought about by the industrial and commercial expansion of Europe the Papacy, to obtain funds for the purposes of the Church, to keep up the splendours of the Roman Court, and to provide the sinews of war for the Papal campaigns, had

come to an agreement with Spain, by which, in return for
half the proceeds of the Spanish gaming tax, perpetual absolu-
tion was granted for the almost continuous excesses and
crimes of the conquistadores in America. Then came the
traffic in Indulgences, the income from which was nominally
devoted to the rebuilding of St. Peter's and a crusade against
the Turk. The Dominican monk, Tetzel, who was put in
charge of the arrangements in Germany, went about his
business of releasing souls from Purgatory (for cash down)
with drum and fife and the general stock-in-trade of a cheap-
jack at a fair.

If dogma played any part in the event, it was very small.
Far more important was the critical situation of many of the
princes of the Church, " who toiled not, neither did they
spin ", but lived on rents and dues. Others of the same rank,
whose possessions assured them constant and comfortable
incomes, fell into a scandalous state of moral decadence.
Finally, the great noble families of Rome, ruined by their
lavish expenditure and the devaluation of money, were
constantly demanding abbeys and bishoprics in Germany
and, to a lesser extent, in France, simply so as to draw an
income from them. The whole system of benefices stood
open to abuse. The highest posts in the Church were endowed
with large material incomes which ended, in the minds of
their possessors, by outweighing the offices themselves. These
incomes had at one time been a just reward for the services
attached to them. Monks had brought much waste land into
cultivation. They had long been the torch-bearers of art,
science and literature. Take, for example, the great Abbots
of Cluny, who were simultaneously feudal lords and bishops,
defenders and inspirers of their flock, and the sponsors in
all Europe of the French Romanesque style of architecture.
But by the sixteenth century their task was finished.

" Three hundred years of jokes about the Pope, the morals of monks and the rule of parish priests, is too much," wrote Michelet in his *Introduction to the Renaissance*. His protest is understandable, but it cannot be denied that abuses, particularly among the higher clergy, did play an important part in bringing about the Reformation.

The nobility and the families of ruling princes suffered equally with the Church from the financial crisis. The nobility had not lagged behind the clergy in acquiring the taste for luxury. It might even be maintained that it was from the nobility that luxury spread to the Church. The nobility, however, was much the harder hit. It became a necessity to sell or to pledge ancestral lands in order merely to live, without taking into account the growing demand for luxury.

Usury had till then been prohibited by the Church, but the force of circumstances made its adoption inevitable. Loans at interest became lawful.

The situation was still further complicated by the prohibition of the export of money decreed by the various states. This prohibition was reasonable, as was that which regulated the interest permissible on loans. There were two kinds of export of money, one in exchange for goods bought, which could become a source of wealth, and the other the export of money solely for the advantages to be derived from it as money. This latter form of export had at that time become an insufferable type of usury, since the monetary variations between countries enabled it to produce vast profits without assisting productive labour, and so impoverished the country which fell a victim to it, by reducing the money in circulation without bringing in return raw materials or merchandise, and simply enriching the speculator.

These were the immediate causes of the Reformation : the economic condition of the country, the revolution in personal property, the speculative export of currency, the straitened circumstances of the greater and particularly of the lesser nobility, the financial difficulties of sovereign princes and the heads of the Church, and the industrial and commercial crisis in the towns. According to Jacques Bainville, "The bourgeoisie and the nobility adhered to the Reformation while the country-people, who had remained untouched by the economic crisis, remained unmoved." Balzac made his Charles IX say : "Every man follows his own interests and religious opinion is only a veil for ambition." Guizot, a great historian and a Protestant, held the same view.

The discontent [wrote Lucien Romier] was widespread among craftsmen, bourgeois, nobles and clerics. By increasing the number of posts, the government had annoyed the members of the Parlements and the fiscal and judicial officers, the people most ready to stand by a social order on which their living depends. Only the soldiers were absent from the chorus of protest. It was easy to see that if they were deprived of employment and pay captains and men-at-arms would be capable of grave disorders.

In those countries which had gradually been converted by martyrs and missionaries, Catholic dogma had taken root and was so firmly impressed upon the minds of the people, that neither the misconduct of the dignitaries of the Church nor the sale of Indulgences had any marked effect, or produced any grave scandal. The practice of religion maintained its prestige and its purity ; it was deep-seated in the popular mind, in which it had been handed down from generation to generation, with gradual modifications universally acceptable.

The countries won for Catholicism by force of arms were in quite another category. Saxony was the storm-centre of Protestantism. Charlemagne had instilled Christianity into the heads of the Saxons with his mace. The process seemed satisfactory, but the religion thus assimilated was merely superficial. In the long run the abstract portions of religion have a deeper effect than its concrete traditions. The abuses which were so profitable to the princes of the Church were bound to cause an outburst as soon as the time was ripe. A single spark was enough to ignite the magazine. Dogma was merely the background on which were drawn the interest, the ambitions and the varying passions of this or that social or economic section of the different countries and provinces. There were in addition a thousand separate causes which each had their effect on the ultimate reaction, private hatreds, interests, and ambitions. Here a city would embrace the reformed religion in the hope of freedom from the oppression of a feudal lord ; there the country became Protestant in opposition to the nearest city which exploited it. England was separated from Rome because the Pope declined to pander to the lust of Henry VIII. In other cases the younger branch of a ruling family turned to the new doctrines in opposition to the elder branch which was in power. The struggle thus became ever fiercer and more barbarous, as is ever the case in religious wars, where the most cogent interests of everyday life are mingled with the best, the deepest and the loftiest sentiments of mankind. Excesses, crimes, even the worst of horrors draw a certain grandeur from this source.

The Renaissance came to an end amid the tumult of religious warfare, rendered horrible by the violence of feelings which by their very sincerity hardened the heart of man against man. Details such as follow can alone give an idea of those horrors. On October 4th, 1564, the Parlement of Paris condemned fourteen Huguenots to the stake. The place of execution was fixed at Meaux, and thither the condemned were brought, together with two doctors of the Sorbonne, Picard and Maillart. The two doctors rode on mules like cardinals, one on each side of those about to die, and as they rode exhorted the heretics to repentance. " Get thee behind me, Satan," cried one of them to Picard, " and leave us to think on our God." When they reached Meaux, they were put to the torture. " Courage ! " cried one of them to his tormentors, " spare not this miserable carcase." The next day, the day of execution, the two doctors of the Sorbonne renewed their pious exhortations. " Confess and you will be spared the cutting off of your hands." Six of the poor wretches gave way, the others were resolute. The executioner cut out the tongue of the first, who tried to murmur " God be praised " with the mutilated stump. Then he and the rest were dragged on sledges to the stake and burnt alive, while the worthy doctors intoned the Salutaris and the Salve Regina.

It is not surprising that two parties, roused one against the other by the heights of faith on one side and the depths of abhorrence on the other, should have committed the wildest excesses under colour of beneficence and virtue. Such men were to be found in both camps, and neither can cast a stone at the other. The same intolerance that animated the Inquisition is to be found in the writings of Luther, Calvin and Zwingli. It was in vain that wise men of good-will such as the Chancellor de l'Hôpital endeavoured to appease the strife ; it was in vain that skilful and intelligent rulers like Catherine dei Medici tried to keep it within bounds. The famous Huguenot reformer Théodore de Bèze held the doctrine of the freedom of conscience to be a " damnable heresy ". Jeanne d'Albret banished all Catholics from her domains, as did Calvin from Geneva and Luther from the Electorate of Saxony.

The following is Montaigne's description of the wars of religion, drawn from his *Essays*.

" Every Frenchman in every hour sees his fortune on the point of being overthrown. A thousand times have I gone to bed in the fear that I would be betrayed and slaughtered that very night." He held it for a miracle that his house " should have remained so long free from the taint of blood, in so long a tempest, so many changes and troubles near by ". The ruffianliness of his age appalled him. " The customs in common use are so savage in their inhumanity and treachery that I dare not think of them without horror."

The principal obstacle to the spread of the Reformation in the greater part of France was the fact that its essentials did not conform to the national genius. Pierre de Vaissière put it strongly : " Protestantism was bound to be rejected by the country itself, whose heart and soul were repelled by the reformed doctrines." In his history of English literature, Taine defined the Reformation as " a Renaissance suited to the genius of the Germanic people "—the converse of de Vaissière's remark.

Renan has very justly and sensibly pointed out that religion was full of good things " which we ourselves put into it ". A religion is the rich, vivid and powerful expression of the moral traditions of a nation, the mirror of its soul, the highest and the visible expression of its moral aspirations.

Francis I showed remarkable tolerance of the new opinions, in which he was encouraged by his hostility to the fanatically intolerant Spaniards. On June 2nd, 1528, however, a statue of the Virgin and Child in a niche in the doorway of the Church of Petit-St. Antoine in St. Germain-des-Prés was badly mutilated. The King, according to a witness, felt this sacrilege as a personal insult. He was as enraged as if it had been an affront to his own mother. The mutilated figure was replaced by another of silver which the King himself piously and humbly placed on its pedestal in the presence of the city fathers and the members of the Parlement. The cult of Mary, at once Virgin and Mother, was perhaps the masterpiece of French genius in its most chivalric mani- festations. It is thus easy to imagine the feelings of revolt and deep indignation aroused by repetitions of this kind of sacrilege all over France at a time when this cult was so deeply rooted in the hearts of the people.

Petit de Julleville has said that the Calvinist reformers reduced religion to sermons. Calvin preached almost every day. About two thousand of his sermons are known and the total number is certainly much higher, but France was saved, not by sermons, but by the beauty of religious ceremonies, the host gleaming white in the golden monstrance, the incense rising to the lofty vaults of cathedrals glowing in the rainbow hues of their windows, the splendour of priestly robes in the harmonious rhythms of the Mass, the statues and images of the saints Christopher and Anthony, Catherine and that Marguerite whose vision inspired Joan of Arc.

The worthy Brantôme was amazed at the idea of exchanging ceremonies for sermons.

Blessed were our fathers of former days [he wrote] when they were kept in simple ignorance and spared the sermons that swarm to-day. Since this madness for preachments and preachers there has been naught but heresy and strife in France instead of belief and following of the commandments of God and the Church, which the simple parish priest could recall to their minds every Sunday at the same time that he announced the holidays for the week and administered the sacraments.

We may sum up in the words of Petit de Julleville : " The Renaissance triumphed in France and Italy, where the Reformation failed, while the Renaissance was stifled wherever the Reformation succeeded."

Humanism had indeed helped Luther and Calvin, but their unadorned and sermon-burdened religion was not calculated to call forth the splendours of art or the lofty flights of poetry. The masterpiece of Renaissance as of mediæval art had been the Virgin in every mood and form, the Virgin of Botticelli, Correggio, Ghirlandaio and a hundred others, the splendid stone Virgins of French cathedrals which the Huguenots condemned and mutilated.

> Stabat mater dolorosa
> Juxta crucem lacrimosa
> Dum pendebat filius . . .

All this, and with it the plain-chant or the music of Pergolesi, was to be suppressed. "Wherever the Protestants were strong, churches were profaned, altars overturned, there was pillage, massacre and destruction of images, books and precious vessels" (Charles Merki).

XVII

CATHERINE DEI MEDICI

CATHERINE DEI MEDICI said in 1586 to the
Vicomte de Turenne, representative of the Protestant
court of Béarn : " The King desires but one religion
in his realm."—" We also," replied Turenne, " but our
own."

Like Francis I, Catherine had been in her early days a
zealous supporter of the doctrines of tolerance and mutual
respect—peace to men of good-will—but the pressure of
events drove her to take repressive measures.

She was born in 1519 at Florence in a palace on the Via
Longa built by Michelozzo Michelozzi. The portrait of her
father Lorenzo has become famous. He is the thinker whose
steady eyes beneath the golden helmet have been immortalized
by Michael Angelo's brush. Her mother was a Frenchwoman,
Madeleine de la Tour, Countess of Auvergne and Lauraguais.
Her mother died in giving birth to her, and her father, the
Duke of Urbino, only survived his wife by a few weeks,
dying at twenty-eight. She was thus left an orphan and a
duchess at the age of twenty-two days. Ariosto addressed
to her some famous lines : " One single branch is green
again with a few leaves. I hover between hope and fear,
asking whether winter will leave or take it."

The child spent her earliest years under the care of Cardinal
Giulio dei Medici, Legate in Tuscany, to whom Leo X,
himself a Medici, had entrusted the government of Florence.

This Giulio dei Medici was later to decide her fate, since it was he, as Clement VII, who arranged her marriage to the son of Francis I. She passed her first years at play in the gloomy, narrow-windowed palace, among the golden marbles of ancient Greece which Michael Angelo came to copy.

She left Florence at the time of the troubles in 1527, when the Medici fell, their coat of arms was broken, and the statues of Leo X and Clement VII were overthrown. She was taken to the famous convent of the " Murati " (the " walled in "), where she was well received and made a favourite. Meanwhile, the troops of Clement VII were marching on the rebellious city, and the siege began on October 24th, 1529. The anger of the Florentines struck at the child. She was too well treated and not well enough guarded with the Murati. She was taken away and placed in Santa Lucia till the time when Florence was compelled to open its gates to the Papal troops. The Pope thereupon removed to Rome the niece on whom henceforward the ambitions and hopes of the family were centred.

A contemporary described her, at thirteen, as gracious, affable and uncommonly distinguished. She was small and rather thin, but coarse-featured. Her eyes were prominent, like those of all the Medici. She was brought up in Rome with her cousin Ippolito dei Medici, who was painted by Titian. The young prince was a fine horseman and made a good figure in tournaments. He was also a poet and translator of Virgil, and a good performer on the organ and the lute. The Duchess fell in love with him, but when Clement VII heard of it he sent her away from Rome, back to Florence.

The Pope had great ambitions for his niece, which were gratified when Francis I asked for her hand for his second son, Henri d'Orléans. Francis was then in the midst of his struggle with Charles V ; the sympathies of the Pope might be of value to him, and, as we have seen, he sought every opportunity to bring France and Italy into closer relations.

Francis I, accompanied by his son, reached Marseilles on October 8th, 1533. Catherine made her entry in great state on October 23rd, riding a chestnut hackney with trappings of gold. The wedding was celebrated on October 27th, the bridegroom and bride each being fourteen years old.

At fifteen the young princess was plunged into the life of the French Court, far from her own people. How did this daughter of " Florentine grocers ", as malicious tongues described her, figure beside Eléonore, wife of Francis I and daughter of Charles V ? All her contemporaries agree in praising her gentle and insinuating cleverness. She became tenderly attached to her husband. She tried to win the sympathy of Francis I, and to please him went hunting and took up the study of Greek and Latin.

In August 1536 her fortunes were subjected to another sudden change ; the death of the Dauphin left her husband heir to the throne and herself prospective Queen of France. She was then only seventeen. Her position was not thereby rendered easier. The daughter of the " Florentine grocers " had not been chosen for her fitness to be Queen. Clement VII died without fulfilling the hopes that the Valois had placed in him, and years went by without Catherine producing an heir. A party was formed about the Court whose avowed object was to " send back the little Florentine girl to her shop ". Among her defenders was Marguerite de Navarre, sister of Francis I.

Catherine gave a foretaste of the political skill she was later to display by the way in which she dealt with this difficult situation. According to the Venetian ambassador Contorini, she went straight to Francis I and told him that she had heard of his intention to provide his son with another wife and that, since it had not pleased God to give her children, she thought it only right that a successor to such a throne as that of France should be by all means assured. As for herself, she was too conscious of the honour the King had done her by his choice not to be prepared to bear the grief of separation rather than displease him, and that she was ready either to enter a nunnery or to remain in the service of her husband's new wife. The Dauphin interrupted her words with sobs and tears.

Francis I was a man of noble feelings. He raised the girl to her feet and said with feeling : "Daughter, since it is God's will that you should be my daughter-in-law and the Dauphin's wife, I would not have it otherwise and perhaps God will grant your wish and mine."

As it fell out, after ten years of waiting, Catherine gave birth on January 15th, 1544, to the first of the ten children she was to give her husband.

Marguerite de Navarre wrote at once to her brother :

Your eyes, I am sure, are full of tears at a joy even greater than that at the birth of your first-born, since this present birth was longer awaited and with less hope. Now I behold your kingdom strengthened as by a hundred thousand men, enriched with infinite treasure. I must be very ill indeed if I were not so far cured as to join the procession of people going to light bonfires.

Three years later, on March 31st, 1547, Francis I died. Catherine dei Medici, at twenty-seven, was Queen of France.

"When Francis I lay on his death-bed," wrote a contemporary, "a woman lay sobbing and desolate. She was Catherine dei Medici. Was it affection for the King that caused her grief ? No, she wept for herself and the fate which awaited her." As Queen of France, she still remained in the background, the Court being dominated by Diane de Poitiers, who was twenty years her senior.

Catherine showed herself a devoted mother, watching over the smallest details of her children's education. She writes letters about their diet and their clothing. She was their first governess. "The Queen," wrote the Cardinal of Lorraine, "takes her two daughters with her, thinking it best to have them sleep in her apartments in the nearest room possible to herself."

She was as good a wife as mother. She loved Henri II with a deep and blind devotion. She wrote to the Constable : "You know my affection for the King and his service is so great that I consider nothing else, and I would sooner die than think he would disapprove of my actions." Later, after the King's death, she wrote to her daughter, now Queen of Spain :

Commit yourself to the care of God, for you have known me happy as you are, never thinking of any other trouble but that the King your father should not love me sufficiently. He honoured me above my deserts, but still, as you know, I had always that fear till God removed it.

Catherine, like the King, rose at seven. While the King gave audience to his counsellors, the Queen dictated her voluminous correspondence to her secretaries. Such of her letters, as are extant—and most of them are certainly lost— are counted by the thousand, and a large number of them are in her own hand.

At ten the Court attended Mass. Only at eleven, when they left the chapel, was the first meal taken, after which audiences filled the time till two in the afternoon. Then came what was called "the Queen's circle", often joined by the King. Afterwards, if the weather was fine, the King played tennis and the Queen went out : if wet, the King played cards or dice and Catherine embroidered, while some

work of literature or science was read to her. At six, dinner :
twice a week, balls.

Brantôme depicted Catherine thus :

> She was a fine figure and very majestic, very gentle when it
> was requisite, good-looking and graceful ; a beautiful face and
> full white bosom ; her hands were the most beautiful I have ever
> seen . . . Her son Henri III inherited these beautiful hands.

He also spoke of her love of needlework. " She spent her
time after dinner in working in silks, in which she had the
most perfect skill."

Thus she presided over the Court of France, or rather
revived and animated it to a splendour till then unknown.
Around her thronged churchmen and nobles in gay attire,
three hundred maids and matrons of honour, each more
beautiful than the last—" the Queen's flying squadron "—
and she saw to it that they were always well dressed in good
taste. " The noblemen of France," said Shakespeare at this
time, " show exquisite taste in dress and a most judicious
tact." And Brantôme wrote :

> The Court of Catherine dei Medici was indeed an earthly
> paradise and school of beauty, an ornament to France. Catherine
> cultivated a distinction and politeness of conversation and manners
> which were handed down after her. I do not believe that she
> brought them with her from Italy, which she left at the age of
> fourteen, but rather that she learnt them from Francis I and his
> sister Marguerite de Navarre, and afterwards perfected them by
> her own personal taste and qualities . . .
> The chamber of Catherine dei Medici, where she gave her
> concerts, was open to every person of breeding. Her ante-chamber
> was not less alluring, being filled with fair young girls with whom
> to talk and pass the time.

Seats were of various heights, making the assembly infinitely more picturesque. The maids of honour, who be-

longed to the best families of the kingdom, sat on cushions on the floor, so that their gay frocks spread out round them like so many gleaming flowers strewn about the room. In the inventory of the effects of Catherine are mentioned more than four hundred of these cushions of various shapes and attractive colouring, kept for this purpose.

We must picture the rooms of the period, painted throughout in bright colours relieved with gilding from the wainscot to the ceiling, which was panelled or cut up by open beams. Or, it may be, the walls hung with Cordovan leather in bright hues, decorated with festoons of flowers and arabesques on a ground of dull gold. The floors were covered with oriental carpets imported by the Queen from Venice. All the furniture was brightly painted and gilt. The apartments in the Louvre must have been a kaleidoscopic harmony of brilliant hues, whose own brightness was subdued by their very number. Nothing struck a jarring note, though each individual tone in itself was striking. Men and women alike went gorgeously clad, in silks, brocades and cut velvets, in lace and jewels and cloths of silver and of gold, and always the same bright colouring. Every face was painted with the crudest of reds. Servants, pages and ushers alike were clothed in a startling livery of parti-coloured red and yellow or green and white. The young nobles wore slit sleeves and puffed hose through which appeared the scarlet or bright yellow of the under-garment, to contrast with the white or pale green of the outer one. The spectacle must have been incomparably splendid in its life and harmony. As Brantôme said, "The world has never seen its like."

It was on this account that the historian de Thou called Catherine " the woman of superb luxury ". She was certainly the richest of French queens.

Amid the feastings which she honoured with her presence

Catherine was developing the mind of a statesman. It was in tragic circumstances that she first revealed what lay beneath her pose of luxurious ease. In 1557 the French army under Montmorency was beaten beneath the walls of St. Quentin. No defensive force remained between the enemy and the capital. A thrill of terror passed through all Paris. It was a dramatic moment in French history, when Henry II wrote to the great Duc de Guise his famous words : " There is nothing to be done save to keep up heart and fear nothing."

Henri II left for Compiègne to attempt to raise a new army. The Queen was left alone in Paris. She succeeded in rallying the terrified people with the cry of " France is in danger ", which inspired instead of further discouraging them. Of her own accord she convoked the Parlement and attended its sittings. She spoke of the country's need and the King's efforts, and of the anguish and also the pride and confidence which should fill all hearts. " The Queen," reported the Venetian ambassador, " spoke with such feeling and eloquence that all hearts were touched." The Parlement, filled with enthusiasm, unanimously voted the required subsidies ; the notables gave 300,000 livres. Then the Queen offered her thanks. " She spoke," said an eye-witness, " with such a combination of gentleness and vigour that tears came to every eye." The Venetian ambassador added, " The sitting ended with such applause for the Queen, and such open satisfaction with her conduct as can hardly be imagined ; her virtues are the talk of the town."

France was saved and the enemy driven beyond the frontiers. The Treaty of Cateau-Cambrésis gave peace to the land, but only two months later followed a second catastrophe which completely altered Catherine's life—the death of the King.

On June 30th, 1559, at a tournament held at the palace of the Tournelles in honour of the marriage of Elisabeth de

Valois, Henri II was to break a lance with the Comte de Montgomery, described by Vieilleville as " a tall and stout youth ". The King took the blow full in the breast : the shock was so great that the lance flew into fragments, one of which knocked up the visor of his helmet and pierced his eye. " I am dying," he murmured as he was carried from the scene. After a moment's silence he added : " No harm is to come to Montgomery ; the blow was a fair one and I forgive him." The Queen, who had been watching the tournament, lay in a swoon.

Henri, equally gifted in character and in intelligence, died at the age of forty, at the moment when France most needed a strong hand to direct its destinies. Catherine lay a whole day, unconscious and unmoving, at the foot of the death-bed. Then she retired to her chamber, there to remain for many weary weeks.

The room in which she took refuge was thus described by the Venetian ambassador :

It was entirely furnished in black, even to the floor. It was lighted only by two candles burning on an altar draped in black. The Queen's bed-hangings were of the same hue. Her Majesty wore garments of the severest cut, a black robe and train, relieved only by an ermine collar. The Queen of Scotland, now Queen of France (Mary Stuart), was in the same room, but dressed from head to foot in white. Then there were Madame Marguerite, the late King's sister and wife of the Duke of Savoy, and the Princesses of France, the Queen of Spain, the Duchess of Lorraine and their young sister Marguerite, all dressed in white, which they were made to wear for forty days.

The ambassador presented to the Queen the condolences of the Republic of Venice.

The Queen replied [he wrote] in the name of her suite, but her voice was so feeble and shaken with emotion that no one could hear what she said, however attentively they listened, since, in addition to the weakness of her voice, she wore a veil which entirely covered her face.

She was to keep this mourning attire throughout her life. Catherine dei Medici was the first Queen of France to wear black in mourning for her husband, in place of the customary white, which had given the Queens-dowager of France their name of "White Queens".

The dying King had forgiven Montgomery, but Catherine's hatred pursued him none the less. Montgomery threw himself into the Protestant revolt. He was besieged in the castle of Domfront and capitulated on the assurance that his life and property were to be untouched. The Queen had been waiting for her moment. Montgomery was brought before the Parlement and sentenced to lose his head. Catherine insisted on watching the execution.

The new King Francis II was fifteen and a half years old, and, according to the traditions of the monarchy, of age. He had married Mary Stuart, a little feather-headed girl, who had once spoken of her mother-in-law as the "merchant's daughter". The sneer was repeated and a hostility awakened which now grew more marked. Francis II was devoted to his pretty wife, and Catherine was the most jealous of women where her maternal authority was concerned. Balzac has described the quarrel which ensued.

Without any suspicion of the tempest of ambition which stirred in the Florentine, the pretty elfin-faced Scots girl perceived that the advancement of her uncle, the Duc de Guise (in whose hands Francis II had placed the executive power), was a source of concealed rage to Catherine. Nothing amused her more than to spy on her mother-in-law, in whom she saw a busybody and a fallen parvenue only desirous of revenge. The faces of the pair were quite different: the one, grave and gloomy, almost terrible in its Italian pallor, which in daylight resembles ivory yellowed with age, but glows with life when the candles are lighted : the other fresh and merry. At sixteen Mary's hair was of the light gold for which she was famous. Her fresh and piquant countenance, her finely-cut features, sparkled with childish malice, which found expression in her regular eyebrows, her lively glance and her pouting lips. Her grace, the grace of a young kitten, remained unchanged throughout her captivity, enduring even to the steps of the scaffold.

The two queens, one in the spring, the other in the summer of life, formed a complete contrast. Catherine was the stately Queen, the enigmatic widow, living only for power : Mary was a frivolous, care-free bride, treating her crowns as playthings. The one foresaw immense disasters, already speculating on the murder of the Guises as the only means of laying low those who might rise above Crown and Parlement ; the other had as yet no inkling that she was the destined victim of a judicial murder.

We have already described the violence of the wars of religion. The Valois held the throne, but at the moment they were represented by sickly children, controlled by their mother. The younger branch of Bourbon-Condé watched the throne with envious eyes, ready to spring if occasion offered. They had become the leaders of the Huguenot movement, to which they brought the prestige of their family and the valour of the Prince de Condé. The Catholics, on the other hand, had found leaders in the Guises, princes from Lorraine who claimed descent from Charlemagne, and were also awaiting the moment when they could bring back into their family the crown of France, of which, as they maintained, they had been most unjustly deprived.

The position of the Guises was immeasurably strengthened by the two great men who were at that time heads of the family, the Cardinal of Lorraine and his brother, " the great Guise ". The ambassador Ricasoli wrote of the Cardinal of Lorraine that he was " Pope and King ". He was thirty-seven, cultured, clever and eloquent. The Venetian ambassador called him " the best political mind of his age ". His brother, François Duc de Guise, was one of the finest soldiers France produced before Napoleon. He had saved Metz for France by forcing Charles V to retreat, and had performed an equal feat in his surprise attack on Calais which had won it from the English. When the great soldier passed through the streets of Paris in his doublet of white satin laced with gold, the whole of France was stirred and the people acclaimed their real sovereign.

François de Guise and his brother dominated the young king Charles IX, and their authority was increased after the conspiracy of Amboise (March 1560), when the vigilance of the great soldier outwitted a party of Protestants, led by La Renaudie, who had planned to carry off King, Queen Mother and the whole Court. This conspiracy, the bloody vengeance that followed it, and the intervention of England, who considered the time ripe for intervention in the internal affairs of France, all combined to increase the violence of the disturbances and the seriousness of the calamities which ensued from them. On the morrow of the conspiracy of Amboise, Throckmorton, English Ambassador in Paris, a fanatical hater of France, wrote to Queen Elizabeth : " The time has come to scatter your money : it will never be spent to better purpose."

If the Protestants recruited their strength from England, Holland and Germany, the Catholics relied on Spanish support, and while the two parties thus tore asunder their own country, it was Catherine, the Florentine, who stood for France. Her policy was at first in word and deed all for peace, unity and conciliation, as was shown by her choice of Michel de l'Hôpital as Chancellor of the Kingdom. He was the Queen's man, and it was as interpreter of her mind that he told the States-General of 1560 : " Let us keep the name of Christians and suppress the names of Lutheran, Huguenot and Papist, which stand only for party and sedition."

It was in this spirit, and in spite of the opposition of the higher clergy and the Sorbonne, that Catherine decided to call the famous " Colloquy of Poissy ". Desgallards, a Protestant, wrote of it to Throckmorton : " The King, the Queen, and the Princes have been pleased to preside over this argument. The Doctors of the Sorbonne who came to-day to St. Germain to oppose it have been unsuccessful." Catholics and Protestants were each to send their foremost speakers to endeavour to find a common ground for compromise, but only the Queen and her minister were sincere in their desire to find it.

On December 5th, 1560, Catherine described the situation in a letter to her daughter, the Queen of Spain : " God took your father whom I loved from me and left me with these small children in a Kingdom divided against itself, without any in whom I could put my trust, with none but had their own private interests."

To the ambassador Chantonnay, who told her that the ill-health of which she complained was due to over-eating of melons, cucumbers and other fruits, she replied : " The melons and fruits which cause my sickness are not grown in gardens."

Events followed one another rapidly, the massacre of Wassy (March 1st, 1562), the battle of Dreux (19th December), and finally the murder of François de Guise by Poltrot de Méré (February 18th, 1563). This last made a deep impression on Catherine's mind. She insisted on questioning the assassin herself, and, immediately afterwards, wrote to the Duchess of Savoy :

He confessed to having had a hundred crowns from Admiral Coligny to do the deed. He said that he did not wish to come, but that Bèze and another preacher had harangued him and assured him that he would go to heaven if he did it, and that the Admiral had sent sixty men to kill M. de Guise, the Duc de Montpensier, Sansac, Sipierre and the Queen, and that she would do well to have herself and her children guarded, for the Admiral hated her infinitely.

Were Poltrot de Méré's confessions sincere ? It is hard to believe so great a man as Gaspard de Coligny guilty of such a crime. Catherine, however, believed them. Her fear of the great Huguenot leader was henceforth to become an obsession which grew in strength as Coligny's authority in the Kingdom reached a pitch at which it might counterbalance the royal power.

Nevertheless Catherine gave one more proof of her magnanimity and conciliatory spirit when she concluded, on March 22nd, 1563, the peace of Amboise, which should have satisfied everyone and, in fact, satisfied nobody.

In September 1567 there was another Huguenot plot to kidnap the Court, this time from the château of Montceaux. Catherine was warned in time to take refuge within the walls of Meaux, but she was deeply stirred. "Never," she wrote to the Duke of Savoy, "could I have believed that such unhappy plans could spring from the hearts of subjects against their King."

This plot, which brought her into the orbit of schemes such as had led to the murder of Guise, was to have a dreadful influence on future events. Catherine had reached a state in which every day she feared to be carried off, perhaps murdered.

The massacre of St. Bartholomew took place on the night of August 24th, 1572. Paris was in tumult : the country within a hair's-breadth of a new explosion which would have led to civil war. The Queen, goaded past endurance by the failure of so many efforts at conciliation, lost her head. Her intention and that of her advisers, the Duc d'Anjou, afterwards Henri III, Birague, Nevers, Tavanne and Gondi, was only to kill Coligny and the other Protestant leaders then in Paris. Charles IX was not admitted to their councils. The popular passions, once unleashed, went far beyond what had been intended and there was general massacre and looting.

On October 1st, 1572, Catherine wrote to the French ambassador in Venice :

I have seen what you wrote to me of the opinion of certain persons that what has happened to Admiral Coligny and his followers was instigated by me and my son the Duc d'Anjou, and of what they have said to you of the harm it has done my son in the eyes of the Protestant princes who all desired to elect him Emperor of Germany. I therefore think it meet to inform you that I have neither done, counselled nor permitted aught but what honour, duty and the love I bear my children commanded me, because the Admiral, since the death of my lord the late King Henri, has shown by his deeds and bearing that he desired the overthrow of this kingdom and the usurpation of the crown of my son the King, to whom, as you know, it lawfully belongs, and because he, instead of avowing himself a subject, did so establish and make himself great within this kingdom that his powers and commandments over those of his faith were equal to the King's, and so far that, being a rebel against his King, he took by force, in the presence of the King and his brother, towns which were held against him and did not hesitate to fight several battles, by which he was the cause of the death of very many people.

Furthermore, since the late peace and edict of pacification he has so grievously conspired against the persons of the King and his brother and my own person, as will soon be proved to the satisfaction of foreign princes and all others at the trial which has now commenced and will soon be decided in the Court of the Parlement of Paris, that I am certain that it will be said that my son the King has only acted within his rights as a sovereign prince, and that the Admiral, strong and powerful as he was in this realm, could not otherwise be punished for his rebellion and disobedience but in the manner after which he and his party have been treated. The King is greatly troubled that in the heat of the moment certain others of the religion were slain by the Catholics, who called to mind infinite evils, robberies and other wicked acts committed upon them during the troubles ; but now at last, all is peaceful, so that there is recognized only one king and one justice rendered to all alike according to duty and equity, since the King is resolved, in view of the evils caused by the diversity of religions, to suffer none but his own.

The reproduction *in extenso* of this letter is justified by its interest as an explanation by the Queen Mother, its instigator, of the massacre of St. Bartholomew, and of the policy which she and her son felt themselves bound to follow in the future.

Henri III succeeded his brother Charles IX on May 30th, 1574. He had always been his mother's favourite. The Venetian ambassador said of him in one of his dispatches : " He is the apple of his mother's eye."

Balzac thus depicted Catherine dei Medici at that time :

Although the habit of dissimulation, as much as advancing age, had given Catherine the abbess-like mask, at once haughty and ascetic, expressionless and profound, discreet yet searching, which so strikes the eye in her portrait, yet the assiduous courtier could see a certain cloudiness in this Florentine mirror. No Queen was ever more stately than she. Her black velvet head-dress, with its widow's peak (for she never went out of mourning for Henri II), gave a touch of femininity to her face, cold and vigorous at all times, though she had the art of investing it with a charm wholly Italian.

Her greatest sorrows were to fall upon her in the reign of her favourite son. One after another she saw her four sons die. They had been the repositories of her most cherished hopes, as she herself had been to her uncles Leo X and Clement VII. The survivor of them all had himself no heir. The power which she had so tenaciously coveted slipped from her hands the moment it lay within their grasp. Henri III was jealous of her authority and ceased to consult her. The murder of the second " Balafré ", Henri de Guise, son of François, which took place against her wishes, was a grave affront to her. The second " Balafré " had gained in France, and particularly in Paris, a popularity which equalled that of his illustrious father, and his power had become a menace to the royal authority. He was murdered on December 23rd, 1588, in the château of Blois, by order of Henri III. Catherine recoiled in horror when her son came to tell her the news. In the evening of her life all the blood that she had shed seemed to call aloud for vengeance.

A few days after the murder the Cardinal de Bourbon met her in a gallery of the château. He was dressed all in red. " Ah ! Madame, this was another of your strokes ; you will kill us all."

Catherine protested with all her strength, then suddenly weakened : " I can bear no more, I must go to bed."

She died on January 5th, 1589, aged seventy, amid general indifference. " She was made no more of than a dead dog," wrote an author of the time.

Balzac's verdict was more generous :

When I realized the difficulties of her position I recognized how unjust history had been to her. She possessed in the highest degree the mental attributes of royalty, which she defended with laudable courage and pertinacity.

As Catherine herself had once written to the Spanish Ambassador : " My principal aim has always been to guard the realm and to see that it did not fall into discontent and division."

XVIII

THE RENAISSANCE AND THE
REVOLUTION

THE rule of Catherine dei Medici may well be said
to mark the end of the French Renaissance.

It remains to determine the actual nature of this
Renaissance. It has been defined in a multiplicity of conflicting ways, each inspired by different opinions and varying
with the points of view of individual writers. The most
frequent mistake has been the consideration from a purely
artistic standpoint of the sweeping change which passed over
Western Europe at the end of the fifteenth and beginning
of the sixteenth centuries. The preceding pages may have
chronicled a deeper and more varied sequence of cause and
effect. The artistic element is indubitably there, and should
not be passed over, but it has already been shown that the
Reformation was one of the main facts of the Renaissance.
No less important are the social and political transformations.

The political changes were produced by a general tendency
toward centralization due to the decadence of local authorities,
and by the birth of national feeling. The social changes were
caused by that separation of the classes which sprang from
the same weakening in local authority. Then there was the
judicial change, the extension of written law and the replace-
ment, particularly in Germany, of customary by Roman
law.

Even in the artistic sphere the most diverse opinions find

expression. Some writers, indeed most, see in Renaissance art a return to classical and in particular to Roman tradition. Nevertheless, Louis Courajod, a scholar who has made a deep study of the arts, sees in it a return to the observation and study of nature in place of the imitation of traditional forms.

Classical art [he writes] remained a dead letter to the Italian Gothic artists till the day when naturalism first freed them from the shackles of tradition and then enlightened them as to the value, the meaning, and the possibility of assimilating that art.

In the same way there is no agreement as to which country was the birthplace of the Renaissance. Walter Pater, an Englishman, Louis Courajod, a Frenchman, and a learned Swedish professor, Johan Nordström, all eminent scholars, hold that the origins of the Renaissance are to be found in France. Pater wrote in the Preface to his Renaissance :

. . . the Renaissance ends also in France, in French poetry, in a phase of which the writings of Joachim du Bellay are in many ways the most perfect illustration ; the Renaissance thus putting forth in France an aftermath, a wonderful later growth, the products of which have to the full that subtle and delicate sweetness which belongs to a refined and comely decadence ; just as its earliest phases have the freshness which belongs to all periods of growth in art, the charm of ἀσχῆσις, of the austere and serious girding of the loins in youth.

The latest historian of the period, Johan Nordström, professor in the University of Upsala, likewise wrote : " The traditional idea that the Italian Renaissance was the influence which moulded our civilization stands in need of complete revision."

We have stressed the importance of economic conditions in the upheaval of the western world, and the preponderant power assumed by money in social life. The mediæval Church had declared money to be a curse ; it now became respectable.

The first characteristic of the Renaissance is a great re-action against the social, political, intellectual and artistic life of the Middle Ages, that is to say, of the period immediately preceding it. The word " reaction " exactly describes the process. Nordström has very clearly shown how much the men of the Renaissance, and particularly the artists and writers, owe to the Middle Ages, and especially the Middle Ages in France. Their work is none the less a determined reaction against the very past which had produced them.

In this respect there is a close parallel between the Renaissance and the Revolution of 1789. In both cases there was the same reaction, directed against the same objects. There was the same centralization, the same attack on clerical abuses, in the arts the same return to classical models, which in painting went so far as to fill the modern canvas with figures modelled on classical statues.

The Revolution, like the Renaissance, placed the middle classes in power, and both periods accentuated class distinctions. Both were distinguished by a sudden spirit of scientific progress, both had the same " touching confidence in the power of reason and the approach of a century of light and progress " (Petit de Julleville).

Both periods produced nationalist movements. Luther, in his contempt for " die Wälschen ", caused the first stirrings of a national spirit in Germany, which the Emperor Maximilian endeavoured to cultivate, " making dearer to every man the soil of his Fatherland ". The Pope sought to drive the French from Italy with the cry of " Out with the barbarians ", and the glow of patriotic sentiment of a later day is already found in the armies which defended the French frontiers in Flanders and Germany.

Though I am recovered from my fright [wrote Rabelais] I am not yet happy—seeing that there has as yet been no success worthy the attempt—and when I consider, throughout the realm of France, on both sides of the Alps, all men diligently training and working, some at the fortification and defence of their country, others in repelling or attacking the enemy, and all so well planned and marvellously organized, with such evident advantage for the future, for in future France will set her frontiers proudly wide and Frenchmen live in peace and security.

There was the same development of bureaucratic rule in both Renaissance and Revolution.

Finally there is the spirit of intolerance. Philip II of Spain and Calvin, the dictator of Geneva, two men as much alike in mind as opposite in position, are exact parallels to Saint-Just and Robespierre. The fearful intolerance of both periods was due to precisely the same causes, centralization and unification of a country subject to one government, governed by one law, one belief and one ideal.

Luther speaks and writes as Marat would have done in his position : the world is full of robbers, and highwaymen are the least guilty among them. The bankers and great merchants are much more to be feared, as robbers on a larger scale. Even worse are the lawyers ; but the worst criminals of all are the priests. Luther wrote to a friend in 1521 : " You know that if any man's earthly possessions ought to be destroyed, it should be those of princes, since it is hardly possible to be a prince without being a robber ; the greater the prince, the greater the robber." The gentle Philip Melancthon, Luther's faithful friend and helper, himself said : " Many men join Luther, not for his religious opinions, but because they see in him the restorer of liberty." They would have found it difficult to define this liberty they so eagerly desired.

A. H. Heinrich has said that " at the end of the eighteenth as at the beginning of the sixteenth century words were everything ". From this standpoint the Reformers offer a striking parallel to the philosophers who derive from Rousseau. They destroy time-honoured and useful realities to make way for abstract theories and nonsensical phrases.

We can fill in a few details on this background. As we have said, there was a reaction against the past. " France," wrote Louis Gillet of the Renaissance, " allowed itself the luxury of beginning again from the beginning." The Renaissance disowned the civilization which had gone before, and only saw a gulf of barbarism between itself and antiquity. As Rabelais said, " From the thick Gothic night our eyes awaken to the glorious light of the sun." Erasmus, in other respects wise and moderate, described the Middle Ages as " a time of darkness, of intellectual slavery ". Again, in the seventeenth century, Fénélon could say : " We have hardly left a state of appalling barbarism."

The Renaissance, like the Revolution, carried out a task of centralization. In the course of the fifteenth century thirteen new territories were added to the French Crown, and the royal power grew not only in extent, but in vigour. For this popular tendencies were more responsible than was the activity or policy of the monarchy. The nation demanded a closer contact with the King as a counter to the tyranny of the local ruler. The same tendencies aided Henry VIII in England, Charles V in Germany and Francis I in France. The Venetian envoy to France maintained that the royal authority there was stronger than it had ever been. No previous ruler had known the people so obedient or so solidly behind him. Thus he was able, by the famous ordinance of Villers-Cotterets (1539), to impose the use of French on every court and every office throughout the kingdom.

In Germany the turbulent " Ritterstand ", the class from

which sprang the robber-knights who kept the country in uproar, lost their power to sovereign princes such as the Elector of Saxony, the Dukes of Brandenburg and Brunswick, the Landgrave of Hesse and the ecclesiastical Electors. It was a great step forward to the present unity of Germany.

Ecclesiastical liberties went the same way. They were destroyed in France by the Concordat, while in Germany the reigning princes took over the headship of their Churches. "Absolutism is everywhere established. The Prince, the temporal ruler, will dominate his clergy as he dominates the rest of his subjects" (Imbart de la Tour).

The vigour which had animated the Church when it possessed a host of small and almost independent lordships was now restrained. The Church became a vast inanimate body, blindly obedient to a single directing will.

We have seen the rise of the idea of nationality among people bound together by moral and economic ties and united by a common tradition. This phenomenon was to extend to the artistic sphere. The Middle Ages had had a common formula, in art as in religion, which extended to all peoples. This was first the Romanesque, widely diffused by the religious orders, and then the Gothic, of which French artists have left splendid examples so far afield as Hungary and Scandinavia. Now, however, a French, a German, a Flemish, an Italian art took shape, until French art succumbed to the flood of Italian importations and German art was stifled by the consequences of the Reformation.

The destruction of local government, as we have seen, entailed the rise of class distinctions. There had been unceasing contact between the old feudal lord and his vassals. As Michelet picturesquely expressed it, "In the worst centuries of the Middle Ages, people and barons still sang the same songs, the 'Dies irae' and the 'Chanson de Roland'."

Literature was popular ; it was the expression of aspirations common to all from the highest to the lowest in the social scale, but when the so-called ruling classes began to isolate themselves socially their literature followed them.

Eugène Baret has written in his introduction to his translation of Lope de Vega :

When the Mysteries and Moralities were destroyed the people of France were entirely deprived of the pleasure and edification to be derived from stage-plays. It is sad but true to say that the further we leave the Middle Ages behind, the more the possibilities of intellectual enjoyment become the preserve of the upper classes.

It was not only a question of enjoyment, but of inspiration. The only valuable literature is that which springs from the soul, the character and the feelings of the people. Corneille and Racine may have produced masterpieces, but—apart from their purely literary talent—they are only valuable for their human element, that is to say, for what contact they have maintained with popular sentiment.

It may well be imputed to the Renaissance as an inexpiable crime that it spoilt for centuries a great part of French art and literature. It was " a complete subjection of the French spirit to Greek and Latin literature and to the influence of classical art and civilization " (Courajod). Except for portraiture, in which the artist is compelled to paint from life, what did the French painters of the sixteenth century produce ? Imagine Poussin or Claude le Lorrain, in the next century, painting French scenes and landscapes. A few artists, such as Le Nain and Dumesnil de la Tour, escaped the fatal tendencies of their day, but their work was not understood. It was left for Watteau and Chardin, in the eighteenth century, to reintroduce French art into France.

What remains that is vital of the literature of the seventeenth century? Precisely that part of it which escaped the contagion of humanism ; that is, Molière, La Fontaine, and Perrault's fairy-tales. England, in its obstinate insularity, kept its head above the rising tide. The English writers of the sixteenth century had the good fortune to remain English. The works of Shakespeare and of the other English dramatists of his day are full of healthy life, sound and fury. Shakespeare dominates them all, as he dominates all else in the theatre. We must go back to Aeschylus and Sophocles, writers who thought and wrote as Greeks, before we find dramatic works worthy to stand by Shakespeare's. Though the men he brings upon the stage be Romans, Italians, Danes, yet Shakespeare remains simply, unshakably English—that is why he is Shakespeare.

We would repeat : "France allowed herself the luxury of starting again from the beginning." When a nation scorns and rejects the work of its ancestors it may commit a crime ; it certainly commits a folly.

Before closing these pages on the Renaissance, we should like to devote a few words to the recent researches which have revealed, alongside the classical and Italian influences, the effect on our civilization of the activity of the Saracens and the Arabs. We refer to the recent work of E. F. Gautier, *Manners and Customs of the Mussulmans.* It is easy to forget what civilization owes to the Saracens ; the mariner's compass and paper which they brought from China, gunpowder, and their astronomical progress, which paved the way for Copernicus. They were the first to place chemistry upon a scientific basis ; to them we owe algebra.

"Let us imagine," concludes M. Gautier, "what the Renaissance would have been without books, without gunpowder, without the compass ; without the use of the heritage of Saracen civilization." When the development of Saracen civilization was arrested, it was Western Europe which profited from its victories and carried on the torch of a new civilization.

INDEX

INDEX

Charles IX, 109, 263, 279, 299, 300
Chartres, 170–1
Chatillon, Cardinal de, 119
Chigi, Agostino, 39, 228
Cibo, Franceschetto, 146
Cibo, Niccolo, 202
Cicero, 65–6, 71, 78, 81, 83, 86, 93, 96, 105
Claude, 309
Clement IV, Pope, 150–1, 159
Clement VII, Pope, 132, 286–7, 301
Clermont-Lodève, Cardinal, 223
Cluny, 277
Coanabo, 17
Coligny, Admiral, 298–9
Collège de France, 92, 104
Colletet, 117
Colombo, Ferdinando, 17
Colonna, Cardinal 143
Colonna, Lorenzo, 143–4
Colosseum, the, 232
Columbus, Christopher, 14–20, 26–7
Columella, 78
Commines, 52, 70, 160, 163, 166
Concordat, the, 262–5, 267–9, 271–2, 308
Condé, Prince de, 295
Constantinople, 39, 58, 83, 147, 154, 184
Copernicus, 14, 20–6, 68, 87
Cordoba, Gonsalvo de, 163
Corneille, 309
Correggio, 284
Cortese, Paolo, 73
Cortona, Domenico da, 167
Cospéan, Bishop, 270
Courajod, Louis, 304, 309
Credi, Lorenzo di, 189
Crillon, 269
Curtius, Quintus, 85

D'Albret, Jeanne, 281
D'Amboise, Cardinal, 169

D'Anjou, René, ex-King of Naples, 150
Dante, 42, 51, 65, 70, 82, 113, 126, 194, 274
Danton, 243
Daudet, Léon, 121
David, the painter, 169
Delft, 89
De l'Orme, Philibert, 175, 269
Demosthenes, 66, 93
De Rohan, 270
Descartes, 68
D'Este, Alfonso, Duke of Ferrara, 206, 222, 228
D'Este, Ippolito, 260
D'Estissac, 117
Diane de Poitiers, 288
Dieppe, 38–9
Dolci, Gaspare, 32
Dolet, 122
Donatello, 50, 74, 171
Dorat, Jean, 107–8
Doria, Andrea, 153
Du Bellay, Eustache, 127
Du Bellay, Guillaume, 125
Du Bellay, Jean, 76, 118–19, 124, 127, 129
Du Bellay, Joachim, 76, 107, 123–9, 304
Du Bellay, Martin, 125
Du Chalard, Joachim, 269
Dumesnil de la Tour, 309
Duns Scotus, 65, 68
Duprat, Chancellor Antoine, 261, 264, 267, 273
Dürer, Albrecht, 34

Elizabeth, Queen, 108, 296
England, 71, 101, 110, 237, 274, 280, 310
Epictetus, 71
Erasmus, 66–8, 70, 72, 81, 86–105, 110, 116–17, 120, 122–3, 138, 164, 218, 236

315